REMAKING UKRAINE AFTER WORLD WAR II

Ukraine was liberated from German wartime occupation by 1944 but remained prisoner to the consequences for much longer. This study examines Soviet Ukraine's transition from war to 'peace' in the long aftermath of World War II. Filip Slaveski explores the challenges faced by local Soviet authorities in reconstructing central Ukraine, including feeding rapidly growing populations in the post-war famine. Drawing on recently declassified Soviet sources, Slaveski traces the previously unknown bitter struggle for land, food and power among collective farmers at the bottom of the Soviet social ladder and local and central authorities. He reveals how local authorities challenged central ones for these resources in pursuit of their own vision of rebuilding central Ukraine, undermining the Stalinist policies they were supposed to implement and forsaking the farmers in the process. In so doing, Slaveski demonstrates how the consequences of this battle shaped post-war reconstruction, and continue to resonate in contemporary Ukraine, especially with the ordinary people caught in the middle.

FILIP SLAVESKI is an Australian Research Council (ARC) Research Fellow (DECRA) at the Alfred Deakin Institute, Deakin University. A historian of the Soviet period, specialising also in East European and German twentieth-century history, he is the author of *The Soviet Occupation of Germany: Hunger, Mass Violence and the Struggle for Peace, 1945–1947* (2013).

NEW STUDIES IN EUROPEAN HISTORY

Edited by

PETER BALDWIN, University of California, Los Angeles
CHRISTOPHER CLARK, University of Cambridge
JAMES B. COLLINS, Georgetown University
MIA RODRÍGUEZ-SALGADO, London School of Economics
and Political Science
LYNDAL ROPER, University of Oxford
TIMOTHY SNYDER, Yale University

The aim of this series in early modern and modern European history is to publish outstanding works of research, addressed to important themes across a wide geographical range, from southern and central Europe, to Scandinavia and Russia, from the time of the Renaissance to the present. As it develops the series will comprise focused works of wide contextual range and intellectual ambition.

A full list of titles published in the series can be found at:
www.cambridge.org/newstudiesineuropeanhistory

REMAKING UKRAINE AFTER WORLD WAR II

The Clash of Local and Central Soviet Power

FILIP SLAVESKI

Deakin University, Victoria

CAMBRIDGE
UNIVERSITY PRESS

Shaftesbury Road, Cambridge CB2 8EA, United Kingdom

One Liberty Plaza, 20th Floor, New York, NY 10006, USA

477 Williamstown Road, Port Melbourne, VIC 3207, Australia

314–321, 3rd Floor, Plot 3, Splendor Forum, Jasola District Centre, New Delhi – 110025, India

103 Penang Road, #05–06/07, Visioncrest Commercial, Singapore 238467

Cambridge University Press is part of Cambridge University Press & Assessment, a department of the University of Cambridge.

We share the University's mission to contribute to society through the pursuit of education, learning and research at the highest international levels of excellence.

www.cambridge.org
Information on this title: www.cambridge.org/9781108794183

DOI: 10.1017/9781108879293

First published 2021
First paperback edition 2024

A catalogue record for this publication is available from the British Library

Library of Congress Cataloging-in-Publication data
NAMES: Slaveski, Filip, author.
TITLE: Remaking Ukraine after World War II : the clash of local and central Soviet power / Filip Slaveski.
DESCRIPTION: Cambridge ; New York, NY : Cambridge University Press, 2021. | Includes bibliographical references and index.
IDENTIFIERS: LCCN 2020029066 (print) | LCCN 2020029067 (ebook) | ISBN 9781108840255 (hardback) | ISBN 9781108794183 (paperback) | ISBN 9781108879293 (ebook)
SUBJECTS: LCSH: Agriculture and state – Ukraine. | Collective farms – Ukraine – History. | Food supply – Political aspects – Ukraine – History – 20th century. | Central-local government relations – Ukraine – History – 20th century. | Reconstruction (1939–1951) – Ukraine. | Ukraine – Economic conditions – 1945–1991. | Ukraine – History – 1944–1991.
CLASSIFICATION: LCC HD1995.45.Z8 S63 2021 (print) | LCC HD1995.45.Z8 (ebook) | ddc 330.9477/0842–dc23
LC record available at https://lccn.loc.gov/2020029066
LC ebook record available at https://lccn.loc.gov/2020029067

ISBN   978-1-108-84025-5   Hardback
ISBN   978-1-108-79418-3   Paperback

In memory of my mother

Contents

List of Figures and Table   *page* ix
Acknowledgements   x
Note on Translation and Transliteration   xii
List of Abbreviations and Translated Terms
  from Russian and Ukrainian   xiii

Introduction   1

PART I THE BATTLE FOR LAND BETWEEN THE PEOPLE
        AND LOCAL AND CENTRAL SOVIET AUTHORITIES   35

1 A Brief Survey of Illegal Appropriations of Collective
   Farmland by Local State and Party Officials   37

2 Taking Land: Officials' Illegal Appropriations and Starving
   People in Raska, Bila Tserkva and Elsewhere   53

3 Taking Land Back: The People and Central Authorities'
   Recovery of Land and Prosecution of Local Party and State
   Officials   84

PART II THE COST OF THE BATTLE FOR LAND TO PEOPLE
         AND THE STATE   119

4 The Cost of Taking Land: The Damage Caused by Illegal
   Appropriations of Collective Farmland to *Kolkhozniki*,
   Communities and the State   121

5 Then and Now: The Shaping of Contemporary Ukraine
   in the Post-War Crises   147

vii

Conclusion 182

*Appendix: Archival Source Locations and Guide for Further
        Research* 191
Bibliography 194
Index 204

Figures and Table

Figures

1	Grave of honour in Raska (2016)	*page* 3
2	Former sowing fields of the Pershe Travnia collective farm in Raska	148
3	Rubbish pits at the Pershe Travnia collective farm	148
4	Dual-language memorial plaque at the grave of honour in Raska	170
5	UPA grave in Myhalky	172
6	UPA monument in Myhalky	172
7a, 7b	October 2016 'Day of the Defender' commemoration at Mykhalky	177

Table

1	Lands Returned to Ukrainian Collective Farms, 1946–1947	79

Acknowledgements

I have accrued significant debts from good friends and better scholars in writing this book. Stephen Wheatcroft has helped me greatly in my research for more than fifteen years, especially on Soviet economic and agricultural matters. David Lowe, Mark McGillivray and Mark Edele read earlier versions of this manuscript, and all provided useful feedback. Yurii Shapoval and I work closely on related projects that provide insights into post-war Ukraine. Hiroaki Kuromiya has always given me good advice and John Merriman his good humour. Jim Collins, as Series Editor at Cambridge University Press, whipped this manuscript into shape, while my commissioning editor, Liz Friend-Smith, has been a joy to work with.

My research assistants in Moscow, Kyiv and Melbourne, all bright scholars in their own right, tied up many loose ends for me between my stints at Russian and Ukrainian archives over the years – Vladislava Gaiduk, Volodomyr Myl'ko and Liudmila Druzenko. It was a pleasure to work with dedicated archivists in making sense of recently declassified and sometimes poorly organised collections across different archives. The deputy director of the State Archive of Kyiv Oblast (DAKO), Galina Boyko, deserves special mention. She opened an archival basement that had closed for the summer so I could work there alone, assisted by the resident archivist, Vera Orlova, to access some of the materials that were most important to my research. In Raska, Valentin Koval'skyi and Zosia Lisovska are the very generous people who helped me connect the past to the present, as did numerous others here and elsewhere.

My annual research at these and other archives, and across Russia and Ukraine more broadly, was made possible by a research grant from the Australian Research Council (ARC) for my project 'The Chaotic and Violent Transition from War to Peace in Soviet-Occupied Europe, 1945–1953' (DE150100969) and support from Deakin University. The generosity from the Higher School of Economics (HSE) in Moscow, the Institute of History in the National Academy of Sciences in Ukraine, and

Sheila Fitzpatrick in Australia in inviting me to share my research at various conferences also assisted my work, particularly the feedback from the participants. In terms of feedback, the most helpful was the 2019 'Recovering Forgotten History' conference in Poland and Ukraine. The Polish Foundation for Civic Space and Public Policy funded my participation at this travelling conference across Polish and Ukrainian cities for two weeks in the summer of 2019 with a few other authors to discuss our forthcoming works at the sites of our research. They organised a panel of five area experts to read this manuscript, line by line, and offer their most valuable feedback over a day-long discussion in Kyiv. I give special thanks to the head of the conference, Andrzej Kaminski, for making this possible, and to my experts, Jan Szumskyi, Natalia Lass, Maryna Bessonova, Juraj Marusiak and especially Marek Wierzbicki.

The deepest debts are invariably personal. My wife, Fleur, maintained the home front so well with our growing family while I was away for long periods. Without her incredible support, this book would not have been possible. I missed the support from my old friend and mentor, John Hirst, who had helped me so much with my work over the years. He died in February 2016. My mother, Hristina Slaveska, died in August the following year. She was born in the long aftermath of World War II, in the crushing poverty of the socialist countryside in post-war Macedonia. She gave me everything, and left me the mystery of how such terrible beginnings can rear such wonderful people, which continues to lead me back to the study of this period.

Any errors made in this book are mine alone.

Note on Translation and Transliteration

I have attempted to translate/transliterate all Polish, Ukrainian and Russian names and placenames to reflect their origin. This can be challenging when the same names are recorded differently in various language sources at different times, sometimes by competing hegemonies mobilising language to establish their authority. Where confusion remains, I have defaulted to the largely Russian or Ukrainian versions of names predominant therein for the sake of clarity. For this same reason, I have used a modified version of Library of Congress transliteration systems for all languages, with some common exceptions.

Abbreviations and Translated Terms from Russian and Ukrainian

antiobshchestvennyi obraz zhizni	anti-social lifestyle
AV BRDA	Archive Department of the Bila Tserkva Raion Administration
besperspektivnyi	unpromising
bezdushnost'	callousness
blank	standard template (form)
Cheka	acronym for the Extraordinary Commission to Combat Counterrevolution and Sabotage, 1917–22
chekist	Cheka member/secret police officer
Chervonyi Khliborob	'Red Farmer/Tiller' collective farm
Chervonyi Pluhatar	'Red Ploughman' collective farm
CP(b)U	Communist Party (Bolshevik) of Ukraine
DAKO	State Archive of Kyiv Oblast
edinolichniki	individual/'private' farmers
GARF	State Archive of the Russian Federation
GKO	State Defence Committee, the chief wartime decision-making body
gorkom	city party committee
gorsovet	city council
HDA SBU	Archive Department of the Security Service of Ukraine
Imeni Lenina	'In the Name of Lenin' collective farm

individual' nye khoziaistva	individual/'private' farms
kolkhoz (sing.), *kolkhozy* (pl.)	collective farm(s)
kolkhoznik (sing.), *kolkhozniki* (pl.)	collective farmer(s)
Komissiia Partiinogo Kontrolia	Party Control Commission (KPK)
krai	administrative territory, larger than an oblast
kraikom	Communist Party *krai* committee
krest'ianstvo	peasantry
kulak	'rich' peasant
militsiia	civil police
mnimye kolkhozniki	'sham' collective farmers
MPVO	Local Anti-Aircraft Defence Organisation
MTS	machine tractor station
NKVD	People's Commissariat of Internal Affairs (All-Union) 1934–46
NKVDisty	mostly Ukrainian colloquial term for NKVD agents
Nove Zhyttia	'New Life' collective farm
ob.	oborot: reverse (back side of a page, especially in an archive document)
obkom	provincial party committee
oblast	province/region, larger than *raion*
obliispolkom	provincial state executive committee
ogorodnichestvo	private horticulture
okolokolkhoznyi element	loosely collectivised elements
okrug	often a military administrative district
otstaiushchie kolkhozy i raiony	collective farms and districts lagging behind
OUN	Organisation of Ukrainian Nationalists
Peremoha	'Victory' collective farm
Pershe Travnia	'First of May' collective farm
pervichnaia partiinaia organizatsiia	lowest-level party cell
pisok	sand
podsobnoe khoziaistvo	subsidiary farming
prispeshnik	collaborator

raiispolkom	district state executive committee
raikom	district party committee
raion (sing.), *raiony* (pl.)	district(s)
RGAE	Russian State Archive of the Economy
RGASPI	Russian State Archive of Socio-Political History
samokritika	self-criticism
sel'skoe khoziaistvo	agriculture
sel'sovet	village council
sobranie (sing.), *sobraniia* (pl.)	farm meeting(s)
Sovet po delam kolkhozov pri Sovmin SSSR	Council on Collective Farm Affairs in the USSR Council of Ministers (the Soviet government)
sovkhoz (sing.), *sovkhozy* (pl.)	state farm(s)
Sovmin	Council of Ministers, replaced Sovnarkom from March 1946
Sovnarkom	Council of People's Commissars (highest body in the Soviet government at republican and all-Union level)
SSSR	Union of Soviet Socialist Republics
strogoe vzyskanie	strong party punishment
Tretii Vyrishal'nyi	'Third Decisive' collective farm
TsDAHOU	Central State Archive of Public Organisations of Ukraine
TsDAVOU	Central State Archives of Supreme Bodies of Power and Government of Ukraine
TsK VKP(b)	Central Committee of the All-Union Communist Party (Bolsheviks)
UkSSR	Ukrainian Soviet Socialist Republic
UPA	Ukrainian Insurgent Army
vygovor (sing.), *vygovory* (pl.)	party reprimand(s)
vzyskanie (sing.), *vzyskaniia* (pl.)	party punishment(s)
zemleustroitel'	land surveyor
zemlianka (sing.), *zemlianki* (pl.)	dirt hovel(s)

Introduction

> There's no point in rebuilding that collective farm. There's no village there, the farm worked poorly in the past and the soil is bad. What's worse, the people there aren't even real *kolkhozniki* – they're just rotten.
>
> Soviet official, Kyiv Oblast, Ukraine, 1948[1]

This is a history of 'rotten' people. Thousands of them returned victorious from fighting against the Germans in World War II to their 'bad soil' in Soviet Ukraine from 1945, but had to keep fighting until the end of that decade. Now they were fighting against their own Soviet government, which obstructed them from rebuilding their villages, farms and what remained of their pre-war lives. These people were not wartime collaborators, forced labourers or other 'traitorous' Soviet citizens whom officials normally discriminated against and slandered after the war. Numerous works have been published on their experiences.[2] The people whom authorities called 'rotten' were decorated war veterans and committed *kolkhozniki*, whom authorities were supposed to assist in, not obstruct from, rebuilding post-war Soviet society. This book examines the struggle between these 'rotten' people and the authorities, which reveals a new fault line in the restoration of Soviet control in parts of the Ukrainian countryside after World War II. The Soviet society that re-emerged in these areas shook chaotically along this fault line in ways we are only beginning to understand.

---

[1] Russian State Archive of Socio-Political History (Rossiiskii gosudarstvennyi arkhiv sotsial'no-politicheskoi istorii – RGASPI) f. (*fond*) 17, op. (*opis'*) 122, d. (*delo*) 316, l. (*list*) 155. *Kolkhozniki* are collective farmers and members of a collective farm (*kolkhoz*).

[2] On the difficulties encountered by displaced persons returning to Ukraine after the war, see Tetyana Pastushenko, 'V'izd repatriantiv do Kyïva zaboronenyi ... ' *Povoienne zhyttya kolyshnikh ostarbaiteriv ta viiskovopolonenykh v Ukraïni* (Kyiv: Instytut istoriï Ukraïny NAN Ukraïny, 2011). For a Soviet-wide history, see Pavel Polian, *Zhertvy dvukh diktatur. Ostarbaitery i voennoplennye v Tret'em reikhe i ikh repatriatsiia* (Moscow: Vash Vybor Tsirz, 1996).

The specific people that authorities called 'rotten' in the above epitaph were soldiers who returned to the land on which their village of Raska once stood. Raska, 90 kilometres west of Kyiv, had been burnt to the ground, the soldiers' murdered loved ones buried beneath it. Like so many of their comrades, in victory the soldiers lost the very things they had fought to protect. On 11 April 1943, German occupation forces and local Ukrainian collaborators launched a pre-dawn raid on this ethnically Polish village in response to the murder of three German soldiers in the area.[3] They herded almost all of Raska's remaining 421 women, children and elderly inhabitants – or 'partisans' as the Germans called them – into a ditch and shot them. Before torching the village, the murderers also killed the visitors who had come to Raska to celebrate a holiday.[4] That is why 'there was no village there'.[5] The soldiers' first task upon their return home after the war was to give their loved ones a proper burial. The soldiers swore an oath to their dead to rebuild the village and collective farm on this 'grave of honour' that can still be visited today (see Figure 1).[6]

Similar oaths rang out across post-war Ukraine. More *kolkhozniki* labelled 'rotten' by authorities swore oaths about 140 km south-west of Raska, outside what remained of the large city of Bila Tserkva. This city, too, was a site of massacres – of Ukrainian Jews in 1941 – and remaining civilian populations especially in 1943 as part of the German forces' 'anti-partisan' war and retreat westwards from the advancing Red Army.[7] Almost the whole of the city's remaining infrastructure was destroyed in

---

[3] State Archive of Kyiv Oblast (Derzhavnyi arkhiv Kyïvskoï oblasti – DAKO) f. 4810, op. 1, d. 3, l. 22.

[4] This is the conservative estimate of total casualties offered by World War II Museum in Kyiv, which is the same as in RGASPI f. 17, op. 122, d. 316, l. 151. This figure, however, does not take into account visitors to the village attending a holiday celebration on that weekend. Locals remaining in Raska have given higher figures inclusive of visitors. On the memorial at the gravesite in the village, 613 victims are listed, 120 of them children. See Chapter 5.

[5] DAKO f. r-880, op. 11, d. 95, l. 7.

[6] A handful of men originally from Raska who had not been drafted into the Red Army worked in the area or fought in partisan units, though most would join the Red Army as it advanced through Kyiv Oblast in late 1943. Some of these men were the first to arrive at the village after its destruction. Small snippets of information, comprising a few pages, about Raska's destruction are found in recollections gathered from some remaining residents in 1973 and later published in a book of poetry (the only such published book found by the author) in Ukraine: L. N. Horlach and I. M. Pal′chik et al., *Dzvony pam′iati. Knyha pro trahediiu sil Kyïvshchyny, znyshchenykh fashystamy u roky viiny* (Kyiv: Radyanskyi pys′mennyk, 1985), 188. For the difference between this 'official information' and the recollections of other survivors of the massacre and the post-war struggle against the authorities, see Chapter 5.

[7] For details of casualties in the German 'anti-partisan' war and the broader 'scorched earth' policy during the retreat from the Soviet Union, see Hamburger Institut für Sozialforschung, ed., *Verbrechen der Wehrmacht. Dimensionen des Vernichtungskrieges 1941–1944: Ausstellungskatalog* (Hamburg: Hamburger Edition, 2002), 387–9.

1 Grave of honour in Raska (2016)

the heavy fighting. The city's pre-war population had been massively reduced. *Kolkhozniki* who had survived brutal German occupation since 1941 joined with those returning from military service to try to rebuild their collective farms and villages where there was little trace of them. Local authorities first obstructed the rebuilding and then tried to liquidate the farms as soon as the *kolkhozniki* were successful in rebuilding them.[8]

Most local authorities tried to fulfil their legal obligations to assist the masses of citizens seeking to rebuild their post-war lives, but it was not unusual to deny it to some people, 'rotten' or otherwise.[9] There was

---

[8] 'Local authorities' refers to village-, city-, *raion*- and oblast-level authorities, unless specifically designated. In Raska, the lowest authority was the local village council (*sel'sovet*), followed by two *raion* authorities representing the state (*raiispolkom*) and party (*raikom*), with the latter usually making decisions carried out by the former. In Bila Tserkva, city authorities comprised the state representative (*gorsovet*) and party arms (*gorkom*) as well as two *raion* authorities, the *raiispolkom* and *raikom*. All reported to their superiors at the oblast level, the state arm (*obliispolkom*) and party arm (*obkom*), who reported to their superiors at the nationwide republican level, who, along with all-Union authorities, are referred to as 'central authorities' unless otherwise designated.

[9] Immediately after the war, most of the Soviet population still lived in the countryside, and the majority of war veterans initially returned to their villages, or what remained of them, after demobilisation. The mass emigration from the countryside to the cities happened after the initial resettlement of the villages following demobilisation. See Mark Edele, 'Veterans and the Village: The Impact of Red Army Demobilization on Soviet Urbanization, 1945–1955', *Russian History* 36, no. 2 (2009), 159–82; Mark Edele, *Soviet Veterans of World War II: A Popular Movement in an Authoritarian Society, 1941–1991* (Oxford: Oxford University Press, 2008); and Robert Dale, *Demobilized Veterans in Late Stalinist Leningrad: Soldiers to Civilians* (New York: Bloomsbury Academic, 2015).

considerable competition for the scant resources on offer, from food rations and building material, to pension payments, loans and housing allocations. In addition to the farms and villages in Raska and Bila Tserkva, 30,000 farms were destroyed during the war and needed to be rebuilt.[10] As many as 8 million Ukrainians may have died from war and occupation among the 28 million Soviet dead.[11] Many returning soldiers, like those in Raska and Bila Tserkva, failed to receive these resources as part of the more generous state assistance to which they were legally entitled, promised to them in the din of war by the state, which had been too impoverished by the war to provide it now.[12] To make matters worse, the consequences of war and occupation continued to unravel years after their cessation. By the time most soldiers returned home in late 1946,[13] the country was hurtling from mass drought to famine, which killed at least a million more people and reversed many of the gains made in rebuilding the countryside upon Ukraine's liberation from late 1943.[14] In this context of enduring material deprivation and massive social disorganisation, the assistance to which people were legally entitled became conditional.[15] 'Rebuilding' or 'reconstructing' the country was by no means a linear process that could be simply facilitated successfully by 'assistance'.

---

[10] This number includes state farms (*sovkhozy*) and machine tractor stations (MTSs) destroyed or pillaged: V. M. Danylenko, ed., *Povoienna Ukraïna. Narysy sotsial'noï istoriï (druha polovyna 1940-kh–seredyna 1950-kh rr.)* (Kyiv: Instytut istoriï Ukraïny NAN Ukraïny, 2010), 7.

[11] S. V. Kul′chyts′kyi, *Chervonyi vyklyk. Istoriia komunizmu v Ukraïni vid yoho narodzhennia do zahybeli*, vol. III (Kyiv: Tempora, 2013), 106. See here too for the broader debate over casualty figures.

[12] There is an emerging literature on authorities failing to assist desperate people as part of their broader inability to negotiate the competing claims for resources among soldiers and other members of society in a period of severe material shortage. This was an enduring problem in the immediate post-war period, even for soldiers, whose status as veterans at this time did not guarantee them the advantages they had been promised by the state. See Edele, *Soviet Veterans of World War II* and Dale, *Demobilized Veterans*.

[13] For demobilisation figures, see Mark Edele, 'A "Generation of Victors"? Soviet Second World War Veterans from Demobilization to Organization 1941–1956', PhD dissertation, University of Chicago, 2004, 102.

[14] Union-wide casualties. On the collapse of the agricultural sector and the famine across the western parts of the Soviet Union in 1946–7, see two major works with varying viewpoints on the state's role in causing and/or exacerbating the famine: V. F. Zima, *Golod v SSSR 1946–1947 godov. Proiskhozhdenie i posledstviia* (Moscow: Institut Rossiskoi Istorii RAN, 1996); and Nicholas Ganson, *The Soviet Famine of 1946–1947 in Global and Historical Perspective* (New York: Palgrave Macmillan, 2009).

[15] It was only in the mid-1950s that *kolkhozniki* in the countryside ate as well as they had done before the war and broader Soviet economic indicators approximated pre-war norms. For comparative pre- and post-war consumption data in each oblast of Ukraine, see the Russian State Archive of the Economy (Rossiiskii gosudarstvennyi arkhiv ekonomiki – RGAE) f. 582, op. 24, d. 430. It is important to remember, however, that these figures are averages.

It was unusual for local authorities, however, to disobey the law and central policy to conspire to obstruct *kolkhozniki* from rebuilding their own villages and collective farms or to try to liquidate operating ones. In Raska, they tore down homes and the school that the soldiers, now *kolkhozniki*, had rebuilt upon their return from the war, and stole their last morsels of food and livestock, before ordering the physical liquidation of the partially reconstructed farm and village. Authorities ejected *kolkhozniki* from their homes and land, and stole farm equipment on the outskirts of Bila Tserkva in their attempt to liquidate the farms as well as in other locations across Kyiv Oblast, where Raska and Bila Tserkva are located. Authorities along the vertical of political power were involved, from the *raion* (district) level – committing the violence on the ground – to the oblast (provincial) level – directing and protecting the former from prosecution. Along this vertical, levels of government were formally separated into party and state bodies, which had different responsibilities for managing agriculture. On the *raion* level, the management lay mainly with the district state committee (*raiispolkom*). The district party committee (*raikom*) was more a decision-making body less involved in day-to-day agricultural affairs. This structure was mirrored at the next and highest level in the oblast with the *obliispolkom* and *obkom*. In practice, there was overlap of personnel and responsibilities between these bodies. This overlap intensified especially around harvest time, in times of food crisis or, in the cases of Raska and Bila Tserkva, when authorities conspired to act against the law and the broader thrust of post-war building to obstruct the *kolkhozniki*.

This obstruction was not simply unusual behaviour: it was potential political suicide for authorities to obstruct the development of the collective farm system – the state's rapacious extraction of food from the countryside to feed the cities and armies and for export. Although this system was economically inefficient, as with most forms of forced labour, it remained the backbone of the entire Soviet economy and economic foundation of Stalinism.[16] The job of local authorities was to make this system work by enforcing the law that bound *kolkhozniki* to their farms and engaged them in work for the state, not kick them off the farms and stop them from operating. *Kolkhozniki* were generally reluctant to work on the farms when they received only a share of the grain or income from produce that remained after the state requisitioned it. This share was often insufficient to keep them alive, so most *kolkhozniki* survived only by

---

[16] Paul Gregory, *The Political Economy of Stalinism* (New York: Cambridge University Press, 2003).

farming the small plot of private land permitted to them, where they could grow their own food.

Soviet officials investigating the crimes committed by these local authorities thus struggled to understand their motivations in obstructing the rebuilding or trying to liquidate farms, especially in regard to Raska. Its inhabitants had been massacred and its collective farm, called 'First of May' (Pershe Travnia), destroyed by German occupiers, making its reconstruction part of the broader narrative of patriotic rebuilding espoused by the state. The *kolkhozniki* too struggled to understand the local authorities' motivations for obstructing them from rebuilding the farms when, unlike many other *kolkhozniki*, they were happy to work on them. By the poor standards of the Ukrainian collective farm sector, the farms in Raska and Bila Tserkva had operated reasonably well by the eve of the war, and *kolkhozniki* earned a decent living, which they all now sought to resume afterwards.[17] Importantly, their commitment to working on their rebuilt farms bound them to the land and to the communities from which the authorities were trying to remove them. Land and lifestyle were entwined for the *kolkhozniki*, and their attachment to both ran deep in these places. Local authorities clearly understood this, but it made no difference to their behaviour.

Leon Koval'skyi (Kowalski), a war veteran and *kolkhoznik* in Raska, best expressed this sense of confusion among *kolkhozniki* over the local authorities' unusual behaviour when he spoke to the investigating officials who visited the farms in the winter of 1948. The officials quickly passed Koval'skyi's plea, made through tears, on to their superiors to address in the highest echelons of Soviet government in Moscow:

> I'm a Red Army soldier. I fought against the enemy for four years while the fascists executed my wife and three children at home. Now I'm back, it's not enough that I cannot be with my family, but I . . . have to put up with the most inhumane treatment [from the local authorities]. What are we asking for? We're asking to rebuild our collective farm . . . on the graves of our murdered loved ones. But the authorities deny us! I can't explain why they're treating us so callously [*bezdushno*].[18]

This book answers Koval'skyi's final question by examining the struggle of *kolkhozniki* to rebuild their villages and farms in Raska, Bila Tserkva and other areas of Kyiv Oblast. These are atypical cases. Nowhere else in Ukraine did local authorities stop *kolkhozniki* rebuilding their farms and villages so violently. Authorities claimed to have rebuilt almost all of the sector's other

---

[17] For data on the pre-war performance of these farms, see Chapter 3.
[18] RGASPI f. 17, op. 122, d. 316, l. 154.

pre-war collective farms by the beginning of 1946, totalling 2,368 farms in Kyiv Oblast and 26,368 Ukraine-wide.[19] Nowhere else did *kolkhozniki* fight for years for the right to rebuild their farms. By the end of the 1940s, life on the collective farms was no longer tolerable, indeed viable, for millions of *kolkhozniki* from Ukraine and across the Soviet Union. Through both legal and illegal means, they fled their farms for new lives in the cities.[20]

Though atypical, these cases teach us a great deal new about the problems of broader post-war agriculture, national rebuilding and post-war Stalinism. They occurred at the extremity of a wider, yet poorly understood process – local authorities' theft of collective farm-land. The answer to Koval'skyi's question, then, concerns not only Raska and Kyiv Oblast, but all of Ukraine. Local authorities in Raska and Bila Tserkva refused to allow the *kolkhozniki* to rebuild their farms so callously because they had taken away the land where their farms were located and given it to others (appropriation). Local authorities appropriating collective farmland that was used to grow food for the state and distributing it for other uses, mostly to factories, institutions and workers to grow food for local consumption, was a widespread practice in wartime across the unoccupied Soviet Union and then in the liberated territories such as Ukraine. There were both legal and illegal appropriations, though the divisions between them in wartime were blurry and not enforced widely. Central authorities succeeded in stamping out illegal appropriations conducted by authorities and by factories, institutions and workers themselves, much of the literature argues, by prosecuting them in a massive political campaign launched in September 1946 called 'On measures to eliminate abuses of collective farm rules'.[21]

[19] For Kyiv Oblast, see DAKO f. r-880, op. 11, d. 95. For Ukraine-wide figures not including west Ukrainian oblasts, which were only forcibly collectivised from 1948, see Yu. V. Arutiunian, *Sovetskoe krest'ianstvo v gody Velikoi Otechestvennoi voiny* (Moscow: Akademia Nauk SSSR, Institut Istorii, 1963), 386.

[20] *Kolkhozniki* engaged in fluid migrations from farm to urban work both legally and illegally. Many were recruited for seasonal urban labour projects by state agencies for short periods after the war and were expected to return to their farms for sowing/harvest periods. Many ended up staying in urban areas permanently and eventually brought their families to settle, especially after 1949. Others left their farms on their own accord. Through both avenues, *kolkhozniki* left the collective farm sector in a massive migratory process across the Soviet Union. Some *kolkhozniki* were prosecuted for engaging in other work without authorisation and especially for failing to return from their urban employment to farm work in the sowing/harvest seasons. They were generally not prosecuted for leaving the farms permanently after 1949, but often lost their membership in them, and thus their claims to private plots. On more detail of the migratory process, see the discussion in Chapter 3 and Zima, *Golod*, ch. 8.

[21] The full title is Postanovlenie Soveta Ministrov SSSR (Sovmin) 'O merakh po likvidatsii narushenii Ustava sel'skokhoziaistvennoi arteli v kolkhozakh' (19 September 1946). From this point onwards, I refer to it as the 'Campaign on Collective Farm Rules'.

This campaign returned millions of hectares of the land that had been appropriated during the war both legally and illegally to the collective farm sector to grow food to supply central rather than local demands.

The atypical – indeed, extreme – cases of Raska and Bila Tserkva, evident from recently declassified Soviet archival sources and survivor testimony, now reveal that local authorities refused to return large tracts of collective farmland in response to the 1946 campaign. Some continued appropriating it, secretly and illegally after 1946, not only here and across Kyiv Oblast, but also in other areas of Ukraine. Without knowledge of these extreme cases, we would have little idea that this problem endured widely after this time. Local authorities left no transparent paper trail of the numerous, less extreme illegal appropriations that remain in the archival record. The extreme cases did leave a transparent and rich trail, because the struggle between *kolkhozniki* and authorities was investigated and recorded.

An examination of this paper trail reveals a conspiracy emanating from the oblast-level state government (*obliispolkom*) in Kyiv to continue illegal appropriations. The heads of various government departments and other leading officials used their positions to spearhead a broader network of subordinates who operated on their orders or at least under their protection. Officials within this network possessed numerous strategies to conduct illegal appropriations, including coercing *kolkhozniki* into accepting the theft of land and concealing and falsifying records of their behaviour. Officials applied these strategies *in extremis* in Raska and Bila Tserkva where they met resistance from *kolkhozniki*. They and officials elsewhere in Ukraine applied them less extremely in other cases of appropriation where they met little or no resistance. Officials recorded these cases falsely in the archival record as legal appropriations reached by agreement between *kolkhozniki* and authorities or simply as mundane land transfers. With knowledge of how this network operated and its strategies of concealment and falsification laid bare, we can now reveal where these 'legal appropriations' conceal illegal ones and thus make transparent the opaque record in the archives. We can begin to understand land theft in Ukraine from its extreme iterations in the cases of Raska and Bila Tserkva to its moderate ones across Kyiv Oblast and elsewhere, committed by other local authorities. In this way, these cases are not limited in what they tell us about post-war reconstruction because they are not typical of general experiences. They shed the greatest insight into general experiences otherwise unknown exactly because these cases are atypical.[22]

Uncovering this hidden aspect of this period of history raises new questions: where *kolkhozniki* could not resist local authorities taking their land, how much of it remained unreturned to the collective farm sector? What impact did this illegal and largely unaccounted-for division in land have on local and central food supply, especially in time of famine and, indeed, on the fate of the post-war rebuilding of the agricultural sector and broader economies in Ukraine? What spurred such illegal conspiratorial behaviour among officials, and how was this resistance to central authorities possible at the local level in Kyiv Oblast and elsewhere? What spurred the resistance of the *kolkhozniki*? What does all of this tell us about the broader problems of post-war Stalinism? By addressing these questions in this book, we can arrive at a much better understanding of the intersections of land, food and power in post-war Stalinism.

*

A clash between local and central authorities over land usage was bound to emerge at some stage in the post-war period. By the end of the war across the entire Soviet Union, hundreds of thousands of factories and institutions, and millions of workers, were in possession of millions of hectares of collective farmland in areas that had avoided German occupation and then in those that had been liberated from it. This was not the case in areas annexed by the Soviet Union in its invasion of eastern Poland from September 1939, including parts of western Ukraine.[23] Former collective farmland was divided into small plots among individual workers and their families, who used it to grow their own food, primarily vegetables and mostly for personal consumption. Land used in this way was called *podsobnoe khoziaistvo*.[24] Local authorities usually made it available to factories/institutions and trade unions; the latter distributed it to their

---

[22] For a discussion of the capacity of local studies to shed insight into more general realities and, broadly, how local conditions can shape central ones, see Allan Pred, *Making Histories and Constructing Human Geographies: The Local Transformation of Practice, Power Relations, and Consciousness* (Boulder: Westview, 1990).

[23] David Marples, *Stalinism in Ukraine in the 1940s* (New York: St. Martin's Press, 1992), ch. 7.

[24] In some cases factories/institutions set up their own farms to feed workforces; see Donald Filtzer, *Soviet Workers and Late Stalinism: Labour and the Restoration of the Stalinist System after World War II* (Cambridge: Cambridge University Press, 2002), 70–5, and, more broadly, T. D. Nadkin, *Stalinskaia agrarnaia politika i krest'ianstvo Mordovii* (Moscow: Rosspen, 2010), 235–51; E. V. Maksimenko, 'Istoriografiia problemy razvitiia individual'nogo i kollektivnogo ogorodnichestva i podsobnykh khoziaistv na iuzhnom Urale v gody Velikoi Otechestvennoi voiny i poslevoennyi period', *Vestnik Orenburgskogo gosudarstvennogo pedagogicheskogo universiteta* 5, no. 1 (2013), 83–6.

workers or factories/institutions. Alternatively, individual workers appropriated the land themselves with or without the consent of the authorities.[25] This land provided a major food source for workers and thus, for local authorities, a basis for the economic reconstruction of their localities in Ukraine from the time of liberation in late 1943. This dependence did not wane in late 1946 when central authorities sought to recover this land. There was thus great impetus for local authorities in the most destitute areas to prevent the return of the land to the collective farm sector, which would have put the land back into state use with the food grown on it to supply mainly the central food supply system, not local demands. The impetus increased in late 1946 as mass famine loomed over the Ukrainian countryside.

Central authorities' decision to recover collective farmland and to begin prosecuting illegal appropriations in late 1946 was part of a broader reversal of a wartime policy of 'self-supply' that had encouraged local authorities to appropriate this land in the first place. Self-supply involved central authorities devolving power to local ones to organise their local economies and food sources, as the central economy was directed towards military consumption.[26] This policy continued in the territories where Soviet power was re-established from late 1943 onwards, such as Ukraine. Once the war was over, central authorities sought to recover the power they had ceded to local levels, along with land and control over food production in the countryside.[27]

This was a difficult process of recovery. Self-supply had worked well in providing food and economic needs on the local level across the Soviet

---

[25] Trade unions usually distributed *podsobnoe khoziaistvo* among their members who worked at the enterprises to which the land was distributed. See Stephen Lovell, *Summerfolk: A History of the Dacha, 1710–2000* (Ithaca: Cornell University Press, 2003), 164–8.

[26] On the devolution of authority to the local level in wartime, see William Moskoff, *The Bread of Affliction: The Food Supply in the USSR during World War II* (New York: Cambridge University Press, 1990); John Barber and Mark Harrison, *The Soviet Home Front, 1941–1945: A Social and Economic History of the USSR in World War II* (London and New York: Longman, 1991); Peter Hachten, 'Property Relations and the Economic Organization of Soviet Russia, 1941–1948', PhD dissertation, University of Chicago, 2005). On the re-establishment of post-war control over liberated territories, see Sanford R. Lieberman, 'The Re-Sovietization of Formerly Occupied Territories of the USSR during World War II', in Sanford R. Lieberman et al., eds., *The Soviet Empire Reconsidered* (Boulder: Westview, 1994), 49–67. On the restoration of central control over the localities, see Oleg Khlevniuk, ed., *Politbiuro TsK VKP(b) i Sovet Ministrov SSSR 1945–1953* (Moscow: Rosspen, 2002); V. Denisov, A. V. Kvashonkin, L. Malashenko, A. Iu. Miniuk, M. Iu. Prozumenshchikov and O. V. Khlevniuk, eds., *TsK VKP(b) i regional'nye partiinye komitety 1945–1953* (Moscow: Rosspen, 2004); and Yoram Gorlizki, 'Ordinary Stalinism: The Council of Ministers and the Soviet Neopatrimonial State, 1946–1953', *Journal of Modern History* 74, no. 4 (2002), 699–736.

[27] Urban residents received smaller plots to use as small vegetable gardens (*ogorodnichestvo*), though this land was generally not affected by the campaign.

Union and continued to work reasonably well after the war. In appropriating the land, local authorities cultivated millions of hectares of state-owned collective farmland not in use by collective farms due to massive shortages of labour, livestock and machinery during both the war and its immediate aftermath.[28] Local authorities were legally permitted to appropriate such 'not in use' farmland in consultation with farm leaders, though they often appropriated whatever land they wanted with or without consultation.[29] Authorities illegally appropriated valuable land close to urban and industrial centres that was required to feed workers and meet local food demands. They also appropriated land either to feed themselves or to generate profit from selling food and agricultural products. In some cases, the utilitarian and corrupt uses of land were difficult to disentangle. Local authorities were supposed to return land to the farms at the end of the war, as self-supply from the agricultural sector gave way to the pre-war norm. Yet some authorities kept it, either because they feared returning the land would reveal their illegal acquisition of it or because they still needed the land they had acquired. In some cases, local authorities continued appropriating more land after the war and even after the 1946 campaign. Either way, it was now mostly illegal for local authorities to keep or continue to appropriate any collective farmland, unless specific authorisation was received from their superiors. As we will see below, this was given less often after the 1946 campaign. We can thus rebrand the continuation of this wartime policy of 'self-supply' in terms of land usage after 1946 as an illegal one.[30]

If the broader clash between local and central authorities over land usage was bound to happen after the war, then it was also bound to happen in the most devastated parts of the Soviet Union, such as the Ukrainian

---

[28] Large tracts of collective farmland were uncultivated due to the destruction of farms and massive losses of agricultural labour. Ukraine's pre-war population was heavily reduced upon liberation due to wartime casualties, conscription, exile and forced labour in Germany, and mass deportations and then population exchanges, which continued into the post-war period. In the capital Kyiv, for instance, the pre-war population of 1 million was reduced to 220,000 by December 1943. See Martin J. Blackwell, *Kyiv as Regime City: The Return of Soviet Power after Nazi Occupation* (Rochester: University of Rochester Press, 2016), 22. On the legal appropriation of collective farmland in Ukraine during the war, see T. V. Vrons'ka, *V umovakh viiny. Zhyttia ta pobut naselennia mist Ukraïny (1943–1945 rr.)* (Kyiv: Instytut istoriï Ukraïny NAN Ukraïny, 1994), 56–7.

[29] On illegal sales and other appropriations of collective farmland, not discussed by Vrons'ka, *V umovakh viiny*, as a major problem in non-occupied areas of the Soviet Union during the war, see Arutiunian, *Sovetskoe krest'ianstvo*, 329–30, and H. Kessler and G. E. Kornilov, eds., *Kolkhoznaia zhizn' na Urale, 1935–1953* (Moscow: Rosspen, 2006), 18. Chapters 1 and 2 discuss the scale of illegal appropriations of collective farmland in Kyiv Oblast.

[30] Specifically, self-supply in the post-war period here refers to the continual use of *podsobnoe khoziaistvo* taken from collective farmland by officials, factories and institutions after 1946.

countryside. Here food and other resource demands were least well met by rationing and other resource distribution systems from the time of liberation in late 1943. This problem was faced primarily by those dependent on *podsobnoe khoziaistvo* and/or food rations to survive, such as workers, clerical employees, schoolteachers and lower-level state officials living in rural areas and especially rural peripheries of cities and urban towns. Local authorities maintained the policy of self-supply on their behalf, and especially on behalf of their factories and institutions that were engaged in the reconstruction of local economies alongside agriculture. These people generally received fewer of the meagre benefits of post-war reconstruction in Ukraine to which they were entitled and of which their compatriots in the major urban areas such as Kyiv received more. With less entitlement to food rations and less ability to access them, rural workers/officials depended also on their *podsobnoe khoziaistvo* to survive.[31]

The opportunity for local authorities in Ukraine to continue pursuing self-supply after the war was also greatest in Kyiv Oblast, which experienced the highest level of disorganisation in the structure of land usage and tenure in all of Ukraine. Confusion reigned over exactly which land had belonged to individual collective farms, and thus which had been stolen from them and was supposed to be returned.[32] Local authorities exploited – indeed, fomented – this confusion to conceal the extent of land they had taken illegally and to continue appropriating more.[33] They undertook the most extensive project across Ukraine to keep it, sometimes violently, after the 1946 campaign sought to identify stolen land and return it to the collective farm sector.

The timing of this clash over land between central and local authorities was precipitated by the failed 1946 summer grain harvest caused by a mass drought across the western parts of the Soviet Union. By September 1946,

---

[31] Post-war reconstruction, though onerous and difficult for everyone, was much more successful from the viewpoint of those sitting atop the hierarchy for food and resource distribution in the cities. They ate relatively well from 1944 onwards and, though accessing the food and resources to which they were entitled was a laborious and competitive task, of which much has been written, there was at least something to fight over. Outside the cities, there was much less. For an account of the successes of post-war reconstruction in the immediate post-liberation period in Ukraine, especially in agriculture, see Vrons'ka, *V umovakh viiny*.

[32] Land tenure established a farm's enduring right to use specific tracts of land and was conferred on farms by the authorities.

[33] This was a difficult and laborious process given that so many of the relevant land records were destroyed during the war in Ukraine, but most of the oblasts – except Kyiv – managed to make great strides towards this reorganisation by 1947. It is not coincidental that this lag accompanied the greatest delays in the return of illegally approved farmland and continuing post-war appropriations after 1946 (see Chapter 1).

the state authorities had collected much less grain from the countryside than they had anticipated and were fearful of famine. They lost all patience with growing evidence of the continuation of self-supply across the Soviet Union. They understood this as symptomatic of the continuation of the 'liberal' wartime practices of local officials, rural workers and *kolkhozniki* with regard to land usage and considered such practices partly to blame for the food crisis. The massive campaign launched in September 1946 forcibly recovered the land appropriated from farms, further criminalised this practice and prosecuted officials for having made egregious appropriations and/or delaying returning the land.

The primary signal of the campaign was directed to *kolkhozniki*: that the repressive pre-war order in the countryside would replace the 'liberal' wartime one. This campaign affected *kolkhozniki* who had lived within the pre-1939 borders of the Soviet Union and less so the non-collectivised rural areas of western Ukraine/eastern Poland that came under Soviet control briefly from September 1939 until the German invasion in June 1941, and then again from 1944.[34] *Kolkhozniki* in the pre-1939 Soviet territories suffered under this campaign because many had illegally expanded the size of their private plot land after liberation in late 1943, that is that land on which they were permitted to grow their own food, by appropriating it from land that belonged to their collective farms and was used to grow food for the state. Many kept their expanded private plot in the post-war period, as it remained their only real food source, often with the connivance of farm leaderships and even local officials until the campaign, when they lost large chunks of it. This did not happen in Raska and Bila Tserkva and some other areas of Kyiv Oblast. Authorities had taken most of the fertile collective farm and private plot land that had belonged to *kolkhozniki* before the war and returned neither in the 1946 campaign.

Although the campaign was directed against *kolkhozniki*, its impact was felt just as keenly by workers/officials in rural areas. Illegal land expansions by *kolkhozniki* across Ukraine accounted for less land illegally appropriated from the collective farm sector than did workers' *podsobnoe khoziaistvo*. Of the almost 1 million hectares of this land slated for return to the collective farm sector by the end of 1946 in Ukraine, more than 70 per cent came

---

[34] The campaign was launched in the very small number of collective farms in these areas, such as in Lviv, which had forty-five farms by the end of 1946. The west Ukrainian countryside was inhabited mostly by individual farmers. See Central State Archive of Public Organisations of Ukraine (Tsentral'nyi derzhavnyi arkhiv hromadskykh ob'iednan' Ukraïny – TsDAHOU) f. 1, op. 23, d. 4805, ll. 13–14.

from institutions and factories, 20 per cent from workers and their families as *podsobnoe khoziaistvo*, and the remainder from *kolkhozniki*'s private plots expanded beyond their legal size.[35] Although there were significant exceptions, *kolkhozniki* often suffered a reduction – though a serious one – in the size of their private plots in the campaign, whereas the entirety of many workers'/officials' *podsobnoe khoziaistvo* was confiscated. Not all, but hundreds of thousands of rural workers/officials in Ukraine thus lost all of the *podsobnoe khoziaistvo* they accessed through their factories/institutions, while 208,000 lost whatever land they had appropriated and cultivated as *podsobnoe khoziaistvo* without authorisation in the countryside.[36]

The timing of the campaign and loss of *podsobnoe khoziaistvo* also could not have been worse for rural workers/officials in Ukraine. Partly as a response to the failed grain harvest, Moscow removed bread ration entitlements for all rural dwellers in the Soviet Union (not *kolkhozniki*, who had never received them) and their dependants in September 1946.[37] This affected more than 2.5 million people in Ukraine, 647,000 of whom Ukraine's leaders feared might die without bread rations.[38] By the end of 1946, workers who had lost *podsobnoe khoziaistvo* could not access bread rations, and those who had lost their ration entitlement could not acquire land to grow food.[39] In short, the state was not feeding its rural workers/officials and was denying them the ability to feed themselves as famine approached.

The clash between local and central authorities over land peaked at this critical point when hundreds of thousands of workers faced starvation in rural areas and urban peripheries. Local officials across Ukraine launched

---

[35] Central State Archive of Supreme Bodies of Power and Government of Ukraine (Tsentral'nyi derzhavnyi arkhiv vyshchykh orhaniv vlady ta upravlinnia Ukraïny – TsDAVOU) f. r-2, op. 7, d. 5032, ll. 219–220.

[36] TsDAVOU f. r-2, op. 7, d. 5032, ll. 219–220 (discussed in Chapter 1).

[37] Across the Soviet Union, pre-famine vulnerabilities among workers were widespread due to limited food supply. As Nicholas Ganson argues, 'problems with [food] distribution, stemming largely from the limitations of the production and trade network, *preceded* the failed harvest of 1946': Ganson, *Soviet Famine*, 56.

[38] TsDAHOU f. 1, op. 23, d. 4023, ll. 209–210.

[39] This affected low-level officials, workers, clerical employees and their families; 27.5 million lost their ration entitlement Union-wide. See Postanovlenie Sovmina no. 380 'Ob ekonomii i raskhodovanii khleba' (27 September 1946) in Filtzer, *Soviet Workers*, 52. Workers dealt with the cut in rations in a number of ways, including increasing their consumption of other available foods (potatoes, cabbage, etc.) from their reserves and purchasing food at their work places. Donald Filtzer argues that workers could stave off starvation in this manner – even if their general health deteriorated significantly – until late 1947 when the food situation improved. More detailed analysis of mortality in the famine may be required to clarify this point. For city workers in Bila Tserkva who kept their ration cards, prices on basic commodities such as bread increased by three times in September 1946, which made the situation difficult also for 'the lucky ones'. See Ganson, *Soviet Famine*, 57.

massive protests with their respective superiors on the workers' behalf, or rather on behalf of the factories and institutions to which rural officials/ workers belonged. They were mainly concerned that the factories and institutions would have to close if their employees lost their food source in land or rations and that broader chaos might result from mass unemployment and starvation.[40] These protests spread up the vertical hierarchy of Ukrainian government from *raion* to oblast level until Ukraine's central authorities, its republican leaders, had little choice but to convey them to Moscow.

While republican leaders, especially the head of the Communist Party (Bolshevik) of Ukraine (CP(b)U), Nikita Khrushchev, were aligned with Moscow on returning land to the sector and establishing control over it, they sided with their subordinates on the matter of the removal of both rations and land from workers in rural areas at the same time. Although it is not widely known, so did 'Iron' Lazar Kaganovich, one of Joseph Stalin's closest allies. Kaganovich was one of the leading officials who had spear-headed the forced collectivisation of the Ukrainian peasantry at the begin-ning of the 1930s. This included the rapacious requisitioning of food from newly established collective farms, which helped to cause, along with a range of other factors, the 1932–3 famine that killed millions of people.[41] Who better than Kaganovich for Stalin to send to Ukraine to pull Khrushchev into line over his 'lax' attitude towards requisitioning food from collective farms during the famine and over his general complaints about the food crisis in Ukraine?[42] Kaganovich replaced Khrushchev as

[40] See TsDAVOU f. r-2, op. 7, d. 5050. For appeals in late 1946 and their continuation into 1947, see d. 5038. See also specific complaints made by local authorities to Kaganovich in O. M. Veselova, 'Pisliavoienna trahediia. Holod 1946–1947 rr. v Ukraïni', *Ukraïnskyi istorychnyi zhurnal* no. 6 (2006), 111. Factories, workers and institutions deemed not to have illegally appropriated land or kept it beyond their wartime agreements were allowed to keep it. Factory farms and other forms of subsistence land generally stayed with factories, though these farms suffered the damaging conse-quences of drought like the others. See Filtzer, *Soviet Workers*, 70–5, on factory farms and 61–2 on railway authorities complaining to state and party bodies.

[41] See a seminal work in the vast literature on this famine, R. W. Davies and S. G. Wheatcroft, *The Industrialisation of Soviet Russia 5. The Years of Hunger: Soviet Agriculture, 1931–1933* (Basingstoke: Palgrave Macmillan, 2004).

[42] *Kolkhozniki* faced starvation too, but not because of the end of bread rationing, as they never were entitled to such rations in the first place. The failed harvest slashed the already meagre wages they received for their collective farm work, often paid in food rather than money, while the reduction of their private plot land lessened their ability to grow their own food. Khrushchev had made appeals to Stalin on behalf of *kolkhozniki* suffering from famine, but most officials were not much concerned with their plight. Kaganovich especially was mostly unsupportive, given his role in the 1932–3 Ukrainian famine and his enduring anti-*kolkhoznik* attitudes evident at the February 1947 All-Union Central Committee Plenum on Agriculture. With regard to aid, Kaganovich was clearly supporting food aid only to enable *kolkhozniki* to at least commence the spring 1947 sowing season,

First Secretary of the CP(b)U from March to December 1947 and did as Stalin expected in continuing to extract food from the collective farm sector with exemplary ruthlessness.[43] But it is clear now from the archives that, at least with regard to rural workers/officials, Kaganovich had softened to Khrushchev's mould by mid-1947. He pleaded with Stalin to restore rations to 647,000 Ukrainian workers, officials and family members in rural areas who were starving. He especially appealed for more food relief on behalf of children in state homes who had been orphaned or abandoned by their starving parents there in the hope that they would be fed. Neither appeal met with much success.[44] Kaganovich, Khrushchev and others at the republican level of government continued to ask for concessions in other areas but understood Stalin's message: to continue to implement the shift away from self-supply, to reduce rural food consumption and to re-establish central control over the collective farm sector. Most officials in the party and state structure at the local level fell into line.[45]

Leading officials in Kyiv Oblast did not. At both the oblast and *raion* level, officials mounted the challenge to their own republican authorities and central ones in Moscow by continuing the policy of self-supply secretly. These officials included *raion*- and oblast-level state and party officials, party secretaries in different *raiony* and, at the top of the hierarchy, the deputy chairman of the state government authority (*obliispolkom*) of agricultural affairs in Kyiv Oblast, S. K. Dvornikov. He was one of the senior officials responsible for the implementation of the 1946 Campaign on Collective Farm Rules that was supposed to return illegally appropriated land to the collective farm sector. Dvornikov and his allies did help

---

as he made clear in his appeals to Stalin. See Ganson, *Soviet Famine*, 110 and 89. For the earlier period, see V. V. Sazonov, 'Povoiennyi holod v URSR (1946–1947 rr.) i derzhavna polityka', in Instytut istoriï Ukraïny NAN Ukraïny, ed., *Holod v Ukraïni u pershii polovyni XX stolittia. Prychyny ta naslidky (1921–1923, 1932–1933, 1946–1947)* (Kyiv: Instytut istoriï Ukraïny NAN Ukraïny, 2013), 133.

[43] Veselova, 'Pisliavoienna trahediia', 105–6.

[44] As was often the case with leading officials pleading for 'humanitarian' assistance from Stalin, Kaganovich found it difficult to do so without implicitly critiquing Stalin's handling of the famine and ration policy. This is one of the reasons why Kaganovich re-drafted his letter to Stalin numerous times with different co-authors before sending it to him. Each draft contained less of an appeal on behalf of 'humanity' of the starving people than the previous one. For the first draft, see TsDAHOU f. 1, op. 23, d. 4023, ll. 209–210. For the second draft with Kaganovich's annotations, see f. 1, op. 23, d. 4026, l. 22, and for the final version sent to Stalin, ll. 63–64. Veselova writes that a letter by Kaganovich and Khrushchev on this matter was sent to Stalin in May 1947 ('Pisliavoienna trahediia', 111). This letter was one of the earlier drafts located in d. 4023. Kaganovich sent a final version of this same letter to Stalin at the end of May with significant changes, but now not with Khrushchev, but Korniets as his co-author: d. 4026, ll. 63–64.

[45] Stalin did accede to seed loans for collective farms per Kaganovich's request – but not on restoring rations for workers in rural areas: Ganson, *Soviet Famine*, 60.

return thousands of hectares to farms in Kyiv Oblast. But it was exactly his role in returning land that enabled him to do the opposite – to allow illegally appropriated land to remain in the hands of those he chose and to continue to make illegal appropriations years after the end of the campaign.[46] It was this 'appropriator in chief' who libelled Raska's *kolkhozniki* as 'rotten' in the epigraph at the beginning of this book, after throwing them out of his office in Kyiv when they came to plead with him to help them fight off the local authorities and rebuild their farm in 1947.[47]

Dvornikov and a network of local officials, working together and independently, kept land that had been illegally appropriated and took more in spite of both the 1946 campaign and the punishments eventually handed down to them for doing so. Their chief motivation was that the appropriated land was far more valuable to them as *podsobnoe khoziaistvo* than as collective farmland. In the pre-war period these farms, located on urban fringes of Bila Tserkva and adjoining factories near Raska, had generated food surpluses after meeting their quota requirements for central supply. *Kolkhozniki* sold this food at nearby collective farm markets for workers and others to purchase as they were located close to urban and light industrial areas. But in 1945 local authorities clearly did not think that these farms could immediately generate food surpluses for workers if they were rebuilt in Raska, and it was clear that those in operation in Bila Tserkva could not do so at this time. If converted to *podsobnoe khoziaistvo*, this land could provide immediate food to workers who had few other sources of food but whose work was essential to regenerating the various economies required to aid in local urban and industrial reconstruction. In Raska the land was projected to supply food to expand light industry in this rural area, while in Bila Tserkva it provided land for the growing urban workforce in the rural peripheries of the city that were slated for urbanisation.

In a period when resources for rebuilding their devastated areas were scarce, local authorities in Kyiv Oblast were thus transforming, hectare by hectare, land here and elsewhere used by central authorities to operate the collective farm system into self-sustaining land to fund local urban/industrial reconstruction, which they valued more than collective farm rebuilding. This strategy was, on the one hand, a logical fulfilment of the basic premise of collective farming – exploiting land and labour from the countryside to provide for urban and industrial needs. On the other hand, this strategy presented a challenge to central authorities' first right to exploit this land and labour.

---

[46] TsDAVOU f. r-2, op. 7, d. 5035, ll. 12–16.   [47] This meeting is discussed in Chapter 2.

This challenge formed an essential tension between the post-war rebuilding strategies of local and central authorities in Kyiv Oblast. It was within this tension that Koval'skyi and thousands of other *kolkhozniki* were caught as they returned from war seeking to rebuild their farms and villages on land that now belonged to and provided essential food to others. Other *kolkhozniki* were also caught within this tension, but not as tightly as those in Raska and Bila Tserkva. Local authorities' more nefarious motivations for continuing sell-supply help explain why this was the case. Officials appropriated the land belonging to the farms in Raska and Bila Tserkva in 1945 and early 1946 illegally, even by the standards of the more relaxed wartime laws on appropriations. They distributed it to officials in industries and institutions among their client networks, which formed the sinews around the muscles of state, party, government and industry in the skeleton of Soviet governance. Due to the risk of revealing the initial crimes and the numerous parties responsible, local authorities could not follow proper channels to petition superiors at the republican level to keep this land from its recovery by the state in the 1946 campaign. For the same reason, these officials could not allow the *kolkhozniki* in Raska and Bila Tserkva to tell their stories to their superior authorities in Ukraine and certainly not in Moscow. It remained imperative for local officials to coerce the resistant *kolkhozniki* into silence and submission through the most callous means available to them, including beating, starving and arresting them. When superior authorities investigated the abuses *kolkhozniki* claimed they had suffered in numerous letters first to Kyiv and then to Moscow, local officials, like Dvornikov and others, dismissed the *kolkhozniki* as 'rotten'. These 'rotten' *kolkhozniki* not only threatened to get local officials into hot water, but also jeopardised their control of the broader client networks upon which their power was based across the oblast.

The local officials' coercion failed. A core group of *kolkhozniki* on each of the farms refused to leave. By 1948, their numerous letters (supplications) requesting help from superior authorities in Kyiv and Moscow drew the attention of representatives of the Council on Collective Farm Affairs (Sovet po delam kolkhozov), the powerful all-Union government body established to drive the 1946 campaign under Minister of Agriculture Andrei Andreev (see Appendix).[48] Council representatives travelled to the farms and championed the case of the courageous *kolkhozniki* in Raska and Bila Tserkva to their superiors in Moscow. Their case was passed on for consideration to the office of the powerful Central

---

[48] The Council's full name was Sovet po delam kolkhozov pri Sovmin SSSR.

Committee secretary Aleksei Kuznetsov, who was the most prominent leading party figure driving the anti-corruption campaign in the state/party structure.[49] By the middle of 1948, the Council and Kuznetsov's office had joined with republican authorities in Ukraine, including Khrushchev, to force Kyiv Oblast's party organisation (*obkom*) to issue a decree requiring the return of all stolen land and goods from all the farms, their full reconstruction, and punishment of guilty officials, even Dvornikov. All other 'legal appropriations' made by these leading local officials now came under suspicion. It seemed as if, at this point, their entire network of resistance to central rule would unravel.

But this network did not unravel. Nor was this the end point in the struggle between *kolkhozniki* and local authorities. According to a classical understanding of how post-war Stalinism operated, it should have been. There was an order emanating first from powerful agencies and individuals in Moscow and then issued locally for authorities to fall into line, and orders like this were implemented, even if they were implemented badly. Instead, oblast- and *raion*-level officials generally refused to assist in the rebuilding of the farms, protected those named for punishment and, on some farms, abused the *kolkhozniki* even more as punishment for having been successful in securing the decree. When these officials were questioned by their superiors the following year on the status of the farms, by no less a figure than Khrushchev, at a CP(b)U Plenum in front of sixty other delegates, they lied, suggesting the farms were doing well. The questions stopped. But the farms were not doing well at all. There are reports in the archival record of this type of behaviour by officials becoming more and more common by end of the decade in some parts of the Soviet Union. But we have little detail and less clarity about how officials were able to conduct it successfully.[50] The cases of Raska and Bila Tserkva provide both, especially in the example of Dvornikov and his department – a leading local official in agriculture charged with recovering land who used his position to steal it. He thus represented both the means of and the greatest obstacles to the 'successful' restoration of central control in the countryside. This, as discussed below, was an old issue in tsarist and Soviet governance, but it was uniquely problematic in many ways by the late 1940s. If an examination of these cases in Raska and Bila Tserkva opens a window into the broader practice of illegal appropriations and the problems of agricultural reconstruction in rural society, then it also opens a

[49] RGASPI f. 17, op. 122, d. 316, l. 160. [50] See the discussion of corruption in Chapter 3.

window into the broader dysfunction in post-war Stalinism at this time and its consequences for people's lives.

*

The view from these windows offers a picture very different from the various ones of post-war reconstruction and Stalinism offered in the wide literatures. None of these literatures offers an adequate explanation for the atypical cases in Raska and Bila Tserkva or answers sufficiently the broader questions on post-war reconstruction and post-war Stalinism that arise from them. I will explore these limitations and work towards their resolution below. Works on ethnic discrimination in the Soviet Union, for instance, explain that the sort of violence directed by authorities towards ethnic Poles in Raska was common and particularly intense in Ukraine from the mid-1930s, and it continued during the war.[51] Ethnic Poles, like those in Raska who lived within the pre-1939 boundaries of the Soviet Union suffered most in 1937–8, when the Soviet state launched a massive operation to imprison and kill people of 'foreign ethnicity'. These were Soviet citizens belonging to ethnicities with a host nation outside the Soviet Union (Poles, Germans, Koreans and Japanese, among others). After years of supporting the rights of people of these ethnicities to develop their own language and cultures within a Soviet framework, the Soviets reversed this support dramatically from the early 1930s. In the paranoia of potential invasion by foreign powers that gripped the Soviet leadership at the time, instead of expecting Soviet allegiance among people of these ethnicities in return for supporting their ethnic development, the leadership now feared these people might betray Soviet interests to 'their' foreign nations when the latter waged war on the Soviet Union, especially Poland and Germany.[52] Ethnic Poles

[51] As these *kolkhozniki* were pre-1939 Soviet citizens, they were not subject to the population exchange between Ukraine and Poland after the war. On the post-war discrimination against Poles living in Ukraine as part of the broader 're-Sovietisation' of the western borderlands, see Alexander V. Prusin, *The Lands Between: Conflict in the East European Borderlands, 1870–1992* (Oxford: Oxford University Press, 2010), 213.

[52] On the nationalities policies and their reversal, especially in Ukraine, see Terry Martin, 'The Origin of Soviet Ethnic Cleansing', *Journal of Modern History* 70, no. 4 (1998), 813–61. The Polish case was unique, given the Soviets' further intent to export the revolution into Poland. After their defeat in the Soviet–Polish war of 1919–20, the Soviets established Polish National Districts (*polraiony*) as 'autonomous' regions in Ukrainian and Belarusian areas from the late 1920s; these acted as prototypes for a planned future Soviet Poland. On the antecedents of state-driven anti-Polish discrimination in Ukraine in the 1930s and the *polraiony*, see Kate Brown, *A Biography of No Place: From Ethnic Borderland to Soviet Heartland* (Cambridge, MA: Harvard University Press, 2003). On the 'Polish' and other operations of 1937–8, see Bodan Musial, 'The "Polish Operation" of the NKVD: The Climax of the Terror against the Polish Minority in the Soviet Union', *Journal of Contemporary History* 48, no. 1 (2013), 98–124. On the impact of the international political situation

occupying state/party positions and those living in Ukrainian areas border-ing Poland were especially targeted during the 'Polish operation' in 1937–8. In total, 111,000 were sentenced to execution and 28,744 to terms in labour camps; their family members, mostly women and children, were deported to remote areas of the Soviet Union.[53] Fourteen of those arrested in this operation were ethnic Poles from Raska, with only one of them returning to the village.[54]

Ethnic Poles who lived outside these pre-1939 boundaries and were subject to Soviet control during the war also came under suspicion by authorities. This time it was for their supposed association with Polish military forces engaged in a broader conflict with Ukrainian nationalist forces and, at different times, with the Soviets. Civilians bore the brunt of this internecine conflict that raged during and in the immediate aftermath of the war.[55] Many Poles openly supported Soviet power as an attempted defence against Ukrainian nationalist forces; tens of thousands of them were killed by these same nationalists.[56] However, the Soviets still deported almost all Poles from their homes in western Ukraine to eastern Poland as part of a border population exchange with ethnic Ukrainians moving the opposite way. Suspicion towards those who remained or settled in Ukraine remained widespread among Soviet officials.[57]

---

on Soviet paranoia, see O. Khlevniuk, *Khoziain. Stalin i utverzhdenie stalinskoi diktatury* (Moscow: Rosspen, 2010), chs. 5–6.

[53] N. V. Petrov and A. B. Roginskiy, '"Pol'skaia operatsiia" NKVD 1937–1938 gg.', http://old.memo .ru/history/polacy/00485art.htm.

[54] Figures are according to the Ukrainian government's official history of the district in which Raska is located: http://piskivska-gromada.gov.ua/s-raska-23-25-00-23-06-2016/.

[55] The following works focus on the mass violence that continued in the enduring insurgencies of the western borderlands after the war along with massive upheavals of demobilisation, population movement, famine and general chaos across large tracts of the Soviet Union: Alexander Statiev, *The Soviet Counterinsurgency in the Western Borderlands* (Cambridge: Cambridge University Press, 2010); Peter Gatrell and Nick Baron, 'Violent Peacetime: Reconceptualising Displacement and Resettlement in the Soviet–East European Borderlands after the Second World War', in Peter Gatrell and Nick Baron, eds., *Warlands: Population Resettlement and State Reconstruction in the Soviet–East European Borderlands, 1945–1950* (Basingstoke: Palgrave Macmillan, 2009), 255–68. The division between war and peace for millions caught within these upheavals was blurry for the years following 1945, encouraging the re-periodisation of wartime and post-war Stalinism among Soviet historians. See Stephen Lovell, *The Shadow of War: Russia and the USSR, 1941 to the Present* (Oxford and Malden, MA: Wiley-Blackwell, 2010); Chris Ward, 'What Is History? The Case of Late Stalinism', *Rethinking History* 8, no. 3 (2004), 439–58.

[56] On wartime allegiance between Polish and Soviet forces as well as positive attitudes among Polish populations towards Soviet power in comparison to Ukrainian insurgents, see Statiev, *The Soviet Counterinsurgency*, 88.

[57] See Chapter 5 for more discussion of this conflict. On the population exchanges, see Timothy Snyder, *Bloodlands: Europe between Hitler and Stalin* (New York: Basic Books, 2010), 313–39, and broadly, Prusin, *The Lands Between*, and John J. Kulczycki, *Belonging to the Nation: Inclusion and*

This suspicion over the allegiance of 'Poles' to Soviet power was clearly evident in the actions of local authorities in Raska. In response to superior authorities' questions regarding the *kolkhozniki*, local ones claimed, falsely, that the latter were 'traitorous'. They drew on the legacy of the 1937 operation and wartime developments noted above to claim, absurdly, that the Poles in Raska were likely to be assisting Ukrainian nationalist forces still operating in Kyiv Oblast in 1945 – the same forces that had been responsible for killing Poles. But xenophobia is only one factor among many explaining the conduct of local authorities in Raska and, importantly, central authorities paid little attention to these arguments and assisted the *kolkhozniki* in any case.[58] Elsewhere, local authorities abused ethnically Ukrainian *kolkhozniki* around Bila Tserkva as well, because, as in Raska, the purpose of the abuse was to realise their more important strategic interests. And these abuses turned violent in both places not because of the ethnicities of the *kolkhozniki*, but due to their resistance and their continual letters to central authorities in Kyiv and Moscow complaining about their treatment and seeking help. These supplications threatened to, and eventually did, drop the local authorities into hot water.[59]

The vast literature on citizens' supplications to central Soviet authorities promises to help us understand the dynamics of this struggle between *kolkhozniki* and local and central authorities in Raska and Bila Tserkva.[60] Supplications to authorities were a central feature of Stalinism, especially after the war, when post-war expectations for improved living conditions among the wartime generation went increasingly unmet. For *kolkhozniki*, they were perhaps the only avenue to plead for assistance from superior authorities when they were hemmed in by a web of local officials

Exclusion in the Polish–German Borderlands, 1939–1951 (Cambridge, MA: Harvard University Press, 2016).

[58] See Chapter 3 for an in-depth discussion of the difference between central and local authorities' attitudes towards ethnic Poles.

[59] Titles most relevant to this study across the literature include: on corruption, James Heinzen, *The Art of the Bribe: Corruption under Stalin, 1943–1953* (New Haven: Yale University Press, 2016); on the antecedents of state-driven anti-Polish discrimination in Ukraine in the 1930s, Brown, *A Biography of No Place*; on abuses of collective farmers in the 1930s, Sheila Fitzpatrick, *Stalin's Peasants: Resistance and Survival in the Russian Village after Collectivization* (New York: Oxford University Press, 1994).

[60] See Chapter 3 for further discussion of supplications. On the political importance of supplications in Stalinism, see Elena Zubkova, *Poslevoennoe sovetskoe obshchestvo. Politika i povsednevnost', 1945–1953* (Moscow: Rosspen, 1999). For veteran supplicants, see Edele, *Soviet Veterans*, chs. 2, 3 and 8; and Dale, *Demobilized Veterans*. For *kolkhozniki*'s letters to authorities, see Kessler and Kornilov, eds., *Kolkhoznaia zhizn'*, 655–67, and the dedicated *fond* for *kolkhozniki*'s letters to authorities in RGAE f. 9476. For ordinary citizens' supplications, see Elena Yurievna Zubkova et al., *Sovetskaia zhizn', 1945–1953* (Moscow: Rosspen, 2003).

representing the different arms of state, party and police control, who conspired to abuse them with impunity. *Kolkhozniki* generally understood how to present themselves as allies of central authorities against local corruption effectively in their supplications. Koval'skyi's charge of *bezdushnost'* against local officials was one of the most prominent made across the Soviet Union at this time. Most supplications went unmet, but those that employed such language had a better chance of superior authorities intervening on their behalf. Central authorities used the same term, *bezdushnost'*, to blame the problems faced by *kolkhozniki* on local officials rather than, of course, on the policies they had directed these officials to pursue. The dynamics in the supplications from Raska and Bila Tserkva and central authorities' responses thus share significant similarities with other cases across the Soviet Union.

But there are significant differences, too, which limit the capacity of the supplication literature to assist our understanding of the dynamics of the struggle in Raska, Bila Tserkva and elsewhere. This literature does not address supplications of *kolkhozniki* asking to rebuild or operate their collective farms against the wishes of local officials and certainly not as a collective of war veterans, at least in Raska, on the site of German atrocities. Most of it addresses abuses of local officials keeping *kolkhozniki* bonded to their land without providing their end of the bargain in wages, good working conditions and lawful behaviour. That is, the literature addresses the problem of authorities keeping *kolkhozniki* working the land, not trying to kick working *kolkhozniki* off it. This failure thus not only limits our understanding of the anomalies in Raska and Bila Tserkva, but also the broader issue from which these anomalies arise – appropriations of collective farmland. This issue remains fundamentally unaddressed or misunderstood in this and the literature on Soviet agriculture, especially that concerning the immediate post-war period.

Historians of Soviet agriculture have written very little on appropriations, especially after the 1946 campaign, and certainly nothing on officials refusing to allow the rebuilding/operation of farms. All reduce appropriations, at least those made by authorities/institutions and factories, to a wartime problem that was more or less resolved by the 1946 campaign with the return of millions of hectares of land to the sector.[61] Their major focus in this literature on the wartime and post-war periods is

---

[61] Arutiunian, *Sovetskoe krest'ianstvo*, 329–30. For this problem in the Urals, see Kessler and Kornilov, eds., *Kolkhoznaia zhizn'*, 18; A. N. Trifonov, 'Sel'skokhoziaistvennye podsobnye khoziaistva Urala v gody Velikoi Otechestvennoi voiny', *Istoriko-pedagogicheskie chteniia* 10 (2006), 293; V. P. Motrevich, 'Vosstanovlenie sel'skogo khoziaistva na Urale v pervye poslevoennye gody (1946–1950

on another major part of the strategy of self-supply – *kolkhozniki* expanding their private plots to supply themselves with food – and the massive post-war recovery of these 'excess lands' by authorities in the 1946 campaign.[62] Along with the pilfering of farm produce and collective farm property by *kolkhozniki* and authorities alike, plot enlargement flourished in response to wartime food shortages and relaxation of state control over the sector. Now central authorities were reasserting this control and hoped to force *kolkhozniki* to spend more time working on the collective farm and less on their private plots, partly by reducing the size of the latter. Unlike the campaign's greater 'success' of returning collective farmland appropriated by factories, institutions and workers, this 1946 campaign was only temporarily successful in returning millions of hectares from these private plots, as *kolkhozniki* resumed expanding them thereafter as well as spending more time working on them than in the collective.[63]

Central authorities were squeezing the countryside in late 1946 to reduce rural food consumption after the failed grain harvest. At the same time as they denied rural workers/officials land and reduced *kolkhozniki*'s land with which they could feed themselves, central authorities encouraged urban residents to do so by allowing them to keep or acquire small plots of garden space to produce food for subsistence (*ogorodnichestvo*). This policy was widespread during the war, and these plots, unlike those for *kolkhozniki* and workers/officials in rural areas, were not recovered for collective farm use in 1946. *Ogorodnichestvo* continued after the end of the first post-war decade as a concession to the reality of continuing urban food shortages. It was a way for urban residents to supplement their food rations at the expense of those who received none or were stripped of the capacity to produce food for themselves from land they had lost. It is indicative of central authorities' commitment to urban welfare at the expense of rural.[64]

gg.)', *Agrarnyi vestnik Urala* 96, no. 4 (2012), 24; and, broadly, M. N. Denisevich, *Individual'nye khoziaistva na Urale, 1930–1985* (Ekaterinburg: Institute of History and Archeology, 1991).

[62] See the seminal post-Soviet works on agriculture including: O. M. Verbitskaia, *Rossiiskoe krest'ianstvo. Ot Stalina k Khrushchevu, seredina 40-kh–nachalo 60-kh godov* (Moscow: Nauka, 1992); and V. P. Popov, *Rossiiskaia derevnia posle voiny (iiun' 1945–mart 1953)* (Moscow: Prometei, 1993).

[63] TsDAVOU f. r-2, op. 7, d. 7024, ll. 83, 86. See Chapter 4 for this discussion.

[64] *Ogorodnichestvo* is widely addressed by historians, though they too usually focus on the war years. Both *ogorodnichestvo* and *podsobnoe khoziaistvo* were intended to combat the massive shortages in the wartime rationing system in urban areas. As these shortages continued well into the post-war period, so did *ogorodnichestvo*, although *podsobnoe khoziaistvo*, which had grown during the war at the expense of collective farmland, was reduced as the land was returned to the farms in the 1946 campaign: Postanovlenie Soveta Ministrov SSSR, 'O kollektivnom i individual'nom ogorodnichestve i sadovodstve rabochikh i sluzhachshikh' (24 February 1949). Those who focus on the post-war years tend to agree on the concession argument (Lovell, *Summerfolk*, 156), and the state's relaxation of its assault on the private trade in foodstuffs (Julie Hessler, 'A Postwar Perestroika?

Those few historians who address appropriations of collective farmland by officials, factories and institutions see it mostly as a method of self-supply in the countryside similar to that of *kolkhozniki*. It was motivated by the breakdown of central supply of food and resources in the war and, indeed, this enduring anti-rural bias over food allocation. These historians focus on how these agents appropriated – or colluded with farm leaderships during the war to 'rent' – collective farmland, paying the farm for the land and using it to feed their workers. This arrangement provided further benefits to the farms in addition to cash, as the reduced sown area of the farm also reduced their obligatory deliveries of foodstuffs to the state. The Soviet sociologist Yu. V. Arutiunian's ground-breaking work in the 1960s on Soviet agriculture put forward this interpretation, which has remained dominant since and has been developed by a few post-Soviet historians who argue that much of this land was returned to farms in the 1946 campaign. These historians locate the major economic consequences of appropriations made by institutions only upon its return to the collective farm sector, as it was accompanied by a proportionate increase in food delivery obligations to the state. The larger amount of land each farm possessed and which was currently under cultivation, the larger amount of foodstuffs it was required to deliver to the state. Unable to farm the land efficiently due to their continuing lack of resources and labour, even after the mass demobilisation in 1946 that flooded the countryside with labour (albeit temporarily), farms were unable to meet these heightened delivery requirements and plunged further into debt and destitution, with some farm leaderships prosecuted heavily. This was a major problem for these farms – but only one side of it.[65]

The analysis of post-war land appropriations in Kyiv Oblast in this book introduces the other side of the problem into the literature and changes the way we need to think about land abuses in the collective farm sector at this time. First, the campaign was not as effective in returning land to the sector

---

Toward a History of Private Enterprise in the USSR', *Slavic Review* 57, no. 3 (1998), 524). On the role of private horticulture in defining public and private space in post-war Stalinism, see Charles P. Hachten, 'Separate yet Governed: The Representation of Soviet Property Relations in Civil Law and Public Discourse', in Lewis Siegelbaum, ed., *Borders of Socialism: Private Spheres of Soviet Russia* (New York: Palgrave Macmillan, 2006), 65–82, and generally, V. V. Kondrashin, 'Krest'ianstvo i sel'skoe khoziastvo SSSR v gody Velikoi Otechestvennoi voiny', *Izvestiia Samarskogo nauchnogo tsentra RAN* no. 2 (2005), 295; A. N. Trifonov, 'Ogorodnichestvo i reshenie prodovol'stvennoi problemy na Urale v gody Velikoi Otechestvennoi voiny', *Istoriko-pedagocheskie chteniia* no. 9 (2005), 214–27.
[65] Arutiunian, *Sovetskoe krest'ianstvo*, 329–30; Trifonov, 'Ogorodnichestvo'. For this problem in the Urals, see Kessler and Kornilov, eds., *Kolkhoznaia zhizn'*, 18, and Motrevich, 'Vosstanovlenie sel'skogo khoziaistva na Urale', 24.

as historians had previously imagined. A much larger amount of land appropriated by local officials, institutions and factories remained in their hands after 1946. Newly declassified sources from the Council on Collective Farm Affairs indicate tens of thousands of hectares of such land in Kyiv Oblast and more across Ukraine.[66] Moreover, they indicate that in Kyiv Oblast local authorities conducted new illegal appropriations after the 1946 campaign until the end of the decade. Second, some *kolkhozniki* did not despair but fought hard for the return of their land across Kyiv Oblast. This land, often the most fertile, was used for both collective and private purposes and had been taken from them forcibly along with their livestock, resources, buildings and machinery. The farms could conduct neither collective nor private farm work properly. In these cases, unlike in most others across the Soviet Union, collective and private work was not mutually exclusive but interdependent. For these *kolkhozniki*, recovering land and resources to become official and functioning farms was essential to their capacity to feed themselves and maintain their rights to their land.

These *kolkhozniki* need to be treated differently from many thousands more who fought to recover their plots of private land, which had been reduced to almost nothing or completely confiscated by overzealous local officials incorrectly implementing the 1946 Campaign on Collective Farm Rules. Only some regions were affected by this problem, as the campaign was never intended to confiscate all private plot land, but only to reduce its size to the legal limit. These *kolkhozniki* too were left with little means to survive as famine approached. But they generally did survive, because this error was readily apparent to other officials, mostly from the Council on Collective Farm Affairs also implementing the campaign. These officials worked hard to get land back to the *kolkhozniki* quickly as the spring sowing period neared in 1947. But those in Raska and Bila Tserkva would have to wait until after the famine to get their land back – and then only part of it – in 1948. In 1946 their farms were not visible to the Council, located as they were outside or on the edges of the collective farm system, along with the most impoverished farms that attracted little attention, let alone assistance from authorities.[67] Here they had least protection or recourse against these debilitating abuses because it was here that local authorities could act with greatest impunity.

---

[66] See Chapter 1 for figures.
[67] See Chapter 3 for a discussion of the self-perpetuating relationship of impoverishment and ignorance in the collective farm sector.

We know least about what life was like for people living on these edges. We know little of how the expansion of city or industrial limits into farm areas affected the many more *kolkhozniki* who remained on the land in the post-war period.[68] This is not only because historians have not addressed the complexities of land abuses in the sector explored here. Their focus in the post-war period has primarily been on how abuses in the collective farm system precipitated its evisceration – on how millions of other *kolkhozniki* across the Soviet Union left the post-war collective farm system, sometimes illegally, to escape its servitude and, indeed, potential starvation during and after the 1946–7 famine. Millions fled to other rural areas or cities to become urbanites and start a new life with greater privileges compared to *kolkhozniki*, hoping to become 'people of the first sort', as one Russian historian puts it, in a better post-war Soviet society.[69] This book examines the thousands of *kolkhozniki* across Kyiv Oblast and in other areas of Ukraine who remained on the land and sought a way back into a collective farm system as a way to survive and recover their pre-war lives.

How could this have happened to these *kolkhozniki* in Stalin's Soviet Union? How could Stalin's local authorities usurp the centre's right to exploit *kolkhozniki* by stopping them from rebuilding or operating the centre's mechanism of this exploitation – the collective farm – and eventually get away with it? More broadly, how could local authorities continue illegal appropriations for years after the 1946 campaign? Some insights into these questions are provided by works published mostly after the opening of the Soviet archives from the late 1980s on local authorities pursuing interests in opposition to or, at least, different from demands from central authorities (localism) as well as works on corruption and post-war transitions in Stalinist society. Their common contention is that dysfunction between levels of government was not an aberration, but a central feature of Stalinism.[70] The problem is that the 'dysfunction' represented by illegal

---

[68] Histories of Soviet 'urbanisation' generally do not address this issue. For a summary of recent works, see Thomas M. Bohn, 'Soviet History as a History of Urbanization', *Kritika: Explorations in Russian and Eurasian History* 16, no. 2 (2015), 451–8.

[69] Verbitskaia, *Rossiiskoe krest'ianstvo*, 18; Elena Zubkova, *Russia after the War: Hopes, Illusions and Disappointments, 1945–1957*, trans. and ed. by Hugh Ragsdale (Armonk, NY: M. E. Sharpe, 1998); Popov, *Rossiiskaia derevnia*.

[70] Donald J. Raleigh, ed. *Provincial Landscapes: Local Dimensions of Soviet Power, 1917–1953* (Pittsburgh: University of Pittsburgh Press, 2001). For local authorities' liberal interpretation of central policies in post-war Kyiv, see Blackwell, *Kyiv as Regime City*, 102–30. On the dangerous though necessary practice of local officials adapting central directives to local conditions, see Kees Boterbloem, *Life and Death under Stalin: Kalinin Province, 1945–1953* (Montreal: McGill-Queen's University Press, 1999), 259; and Karl D. Qualls, *From Ruins to Reconstruction: Urban Identity in Soviet Sevastopol after World War II* (Ithaca: Cornell University Press, 2009). Other notable local

appropriations looks very different from the dysfunction addressed in these works and, again, limits their capacity to explain it.

These newer works on localism develop an older tradition of examining the 'independent' and often illegal actions of local officials evading central policies whose fulfilment would be injurious to their localities, focusing mainly on the 1930s.[71] Local officials struggled to balance the impossible demands made of them by their superiors with their local responsibilities.[72] These 'revisionist' historians worked against the 'totalitarian model' predominant among Western historians in the aftermath of World War II.[73] This model understood Stalinism as an all-powerful regime imposed on a powerless and passive society, which ruled through violence and propaganda and governed via a network of local authorities that fulfilled central authorities' orders unquestioningly. Post-war or 'late' Stalinism was not very different from pre-war Stalinism, but only a late chronological stage of a political system that re-emerged after the interregnum of war to pursue its totalitarian aims with more vigour.

At least the view of centre–local relations within this model has been eroded by the barrage of newer local studies based on available Soviet archival material that focus on dysfunction in Stalinism.[74] This dysfunction peaked in the post-war period, which was not only a 'stage' of

studies include Jeffrey W. Jones, *Everyday Life and the 'Reconstruction' of Soviet Russia during and after the Great Patriotic War, 1943–1948* (Bloomington: Slavica Publishers, 2008). Recent Russian studies examine the post-war *nomenklatura*'s rise to power and how they shaped post-war society in the Urals: Oleg Leibovich, *V gorode M. Ocherki sotsial'noi povsednevnosti sovetskoi provintsii* (Moscow: Rosspen, 2008).

[71] For early revisionism, see Merle Fainsod, *Smolensk under Soviet Rule* (Cambridge, MA: Harvard University Press, 1958), and Sheila Fitzpatrick, *The Commissariat of Enlightenment: Soviet Organization of Education and the Arts under Lunacharsky, 1917–1921* (Cambridge: Cambridge University Press, 1970).

[72] Graham Gill argues that Stalinism placed Soviet cadres in an impossible position, demanding they pursue the transcendent final goal of communism but also follow party and state laws often inimical to its realisation. If cadres broke these laws in pursuit of this transcendent goal, 'they could be accused of breaching party discipline, but if they adhered to those instructions and failed to achieve the goals that had been set down, they could be accused of political failure': Graham Gill, 'The Communist Party and the Weakness of Bureaucratic Norms', in Don K. Rowney and Eugene Huskey, eds., *Russian Bureaucracy and the State: Officialdom from Alexander III to Vladimir Putin* (Basingstoke: Palgrave Macmillan, 2009), 123. Donald Filtzer also argues that Stalinism imposed impossible demands on cadres and its citizenry, requiring them to act illegally for it to function and then punishing them for it, making criminals of the bulk of its citizenry. See his thesis on the 'psychology of circumvention' in Filtzer, *Soviet Workers*, 250.

[73] For classic 'totalitarian' texts, see Carl J. Friedrich, ed., *Totalitarianism* (Cambridge, MA: Harvard University Press, 1953); Carl J. Friedrich and Zbigniew Brzezinski, *Totalitarian Dictatorship and Autocracy* (Cambridge, MA: Harvard University Press, 1956).

[74] On the broader state of these schools and 'post-revisionism', see Sheila Fitzpatrick, 'Revisionism in Soviet History', *History and Theory* 46, no. 1 (2007), 77–91, and M. Rendle, 'Post-Revisionism: The Continuing Debate on Stalinism', *Intelligence and National Security* 25, no. 3 (2010), 370–88.

Stalinism, but a 'phenomenon in its own right'.[75] Although formal control was re-established by central authorities, their capacity to administer the country in the way they desired was diminished in comparison to the 1930s. Wartime exigencies of mass violence, insurgency, hunger and massive population dislocations endured into this chaotic post-war period when Soviet society was shifting from wartime to post-war economic and social settings.[76] In this literature, local authorities traverse, often successfully, the tangled webs of state and party structures in their dealings with the centre to pursue independent policies and practices. When questioned by their superiors about their failure to follow concrete laws and policies, local authorities typically justified their independent conduct with reference to broader political loyalties. Central and local authorities shaped one another through their interactions, within a clearly dynamic relationship.[77]

Corruption is perhaps a key platform on which centre–local relations shaped one another in this period. We now know that Moscow allowed corrupt leadership networks embedded in party institutions to operate after the war, in exchange for their loyalty to the centre. Such 'deals' between centre and periphery, and tolerance of corrupt activity among officials everywhere in exchange for political loyalty, developed after Moscow had launched massive and ultimately futile anti-corruption campaigns in the post-war period.[78] The premise of much of this literature is that central policies had engendered the very criminal practices in governance on the local level about which central authorities complained or which they came to accept.[79] Criminality was begat by the criminal political system, whose largest footprint was made in the last years of Stalin's rule.

There is much evidence to support this argument in the case studies covered here. This book thus joins the barrage of 'revisionist' archival-based 'local histories' flung against the totalitarian models of Stalinism, but from a new trajectory fundamentally different from the others. Officials in

---

[75] Juliane Fürst, 'Introduction', in Juliane Fürst, ed., *Late Stalinist Russia: Society between Reconstruction and Reinvention* (Abingdon, UK: Routledge, 2006), 1.

[76] Ibid., 7. Moshe Lewin, *The Soviet Century* (New York: Verso, 2005), ch. 4; Denisov et al., eds., *TsK VKP(b) i regional'nye partiinye komitety*.

[77] See Donald J. Raleigh, 'Introduction', in Raleigh, ed., *Provincial Landscapes*, 1–13.

[78] Denisov et al., eds., *TsK VKP(b) i regional'nye partiinye komitety*, 6, 123; Heinzen, *The Art of the Bribe*; Cynthia Hooper, 'A Darker Big Deal: Concealing Party Crimes in the Post-Second World War Era', in Fürst, ed., *Late Stalinist Russia*, 142–64; and Juliette Cadiot and John Angell, 'Equal before the Law? Soviet Justice, Criminal Proceedings against Communist Party Members, and the Legal Landscape in the USSR from 1945 to 1953', *Jahrbücher für Geschichte Osteuropas* 61, no. 2 (2013), 249–69.

[79] Heinzen, *The Art of the Bribe*, 1. For further works and discussion on corruption, see Chapter 3.

Kyiv Oblast did not arbitrate between local needs and central demands with the type of deal making and negotiation among political networks that was common in Stalinism. Fundamentally, they mobilised these networks not to pursue self-enrichment via corruption, but to attack the system's economic base of collective farming to continue a wartime strategy of economic survival in the post-war period once it had been declared illegal. Central authorities understood this not only as a crime, but also as a challenge to their authority, and handed down punishments to officials. These officials nonetheless mobilised their networks to avoid serving their punishments and continued to commit such crimes until the end of the 1940s in Kyiv Oblast and, importantly, in other areas as well. This behaviour is fundamentally different from the activities covered in these works on post-war localism and sits outside the conceptual framework of dynamic, contested centre–local relations that shaped one another through their exchange. This behaviour was an abrogation of exchange, not an expression of it.

To make sense of this behaviour, we cannot simply locate it within a context of massive transitions in Soviet society in the immediate aftermath of the war, as others do. We need to locate this behaviour at the disjuncture between different understandings of the meaning of this transition from wartime to post-war economic and social settings held by central and local authorities. This disjuncture was most severe in late 1946, as mass drought threatened to turn into famine. As this point in October 1946, Andrei Zhdanov, a key figure in the central Soviet leadership, told an audience of party/state leaders and bureaucrats in Moscow that famine could be avoided only if local authorities were forced into making the transition into the post-war period by ending self-supply and reducing 'wasteful' food consumption. Essentially, famine could be avoided only by the restoration of the pre-war economy and central control over the countryside.[80] For *raion-* and oblast-level authorities in Kyiv Oblast, these famine-prevention

---

[80] On the broader pre-war restoration project, see Lewin, *The Soviet Century*, 127 and Lewin, 'Rebuilding the Soviet *Nomenklatura* 1945–1948', *Cahiers du monde Russe* 44, nos. 2–3 (2003), 219–52. For the reconstruction of the Ukrainian political class, see Blackwell, *Kyiv as Regime City*, 73–101, and Danylenko, *Povoienna Ukraïna*, 139–62. For the legacy of collaboration in rebuilding Soviet power in western Ukraine, see Amir Weiner, *Making Sense of War: The Second World War and the Fate of the Bolshevik Revolution* (Princeton: Princeton University Press, 2001). On the re-establishment of Soviet police structures after the war, but also changes in repressive policies – from broad campaign justice targeting entire groups before the war to judicial-bound repression of individuals after it – see David R. Shearer, *Policing Stalin's Socialism: Repression and Social Order in the Soviet Union, 1924–1953* (New Haven: Yale University Press, 2009). Some historians argue that divergent options were available to the Soviet leaderships upon victory in the war: that of returning to a more repressive regime or that of pursuing a more liberal political course. See Sheila Fitzpatrick,

measures threatened to bring it straight to their doorstep. They had long been dealing with the challenge of supplying food to workers in rural areas and urban peripheries with the same strategies, such as self-supply, that had proved effective in wartime. Central authorities' attempt to end self-supply at this time made it more essential for local authorities to continue it. At the October meeting, Zhdanov expressed central authorities' frustration with this disjuncture between central and authorities, asking his audience of 'centralists' rhetorically:

> Everyone is still fighting the war . . . Leningrad is still under blockade (audience laughter). That is why we are wasting bread and produce . . . So even though the war is over, wartime practices continue to affect the entire period of peaceful reconstruction. Why?[81]

By answering Zhdanov's rhetorical question literally in this book, I situate our understanding of the behaviour of local authorities in Kyiv Oblast at this disjuncture of where war ends and 'peace' begins. This enables us to explain why their continuation of self-supply was different from the deal making and negotiating behaviour addressed in the literature and, more importantly, to understand how this disjuncture, the key pressure point in the broader context of post-war transition, produced this difference. As with interrogating 'legal' land appropriations in the archival record to reveal their 'illegal nature', understanding this progenitive pressure point encourages us to identify new or review other possible behaviours which appear as corruption or traditional localism in the archival record, but may actually represent local authorities 'correcting' post-war central policy by continuing its previous wartime iterations. In this way, the story in Kyiv Oblast may have a broader relevance beyond Ukraine, across the Soviet Union and the emerging Soviet empire in Europe.

Similarly, thinking about this disjuncture in understanding where war ends and 'peace' begins can bring this Ukrainian and Soviet story into a thoroughly Europe-wide context. Much of the wider literature on the difficulties of post-war transitions across Europe after the world wars of the twentieth century sees war's end as a process rather than a moment in

On Stalin's Team: The Years of Living Dangerously in Soviet Politics (Princeton, NJ: Princeton University Press, 2015), 171. Others are more sceptical about the possibilities of pursuing anything other than a return to pre-war economic norms among the leadership, largely due to the leadership's own power bases being rooted in heavy industry, which required cutting back on civilian consumption.

[81] RGASPI f. 17, op. 121, d. 460, l. 121.

time. French historians of World War I have developed a useful term, 'exiting war', to describe this process, which was experienced differently by everyone in the multiple centres and peripheries of any country.[82] For millions of Europeans, 'the war did not end with the end of the war'.[83] There are obvious parallels between the shared experiences of Europeans and Soviet citizens, which prevented their 'societies from settling down' beyond the physical devastation of war: continued population dislocation wrought by deportations and flight, forced repatriations of citizens to their 'home countries', and soldiers becoming civilians again after the brutalities of war.[84] Rural and urban experiences of the severity of these problems could be different within Europe as they were within the Soviet Union, especially evident in the case studies presented here in Kyiv Oblast. As the Soviet Union expanded its empire towards central Europe after the war as well, the similarities in these shared experiences became more prevalent among old Soviet citizens, new ones and those who had recently come under Soviet rule via their own governments being installed or controlled by Moscow.[85]

However, the differences between their experiences and especially those outside the Soviet sphere of influence are stark. The experience of many Soviet citizens and especially Ukrainians, at least until the end of the 1940s, was marked by vacillations in the severity of enduring wartime conditions not seen in the rest of Europe, mostly mass violence from the insurgency in western Ukraine and death from mass famine. In Kyiv Oblast, these wartime conditions continued to unravel not only at a disjuncture of understanding of where war ended and peace began, but where different levels of government contested it. The

---

[82] Recent years have seen a transformation in the literature of post-war 'transitions': Richard Bessel and Dirk Schumann, eds., *Life after Death: Approaches to a Cultural and Social History of Europe during the 1940s and 1950s* (New York: Cambridge University Press, 2003); Frank Biess and Robert G. Moeller, eds., *Histories of the Aftermath: The Legacies of the Second World War in Europe* (New York: Berghahn Books, 2010). On French historians, see Henry Rousso, 'A New Perspective on the War', in Jorg Echternkamp and Stefan Martens, eds., *Experience and Memory: The Second World War in Europe* (New York and Oxford: Berghahn Books, 2007), 5. Recent works on post-World War II Germany and eastern Europe share elements of this approach, though they are coloured by a unique continuation of mass violence in these countries that is absent in the western part of the continent. See Snyder, *Bloodlands*; Prusin, *The Lands Between*; and Kulczycki, *Belonging to the Nation*.

[83] Jorg Echternkamp and Stefan Martens, 'The Meanings of the Second World War in Contemporary European History', in Echternkamp and Martens, eds., *Experience and Memory*, 246.

[84] Ibid.

[85] On the post-war transition in Soviet-occupied Germany, see Filip Slaveski, *The Soviet Occupation of Germany: Hunger, Mass Violence and the Struggle for Peace, 1945–1947* (Cambridge: Cambridge University Press, 2013).

historical asymmetry in Ukrainian and European experiences is key to understanding how Ukraine's experience of a longer, more severe war continues to cast the longest and darkest shadows over its contemporary experience.

*

This book comprises five chapters that look at the clash of local and central Soviet authorities in Kyiv Oblast from 1944 to 1950, but also the consequences of this clash and broader ramifications of the war for years afterward to the present day. The first chapter, 'A Brief Survey of Illegal Appropriations of Collective Farmland by Local State and Party Officials', provides a historical background to the enduring devastation of the postwar agricultural sector that encouraged appropriations to persist in Ukraine after the war and 1946 campaign. Chapter 2, 'Taking Land: Officials' Illegal Appropriations and Starving People in Raska, Bila Tserkva and Elsewhere', analyses the various methods used by authorities to appropriate land illegally from the collective farm sector and to hide these attempts from superior authorities; it begins to trace the scale of this activity across Kyiv Oblast and Ukraine. Chapter 3, 'Taking Land Back: The People and Central Authorities' Recovery of Land and Prosecution of Local Party and State Officials', examines how *kolkhozniki* and their supporters in the state and party structure went about recovering land and resources taken from them and punishing the local officials responsible. Similarly, examining how local authorities avoided punishments handed down to them for illegal appropriations offers insight into broader difficulties faced by central authorities in re-establishing control over the post-war agricultural sector.

Chapters 4 and 5 address the short- and long-term consequences of illegal appropriations, respectively. Although independent initiatives like appropriations by local authorities were pursued to deal with food crises, instead, they may have exacerbated them. Chapter 4, 'The Cost of Taking Land: The Damages Caused by Illegal Appropriations of Collective Farmland to *Kolkhozniki*, Communities and the State', demonstrates that this problem was caused mainly by officials in Kyiv Oblast continuing with this policy when they did not need to. From 1948 central pressure eased on food collections across the Ukrainian countryside, and this reduced the need for continuing self-supply at the local level. Continuing to keep appropriated land, and refusing to assist farms in this period where their successful reconstruction was more feasible than before, imperilled the farms and the broader localities of which they were part long after the crisis in workers' food allocations had passed.[86] Chapter 5, 'Then and Now: The Shaping of Contemporary Ukraine in the Post-War Crises', reflects on the long-term impacts in contemporary Ukraine of the post-war developments described throughout the book. It traverses between contemporary accounts of the areas discussed in this book and their post-war developments, which look very different in Raska and Bila Tserkva. All of the farms reconstructed in 1948 began folding from 1950 onwards. They were swallowed up as part of Khrushchev's 1950 campaign to amalgamate small farms into larger ones, abandoning them to the fate from which he and the Council on Collective Farm Affairs had saved them two years earlier. In Raska at least, the *kolkhozniki* kept their homes, land and graves, while many in Bila Tserkva were not so lucky. This set these areas on divergent historical paths that this chapter follows into the present.

---

[86] The general end of rationing in 1948 affected urban dwellers more than it did rural areas as in 1946. Central authorities expanded *ogorodnichestvo*; see Hessler, 'A Postwar Perestroika?'

PART I

The Battle for Land between the People and Local and Central Soviet Authorities

A Brief Survey of Illegal Appropriations of Collective Farmland by Local State and Party Officials

Most of the soldiers who left Raska at the beginning of the war in 1941 had no knowledge of the destruction of their village and murder of their loved ones in 1943 until they returned after the end of the war. The few soldiers from Raska who lived under German occupation and were mobilised into the Red Army after the massacre, as it swept through Kyiv Oblast from late 1943, carried this pain with them to the front and back home again. All of the soldiers began to arrive home from late 1945 as they were demobilised. Some left the village shortly afterwards, their families dead, to start new lives elsewhere.

But most stayed and joined the handful of survivors of the massacre to start rebuilding their village and farm after the war in earnest. Like other returned soldiers who resumed their lives as *kolkhozniki*, they sought state assistance, to which they were legally entitled, to rebuild their farm and village. They travelled to the town of Borodianka, where the office of the state representative of the *raion*-level authorities, the *raiispolkom*, was located. The *kolkhozniki* left the office after the *raiispolkom* secretary assured them that he would look into what money and material he could offer them to rebuild but, as the *kolkhozniki* left, other *raiispolkom* officials sequestered the five horses and carts that they had arrived on, leaving them to walk the twenty-some kilometres home. Shortly thereafter, the same official who promised to 'look into the matter' helped pass a *raiispolkom* decree and organised for it to be passed by the party organisation in the district, the *raikom,* to liquidate the farm and village before they had even been fully rebuilt.[1]

---

[1] DAKO f. 4810, op. 1, d. 3, l. 5. See also a previous report, issued by oblast-level authorities in early 1946, stipulating that Raska's lands were empty, that the farm could not be reconstructed and that its lands should be given to other users, especially the military: DAKO f. 4819, op. 14, d. 2, ll. 6–7. The decree liquidating the farm and village at the oblast level was issued in September 1947: DAKO f. r-880, op. 9, d. 17, ll. 170–171.

Raska's *kolkhozniki* continued to rebuild despite authorities enforcing this decree by periodically raiding the village for livestock, timber, seed and food over the next couple of years. Authorities dismantled anything the *kolkhozniki* built, including a school for their children, and threatened to arrest them for conducting any more building works. The fourteen factories and institutions already using Raska's pre-war land-holdings to feed their workers wanted more of it.[2] As long as the *kolkhozniki* remained on what was left of their land, *raion* authorities would try to starve them into leaving it. When the *kolkhozniki* began seeking help from Moscow to deal with local authorities, the *obliispolkom*, the state authority superior to the *raiispolkom*, passed another decree, in 1947, not only liquidating both farm and village, but also now stipulating the evacuation of the villagers.[3]

One hundred and forty kilometres away, *kolkhozniki* on the outskirts of Bila Tserkva were being beaten by *militsiia* (Soviet police). The *kolkhozniki* had conducted a sit-in demonstration at one of their farm warehouses that the local city council (*gorsovet*) had sequestered. The police advanced on them and threw them and all of their possessions out on to the street.[4] The *gorsovet* and *militsiia* then sequestered houses here and on neighbouring farms belonging to the *kolkhozniki*. The authorities also took their food and land – thousands of hectares of the farm's pre-war land-holdings and, in some cases, all of their private plots. The *gorsovet* parcelled this land as *podsobnoe khoziaistvo* to factories and workers or as garden plots to urban residents to grow food as the city expanded. While taking food and land, both city authorities, the *gorsovet* and *gorkom* (the city's political authority), refused to provide *kolkhozniki* with even the most basic of farm equipment to replace what had been destroyed in the war and was now required to sow and harvest crops. As in Raska, they threatened to arrest the more troublesome *kolkhozniki* who protested, but here the remaining *kolkhozniki* left the farms in their droves. City authorities then passed decrees, citing labour shortages and incapacity of the farms to utilise their land to justify the land grab. Like *raion*-level authorities in Raska that sought to evacuate the *kolkhozniki* to beget the reality of their decree claiming the land was uninhabited, city authorities in Bila Tserkva tried to create the conditions they had anticipated in their planning.

The theft of food from the countryside was the fundamental characteristic of the collective farm system. Authorities employed violence both to extract resources and to coerce *kolkhozniki* into remaining on the farms

---

[2] DAKO f. 4810, op. 1, d. 3.   [3] DAKO f. r-880, op. 9, d. 17, ll. 170–171.
[4] RGASPI f. 17, op. 122, d. 317, l. 11, and DAKO f. 4810, op. 1, d. 1.

within the system's abusive clutches. This was their job in the 1930s and especially after the war, when they needed to re-absorb millions of *kolkhozniki* into the system to rebuild it.[5] Why, then, did authorities in Raska, Bila Tserkva and other areas mobilise violence to drive these *kolkhozniki* from their farms and from the broader collective farm system? This book addresses this question over the next two chapters, first by a broad survey of local authorities' illegal appropriations of collective farmland in this chapter and then a detailed examination of events in these areas in the next.

Antecedents of Appropriations

In taking collective farmland and putting it to other uses, authorities were continuing in post-war Raska and Bila Tserkva what they had been doing continually elsewhere from the beginning of the war. That is, they took land from mostly smaller and poorer collective farms adjoining urban or industrial areas to facilitate their expansion. This land was transformed into *podsobnoe khoziaistvo* and *ogorodnichestvo* for workers and urbanites by local authorities, who did this on behalf of factories and institutions or in league with them, or allowed them to do so on their own. Although this practice diminished the collective farm system, it reflected the deeper bias inherent within it of prioritising urban food supply at the expense of the rural. In this way, local workers often overcame the problem of poorly operating farms not being able to immediately generate enough food surpluses, which they could purchase to supplement their rations. At this time, *podsobnoe khoziaistvo* was often more direct and effective in producing food for workers than collective farms.

The mass devolution of authority to the local level and constriction of central food rationing in wartime encouraged local authorities to appropriate more land from the collective farm sector for local use in the broader establishment of self-supply. In most cases, authorities took parcels of land from farms for *podsobnoe khoziaistvo* and *ogorodnichestvo* but left them operational. In others, authorities evacuated *kolkhozniki*, usually from smaller, struggling farms to nearby larger farms, which took control of all the farmland. This consolidated scarce labour and machinery to cultivate larger areas. These farm 'amalgamations' were usually temporary, and the individual farms were reconstructed after the war when the *kolkhozniki*

---

[5] Davies and Wheatcroft, *The Industrialisation of Soviet Russia 5*; and Lynne Viola et al., *The War against the Peasantry, 1927–1930: The Tragedy of the Soviet Countryside* (New Haven: Yale University Press, 2008).

returned after demobilisation (Raska, Bila Tserkva and others discussed later being the exceptions). This strategy of amalgamating farms and freeing up land had proved largely effective in helping both to keep collective farms operational and to supply additional land for food for an increasing urban working population from a strained and underpopulated agricultural sector in unoccupied and then liberated areas of the Soviet Union.[6]

Wartime decrees issued by central authorities in 1942 and 1944 ratified this practice of appropriating collective farmland for *podsobnoe khoziaistvo*, which was widespread around the country. These decrees established clear rules to appropriate only collective farmland that was 'not in use' and by agreement with the farm leaders; the land must be returned to the farms at the end of the war. But, as we will see, these conditions were often not met by appropriating officials, whose behaviour often exceeded the official scope provided to them to organise the self-supply of food for survival, as state and broader structures of economic exchange broke down during the war.[7]

Officials in Kyiv Oblast were experts in self-supply and operating beyond the scope established by the decrees, having cut their teeth in wartime governance by helping to implement this strategy in the areas to which they had been evacuated in 1941, mostly Kazakhstan and the Urals. The Urals were one of the greatest sites of the wartime self-supply experiment. Decrees passed in major cities in the Urals to ratify the decrees passed by Moscow on self-supply in 1944 stressed:[8]

> The industrial centres of the Urals cannot grow unless they develop a self-sustaining potato/vegetable supply base around their periphery. We must increase the role of *podsobnoe khoziaistvo* to supply cities and industrial centres.[9]

This urgency was partly a response to the skyrocketing demand from workers and urban residents for more and more land. In the three Ural oblasts of Cheliabinsk, Sverdlovsk and Perm, the number of workers occupying *podsobnoe khoziaistvo* rose from 655,000 in 1940 to almost

---

[6] Kondrashin, 'Krest'ianstvo i sel'skoe khoziaistvo SSSR'; Trifonov, 'Ogorodnichestvo'; Denisevich, *Individual'nye khoziaistva na Urale*. There were exceptions to this success, especially in the famine period in Siberia at the beginning of the war.

[7] Sovnarkom SSSR i TsK VKP(b) 'O merakh po dal'neishemu razvitiiu podsobnykh khoziaistv promyshlennykh narkomatov' (18 October 1942).

[8] Postanovlenie Gosudarstvennogo Komiteta Oborony (GKO), 'O meropriiatiakh po usileniiu prodovol'stvennoi bazy promyshlennykh tsentrov Sverdlovskoi oblasti' (25 March 1944). Sovnarkom issued analogous decrees for Cheliabinsk (29 May 1944) and Perm (11 August 1944) Oblasts.

[9] Trifonov, 'Sel'skokhoziaistvennye podsobnye khoziaistva', 293.

1.8 million in 1945; the total land in their possession increased from 44,300 to 112,000 hectares in the same period.[10]

This land had to come from somewhere. The relevant central decrees in 1942 and 1944 allowed for unused land and unoccupied state land around urban areas to be turned into *podsobnoe khoziaistvo* for workers or gardens for civilians, as was collective farmland not in use with the permission of farm leaderships.[11] But even in the open spaces of the Urals with the mass reduction in collective farm labour, capacity and sown area in wartime, there still was not enough unused land to meet the growing demand. Or, to be more specific, there was not enough land suitable for food growing in close enough proximity to urban centres to meet demand. In Kyiv, the best 'unused land' near the city was snapped up quickly upon liberation in late 1943 by workers and residents.[12] The rest of it was poor for growing, and authorities, workers and their bosses, many of whom had some connection to village life, knew the difference between good land and bad. Collective farmland 'in use' that was close to urban populations and more fertile than unused state land thus became most attractive for appropriations. Some farms in Kyiv Oblast were even more attractive to authorities because their major crops better served urban demand, namely vegetables rather than grain, whereas farms in the Urals needed to convert from grain to vegetable crops.[13] In the Urals and Kyiv Oblast, authorities interpreted the term 'not in use' loosely, or simply applied this designation to the land they wished to appropriate in the agreements with collective farm leaders.[14] In Sverdlovsk Oblast alone, 22,572 hectares of collective farmland illegally appropriated during the war by state/party institutions and industrial

[10] Trifonov, 'Ogorodnichestvo', 224. Trifonov stresses that authorities gained valuable experience in implementing this policy 'on the ground', and *obkom*s and *obliispolkom*s prepared plans for the development of allotment gardens in detail before the beginning of each spring sowing season, especially from 1943 onwards.

[11] In September 1946; the Sovmin order launching the campaign is Postanovlenie Sovmina i TsK VKP(b) SSSR no. 2157, 'O merakh po likvidatsii narusheniia Ustava sel'skokhoziaistvennoi arteli v kolkhozakh' (19 September 1946). This order nullified previous Sovnarkom orders in 1942 in which allotment gardening was allowed to develop from unused collective farmlands, especially Postanovlenie Sovnarkoma TsK VKP(b) SSSR (7 April 1942), and demanded the return of all former land to the collective farm sector by 15 November 1946. (Sovnarkom became Sovmin, the Council of Ministers in 1946.)

[12] Vrons'ka, *V umovakh viiny*, 56–7.

[13] Motrevich, 'Vosstanovlenie sel'skogo khoziaistva na Urale', 25.

[14] Some collective farm leaders were amenable to land reductions. The less land they had under cultivation, the lower the amount of food they were required to deliver to the state. These amounts were often unrealisable, especially in times of crisis: Kessler and Kornilov, eds., *Kolkhoznaia zhizn'*, 639–46.

enterprises were returned by the 1946 Campaign on Collective Farm Rules.[15] As we will see below, in Kyiv Oblast, geographically much smaller, this figure was significantly higher. In any case, more food had been kept in the area for local consumption rather than delivered to the state when it really mattered in wartime.

It is unsurprising that self-supply and the transgressions against the rules of appropriating land were enacted by Soviet officials in territories liberated from German rule from late 1943 onwards, such as Ukraine. The wartime challenges in the Urals and post-liberation Kyiv Oblast were similar, especially the demand from rapidly growing populations for scarce fertile land close to urban centres for growing food. Ukrainian officials who returned to *raion*- and oblast-level positions from evacuation from late 1943 implemented self-supply to deal with these challenges. In the immediate post-war period, these 'old hands' tended to exercise more power than did the waves of new recruits and officials from other areas of the Soviet Union, who had less experience of local conditions and possessed less-established political networks.[16]

The rapid repopulation of Kyiv city and its outskirts by wartime returnees, evacuees from the Far East and 'illegal' entrants saw the urban population skyrocket after liberation. It nearly tripled from about 220,000 in December 1943 to 600,000 by March 1946.[17] By 1945 almost 100,000 urban residents in Kyiv had petitioned local authorities to provide them with land as *ogorodnichestvo* as the fertile 'unused state' land had already been gobbled up upon liberation earlier.[18] Oblast-level authorities tried to regulate the large influx of people moving into Kyiv from 1944 onwards, mostly from the east, and then with the massive influx of demobilised soldiers, repatriates and others from the west in 1946. Oblast authorities established a fifty-kilometre zone around the city centre from which they would regulate entry. In practice, the radius of this 'zone' varied in different places, as did its level of security; until late 1946, this control was poor and did little to ease demand for land and food.[19]

[15] Ibid., 645.
[16] Lieberman, 'The Re-Sovietisation of Formerly Occupied Territories'; Lewin, 'Rebuilding the Soviet Nomenklatura'. On the calibre of post-war party officials in Ukraine, see V. Krupyna, 'Osvitn'o-kul'turnyi riven' partiinoï nomenklatury UkSSR (druha polovyna 1940-kh–pochatok 1950-kh rr.)', *Ukraïnskyi istorychnyi zbirnyk*, no. 12 (2009), 207–14.
[17] The largest influx of war veterans returned over the winter of 1945–6. From 1 December 1945 to 1 January 1946, 1,212,782 demobilised men returned, which brought the total number of soldiers demobilised since November 1945 to 4,551,934. See Edele, 'A "Generation of Victors"?', 102.
[18] Blackwell, *Kyiv as Regime City*, 113.
[19] Danylenko, *Povoienna Ukraïna*, 265; on the ineffectiveness of migration controls in Kyiv until late 1946, see Blackwell, *Kyiv as Regime City*. On the widespread nature of this problem, especially of 'one-way' migration to other cities during the summer months, see RGASPI f. 17, op. 121, d. 460,

Industrial managers with swelling workforces also made greater and greater demands for land to provide to their workers as *podsobnoe khoziaistvo* in Kyiv and other cities and urban/industrial areas. By 1944, Ukrainian workers had gained 200,000 hectares of land as individual or collective *podsobnoe khoziaistvo* and, by 1945, 2.63 million of them occupied 385,000 hectares or almost 0.146 hectares each on average.[20] There were clearly more workers than available land; as a result, most only possessed a sliver of it, which they used for vegetable growing, especially potatoes. But it was rarely their only food source, and workers balanced food income from different sources to survive and provide for their families: from *podsobnoe khoziaistvo*, rations at their workplaces and what they could purchase. Those workers in rural areas like Kyiv Oblast tended to have larger allotments and less access to food rations than those in urban ones closer to Kyiv city. Kyivans' *podsobnoe khoziaistvo* came from the city's rural peripheries or oblast areas adjoining it, especially from late 1943 to late 1946, when the oblast began repopulating at a much faster rate and these people began recovering their former farmland in use by Kyivans and others, even before the 1946 Campaign on Collective Farm Rules mandated its return.[21] The incomers were mostly demobilised soldiers or those returning from forced labour.[22] Of the 156,000 people taken as forced labour from the oblast, 115,000 had returned by February 1946. By July, the total of all types of returnee was approximately 230,000.

The growth of self-supply and particularly *podsobnoe khoziaistvo* in Kyiv was a massive wartime achievement. It was even a greater achievement in the city's outskirts and the oblast where most workers, unlike in Kyiv, were not as well supplied by the strained wartime rationing system. Here

---

l. 52. This problem further strained the food rationing system even in Moscow, which like Kyiv had strong restrictions in place for inward travel. In summer 1946, upon the arrival of another 50,000 non-Muscovites to the city, institutions put in requests for an additional 50,000 ration cards to feed them, but authorities from the places these people had come from did not declare a reduction in their ration card needs. This contributed to duplications in the food rationing system as well as giving rise to other abuses.

[20] V. A. Smolii, *Ekonomichna istoriia Ukraïny. Istoryko-ekonomichne doslidzhennia v dvokh tomakh* (Kyiv: Nika-Tsentr, 2011), 361. This was still less than the pre-war total of *podsobnoe khoziastvo*, but there were more workers at that time. In 1938, 406,000 hectares were in use as *podsobnoe khoziaistvo* in Ukraine: GOSPLAN, *Posevnye ploshchadi SSSR v 1938* (Moscow and Leningrad: Gosplanizdat, 1938), 25.

[21] Population figures are calculated from Kyiv demographic data in RGAE f. 1562, op. 329, d. 2641, noting the faster and greater repopulation of urban areas in Kyiv compared to rural areas, as well as the broader context of fluid migrations between urban and rural areas by demobilised soldiers and others.

[22] During the latter stages of the war, there was often a shortage of suitable land close enough to urban settlements in Kyiv city for use as *podsobnoe khoziaistvo*. See Vrons'ka, *V umovakh viiny*, 56–7.

podsobnoe khoziaistvo had proved most necessary to supplement this system and the devastated Ukrainian agricultural sector that supplied it – and not only in wartime. *Podsobnoe khoziaistvo* remained essential to workers afterwards, when the consequences of wartime damage to the sector continued to unravel, climaxing in 1946–7 with famine.

War and occupation had reduced this sector to rubble. Approximately 30,000 collective and state farms and MTSs had been destroyed, along with most of the tractors, machinery and livestock.[23] Ukraine's population fell from 40.9 million in 1941 to 27.3 million in 1945.[24] Most of these losses were due to death, military service, evacuation or conscription into forced labour in Germany. Post-war insurgency in western Ukraine, mass deportations and large-scale population exchanges between western Ukraine and eastern Poland compounded these losses. The German occupation administration had toyed with relaxing the conditions of collective farming and affording greater private land to *kolkhozniki*, but mostly sought to continue and, indeed, intensify the practice of collective farming in wartime. Although the Germans did not upset the basic socio-economic structures of collective farming in the countryside, by the end of 1943 the farms were barely functioning.[25]

Impressive advances were made in rebuilding what remained of the sector the following year, but these were short-lived and could not withstand the ravages of drought from mid-1946. These advances were impressive in spite of central authorities' paltry investment in agricultural reconstruction in money and equipment, which were minuscule in comparison to the damage suffered. More useful was the influx of agricultural personnel into Ukraine and the redirection of farms' food delivery obligations from the state directly to military formations moving westwards.[26] The harvest in 1944 was thus much improved but was swallowed up primarily by these military forces fighting beyond Ukraine, and by the major cities.

---

[23] By 1945, cattle numbers were at 43 per cent of the pre-war level, horses at 30 per cent, sheep and goats at 26 per cent and swine at 11 per cent. The sowing field area had been greatly reduced as had the amount of agricultural technology. See Danylenko, *Povoienna Ukraïna*, 7.

[24] Kul'chyts'kyi, *Chervonyi vyklyk*, 104.

[25] On the countryside under German rule, see Karel Berkhoff, *Harvest of Despair: Life and Death in Ukraine under Nazi Rule* (Cambridge, MA: Harvard University Press, 2004), ch. 7, and on the state of Ukraine at the end of German occupation, ch. 12.

[26] In 1943, the Soviet government allocated 15 million roubles for the reconstruction of agricultural infrastructure and 34 million roubles for rebuilding of MTSs and associated facilities. In 1944, this rose to 314 million roubles in agricultural infrastructure and in 1945 to 429 million roubles. On the supply to military formations from Ukrainian collective farms, see O. Perekhrest. 'Sil'ske hospodarstvo Ukraïny v 1943–1945 rr. problemy ta rezul'taty vidbudovy', *Ukraïnskyi istorychnyi zhurnal* no. 3 (2010), 99–100.

Food provisions for *kolkhozniki* and rural populations remained much lower than before the war, but *kolkhozniki* put their shoulders to the wheel. For many, their efforts were fuelled by a genuine desire to help win the war and to rebuild after the horrors of occupation as well as by the hope that their efforts would ease the authorities' derision towards them. They remained civilians, neither evacuating before nor actively resisting the German occupation, as the Soviet regime had expected.[27] This boost in morale was dashed by the disappointing 1945 grain harvest, which was about half the 1940 level, and more so by the 1946 drought-affected harvest, which was only about a third of the 1940 level. This poor harvest coincided with a massive influx of hungry soldiers and repatriates from demobilisation, meaning there was now less food to feed more people.[28] The returnees were supposed to help address the sector's major labour shortage problem, but came too late to assist much with the spring sowing. Instead, they arrived mostly at harvest time to gather and consume the much lower amount of food available.[29] Until the demobilised returned to work in the fields – and many only stayed for a short while – women and children made up 80 per cent of the sector's workforce.[30] With mass shortages of machinery, fuel and livestock, they had performed the majority of ploughing and hard farm labour by hand.[31]

Re-establishing Control over the Post-War Agricultural Sector

With the agricultural sector on its knees by late 1946 and famine threatening, central authorities launched a massive campaign to re-establish control over it. Fearing mass starvation in the cities and the depletion of their own state reserves, they tried to reverse the direct flow of food from land to rural

[27] Danylenko, *Povoienna Ukraïna*, 304. Evacuation was hardly a choice for *kolkhozniki* in many cases, given the speed of the German advance and collapse of Soviet forces, as well as their limited mobility.
[28] Grain production figures (barn yield) taken from RGAE f. 1562, op. 324, dd. 5295–5301. Stephen Wheatcroft makes sense of these figures in 'The Soviet Famine of 1946–1947, the Weather and Human Agency in Historical Perspective', *Europe–Asia Studies* 64, no. 6 (2012), 987–1005.
[29] Pay for labour days was often symbolic at this time. In the worst-affected areas, the most *kolkhozniki* could hope to receive was probably 100 grams of bread in comparison to the more than 400 grams they had received in 1940, depending on the farm. *Kolkhozniki* supplemented these starvation-level rations with food from their private plots, but this became more difficult as central authorities recovered land from these plots and taxed them more heavily from September 1946, as famine approached.
[30] On soldiers' population movements from city to village and vice versa, see Edele, 'Veterans and the Village'.
[31] V. K. Baran and V. M. Danylenko, *Ukraïna v umovah systemnoi kryzy (1946–1980)* (Kyiv: Al'ternatyvy, 1999), 37.

dwellers via self-supply and redirect it into state coffers.[32] This campaign was primarily directed against *kolkhozniki*, many of whom in the unoccupied parts of the USSR had exploited the relaxation of wartime rules on the collective farms to expand their private plots beyond the size allowed by law. These *kolkhozniki* continued to spend more time working on these plots than on collective farmland after the war, as food grown on these plots, not food received from the state, remained their primary resource for survival. Authorities hoped that, by reducing the size of these plots, they would force *kolkhozniki* back into collective farm work. In the unoccupied parts of the Soviet Union this campaign had some rationale, but it was equally applied to liberated areas such as Ukraine where the situation was different, and *kolkhozniki* were far more destitute. With the state having already procured from the farms most of the grain gathered in the disastrous 1946 harvest along with the remaining seed, the reduction of private plot size hindered the capacity of *kolkhozniki* to reproduce the food taken from them in the areas hit hardest by drought in mid-1946. Some responded by leaving the farms in search of food or with other forms of passive resistance, which drove down food production and exacerbated the problems that the campaign was trying to address.[33] This helped thrust the sector into famine.[34]

Historians have focused less on the consequences of the other two-pronged attack against workers in rural areas: the end of rationing in September 1946 and the confiscation of land used as *podsobnoe khoziaistvo* – the two sources of their survival. There was not much workers could do to recover bread rations after September 1946. Certainly, the factories and institutions to which they belonged could work with local authorities to stop or at least delay the return of land required for their survival. Some authorities led or sponsored these attempts as they had a vested interest in prioritising workers' and urban needs over those of collective farms, particularly poorly performing ones in time of famine. After the war, it

---

[32] RGASPI f. 17, op. 121, d. 460, l. 121.

[33] This migration, albeit temporary, increased urban populations. These exiles from the countryside rarely gained access to state rations unless they found official employment, but their presence added to the existing urban food, disease and housing crises, exacerbated by the famine, which authorities were desperately trying to address. The incorporation of greater territory and population, especially in the western part of the Soviet Union after the war, compounded this imbalance between food producers and urban recipients.

[34] The campaign's punitive aspects continued over the winter. For instance, one investigation focused on nine oblasts in Ukraine and concluded that, by the third quarter of 1947, collective farm chairmen had been replaced for abuses of collective farm rules on only 452 of all farms (14,703) or 3.1 per cent. This compared to their replacement on 4,316 farms or 29.4 per cent at the height of the campaign at the beginning of the year. See TsDAVOU f. r-2, op. 7, d. 7024, l. 67.

was generally more profitable for them to direct what scant resources they had to local industry, which kept produce local and provided a pretext for appropriating collective farmland, whose produce was otherwise taken away by central requisitioning. There was always a balance to be struck, as local officials were still answerable to their superiors for collecting the set amount of food from collective farms under their control. As discussed later, they made up this total by over-collecting elsewhere. After the 1946 Campaign on Collective Farm Rules, institutions and factories still legally acquired *podsobnoe khoziaistvo* via oblast-level authorities, but it became more difficult for them to do so from collective farmland without more rigorous examination from superior authorities. The pertinent questions here are: how do we identify oblast-level government interests in expanding *podsobnoe khoziaistvo* at the expense of collective farming? And through what means, particularly illegal, did authorities act on them?

The campaign to return land to collective farms in September 1946, 'On measures to eliminate abuses of collective farm rules', was driven by the newly formed Council on Collective Farm Affairs under Minister of Agriculture Andrei Andreev. This decree was similar to previous ones issued in 1935 and 1939,[35] in that it focused primarily on recovering land from illegal *kolkhoznik* land expansions. This Council eventually mobilised almost 16,000 commissions in Ukraine alone to investigate collective farm abuses. These commissions worked with local authorities to identify 998,000 hectares of land for return to collective farms in Ukraine. Of this total, 45,200 hectares were being used illegally by 789,800 collective farm households; 46,700 hectares were being used illegally by 208,000 workers and non-collective farm members as *podsobnoe khoziaistvo*; 398,600 hectares remained in the hands of institutions, factories and various other bodies.[36] Some of the 398,600 hectares had been officially slated for return to farms earlier, as they had been appropriated by agreement between the farm and the institutions/factories for *podsobnoe khoziaistvo*.

The post-war return of some of this land was delayed by two factors. First, there was continuing disorganisation in the agricultural sector, particularly documentation, and the complex logistics of farm reconstruction where *kolkhozniki* were in the process of re-forming their farms or amalgamating with others. Second, some factories protested the return of land at the end of the war as the law demanded and, as long as the protest

---

[35] Postanovlenie TsK VKP(b) i SNK SSSR, 'O merakh okhrany obshchestvennykh zemel' kolkhozov ot razbazarivaniia' (27 May 1939).
[36] TsDAVOU f. r-2, op. 7, d. 5032, ll. 219–220.

was being considered via bureaucratic channels all the way up the republican level, the land usually remained with the factory.[37] Eventually, republican-level officials, including Khrushchev, decided to hand back the land to the farms in most cases.[38]

Of the 398,600 hectares, the Council identified 56,800 as having been taken illegally by officials, institutions and factories, that is, without the agreement of farm leaderships. This was only an estimate of the total land mass, as identifying illegal appropriation was most difficult for the commissions. They first needed to determine which of the land taken had actually belonged to specific collective farms. This was difficult to do with any great certainty because almost the entire documentary base of the sector – outlining the land boundaries of individual farms and tenure arrangements for who had the right to use it – had been destroyed during the war and the occupation.[39] The commissions were trying to re-establish a pre-war agricultural sector in Ukraine with little detailed idea of what it had previously looked like on the ground. The 56,800 figure, as the commissions bemoaned in their reports to republican authorities, was lower than the actual total.[40]

The recovery of *kolkhoznik* land expansion suffered less from this lack of documentation than did the recovery of illegally appropriated *podsobnoe khoziaistvo*. *Kolkhoz* households were afforded a legal allotment of private land, usually between 0.25 and 0.5 hectares dependent partly on where they lived. Commissions could determine which *kolkhozniki* were using more than this allotment often 'by eye' in their investigations and return the land to the collective. This arbitrary process often took the best land and more of it from *kolkhoznik* plots and was relatively speedy. This could leave *kolkhozniki* with a legal-sized allotment of land that could be useless in providing them with food necessary to supplement their poor, sometimes non-existent food wages. Recovering land from workers or other non-collective farm population too was speedy and legal, as officials deemed they often had no right to this land in the first place. Working out which land the institutions and factories had appropriated by agreement with farm leadership was not difficult either. In fact, the significant advance in establishing land records for farms by late 1946

---

[37] See records of correspondence in TsDAVOU f. r-2, op. 7, d. 7008.

[38] TsDAVOU f. r-2, op. 7, d. 5032, ll. 219–220.

[39] Land and tenure records – which recorded land boundaries and established the right of farms and others to the use of farmland – were lost in 98.2 per cent of farms: Perekhrest, 'Sil′ske hospodarstvo Ukraïny', 97.

[40] Large numbers of reports sent to republican authorities in the winter of 1946–7 indicate this discrepancy: TsDAVOU f. r-2, op. 7, dd. 5032, 5034–5037. For the continuation of this problem in Kyiv Oblast into 1948–9, see DAKO f. 4810, op. 1, dd. 1, 3, 27, 33, 37.

across Ukraine was assisted in no small part by the wartime agreements. Commissions used these agreements, if they were recorded on paper, as a starting point to discover recoverable land because they outlined how much land 'in use' had been taken from farms – even if this amount was inaccurate.

The real problem faced by these commissions was to identify and return land appropriated without agreement, sometimes forcibly, by state officials, institutions and factories. Lack of documentation enabled the appropriators to avoid discovery by the commissions or, if questioned by them, pass false decrees claiming that the land did not belong to collective farms or was part of their own pre-war land-holdings. To work through these cases and pursue their investigations, the commissions required the assistance of local authorities with on-the-ground knowledge of pre-war or even farm arrangements. In most oblasts in Ukraine this was a given, but less so in Kyiv Oblast. Here the lack of clarity in land records provided a platform for the resistance of local authorities to keep their illegally appropriated land and to continue to appropriate more as *podsobnoe khoziaistvo*.

In January 1947, the Council on Collective Farm Affairs prepared a series of reports on the results of the 1946 campaign. It provided a short summary of the amount of land returned to the collective farm sector in the Ukrainian oblasts in which the campaign was implemented. These reports followed a standard template (*blank*) which the Council had for reporting to authorities. The report on Kyiv Oblast strayed from the norm: it did not provide a summary of land returns but indicted the *raion*- and oblast-level leadership for their failure to take seriously the restoration of land records and the broader campaign. This failure encouraged the massive land abuses taking place in Kyiv Oblast.

This report was picked up by the republican-level party bureaucracy and sent directly to Khrushchev, especially targeted to grab his attention. It was addressed to him as Central Committee secretary of the CP(b)U, not as head of the Ukrainian government (Council of Ministers, or Sovmin) through which most correspondence between the Council and republican-level government took place. This move clearly represented the bureaucracy's attempt to seek assistance from him to prosecute the offending officials, especially at the oblast level, for their political failures.[41] These failures – localism in food supply and corrupt cliques protecting their own from prosecution – were of great concern to the republican leadership during the implementation of the 1946 campaign. Moscow officials had

---

[41] TsDAHOU f. 1, op. 23, d. 4805, ll. 10–11.

specifically outlined these political failures to Khrushchev as a major problem in Ukraine in the previous year when Khrushchev had failed to supply Moscow with sufficient food from Ukraine.[42] Now he was being reminded again that his government's effective implementation of the campaign was threatened by the same political problem. On these points, the interests of the Council and republican leadership aligned, and the Council could generally count on Khrushchev's support (see Chapter 3).

The mass of correspondence between the Council and Sovmin confirms these claims of the officials' failure to assist them.[43] One of these reports was also prepared for Lazar Kaganovich in his new role as head of the CP(b) U in April 1947. This report, like the one sent to Khrushchev mentioned earlier, again stressed that by every measure of the campaign Kyiv Oblast was the worst of the oblasts in which the commissions implemented it. Due to staff shortages, mostly of local officials not taking part in the campaign, commissions failed to assess land usage in almost a third of the 2,378 farms in Kyiv Oblast, which was well below the Ukrainian average. Later investigations found that commissions in Kyiv Oblast failed even to assess many of the farms they had claimed, instead delegating the work to other people, often those who were engaged in the land abuses the commissions were supposed to identify.[44]

The capacity of anyone to assess land usage accurately was greatly diminished in any case, because Kyiv Oblast was slowest to restore land documentation that established the boundaries of each farm. This documentation was required for farms to receive land tenure, which gave them legal protection over land and resource usage. More than a third – 817 of the 2,378 farms – had not received it by April 1947, whereas most farms in other oblasts had. There were only two oblasts in Ukraine that lagged behind even Kyiv in conferring tenure (Odesa and Mykolaiv), and this was mainly because they were worst affected by the famine, with agricultural sectors that were in a general state of collapse. Council on Collective Farm Affairs representatives began to stress that the ongoing lack of clarity in land boundaries and delays in affording tenure to farms enabled appropriators to keep land they had appropriated illegally in these oblasts. In Kyiv Oblast especially, this lack of clarity encouraged them to continue taking more. Council representatives accepted authorities' excuses of staff shortages in these oblasts for both the failure to assist in the campaign and the

---

[42] TsDAVOU f. r-2, op. 7, d. 1748, ll. 127–129.

[43] See TsDAVOU f. r-2, op. 7, dd. 5032, 5050, 5051, 5059 and 5064.

[44] TsDAVOU f. r-2, op. 7, d. 5032, l. 220. Investigations found that this problem was widespread in Chernihiv Oblast as well, but not across Ukraine.

delay in undertaking the important land documentation/tenure work.[45] They did not suggest, at least at this early stage, that the shortages and delays were the intention of the oblast-level leadership, but argued that the lack of certainly in land boundaries and rights established by tenure encouraged illegal appropriations. This changed by 1948, as discussed later, when staffing shortages were no longer an issue and even the famine-affected oblasts improved their land documentation and tenure conferral rates, while Kyiv's remained poor.[46]

The case studies in the following chapter demonstrate that these reports were too diplomatic in 1946. The delay in restoring land documentation and tenure at this time was indeed the intention of oblast-level authorities. They were not disinterested parties, but agents driving illegal appropriations and protecting from prosecution their acolytes on the ground, who were acting directly on their behalf or in the spirit of illegal appropriations. They did this to protect and expand the food sources of workers and low-level officials in urban peripheries and rural areas at the expense of weak, poorly performing farms at a time when food supply was low and, by late 1946, severely depleted. The highest state authority in the oblast, the *obliispolkom*, was the key player in the drama. Its deputy secretary for agricultural affairs, Comrade Dvornikov, was responsible for the implementation of the 1946 campaign to return illegally appropriated land to collective farms in Kyiv Oblast and used this position to leave this land in the hands of some, while taking it from others. He and the *obliispolkom* were clearly pursuing a policy of selective land recovery, leaving land as *podsobnoe khoziaistvo* in some areas where they felt it was needed most, or at least in the hands of members of their broader networks with whom they continued to illegally appropriate land after the campaign.

The key statistics of land recovery relevant to this investigation are not the total amount of land identified and then returned to farms in Kyiv Oblast compared to others. These figures are similar to those in other oblasts. The campaign in Kyiv Oblast recovered 36,000 hectares from 2,980 institutions and factories, 16,822 hectares from workers, independent peasants (*edinolichniki*)[47] and others, and 10,665 hectares from 69,194 expanded plots. Dvornikov claimed that the 36,000 figure referred to land illegally obtained by institutions and factories. This would have made it account for the bulk of the whole Ukrainian total of 56,800. But

---

[45] Odesa had failed to confer tenure on 638 farms and Mykolaiv on 269: TsDAVOU f. r-2, op. 7, d. 5032, ll. 74–75.

[46] TsDAVOU f. r-2, op. 7, d. 7024, l. 88.

[47] Individual farmers were legally not part of the collective system.

his figure included both institutions and factories that had appropriated the land illegally as well as those that had simply kept it beyond their legal wartime agreements.[48] Dvornikov did not differentiate between these categories and likely could not do so at the time. What is key to this analysis is understanding how the co-ordinating role played by Dvornikov and broader oblast-level authorities in illegal appropriations ensured that the actual scale of land taken by officials, factories and institution before the campaign was higher than they had identified. This pattern is evident in the case studies at the local level in Raska and Bila Tserkva as well as across the oblast and, with some distinctions, in other areas of the Soviet Union addressed in the following chapter.

[48] TsDAVOU f. r-2, op. 7, d. 5035, l. 12.

CHAPTER 2

Taking Land: Officials' Illegal Appropriations and Starving People in Raska, Bila Tserkva and Elsewhere

We would have little sense of how widespread officials' illegal appropriation of collective farmland was in Kyiv Oblast and across Ukraine if not for the resilience of *kolkhozniki* in Raska and Bila Tserkva. Their battles with local authorities over their small parcels of land have left the necessary paper trail in the archives that points researchers to the much broader problem beyond their farms. Evidence of illegal appropriations would otherwise have remained obscured in the archival record by the falsifications and concealments made by the perpetrating officials at the time. By conducting these case studies in Raska and Bila Tserkva, we gain insight into how to reveal these falsifications and concealments to reconstruct partially the true scale of illegal appropriations of collective farmland in Kyiv Oblast and across Ukraine. We can begin to trace its consequences on the thousands of people involved and the development of the post-war agricultural sector.

This discovery of the scale and consequences of illegal appropriations unsettles the dominant orthodoxies of the literature on Soviet agriculture in the post-war period. This literature has understood land abuses in the collective farm sector in terms of the illegal expansion of private landholdings by *kolkhozniki* or, to a lesser extent, on that practice's inverse – the theft by officials as part of a broader embezzlement of farm resources.[1] The overriding assumption has been that appropriations were part of a broader web of corruption in the sector spun by officials seeking personal gain. Some works mention the illegal 'renting' of collective farmland by farm leaderships to local industries and factories by mutually beneficial agreement but assume that, like this 'renting', most transgressions were reined in

---

[1] For broader abuses in the sector, see the seminal post-Soviet works on agriculture including: Verbitskaia, *Rossiiskoe krest'ianstvo*, and Popov, *Rossiiskaia derevnia*.

by the 1946 Campaign on Collective Farm Rules.[2] The new cases of Raska and Bila Tserkva, on the other hand, point to coercive appropriations executed but not motivated by corruption: this book is the first attempt to provide such an account of this widespread practice.

Raska and Bila Tserkva

Local authorities in Kyiv Oblast, led by Dvornikov, were most resistant to the 1946 Campaign on Collective Farm Rules compared to others in Ukraine. Everywhere officials at the oblast and *raion* level refused to return some collective farmland, but few outside Kyiv Oblast continued to appropriate so much more after the war in much the same way as they had done during it. On the extreme end of the scale, this included refusing to allow those farms liquidated or amalgamated during the war to reconstruct afterwards, when the *kolkhozniki* had returned. In the cases of Raska, Bila Tserkva and elsewhere discussed below, *kolkhozniki* fought back against the authorities' conduct with the law on their side.

The Council on Collective Farm Affairs and central authorities in Kyiv and Moscow understood this broader practice of illegal appropriations as one committed by corrupt officials pursuing personal gain. This understanding was reflected in the 1946 decree launching the Campaign on Collective Farm Rules, which, for the first time in Soviet history, listed land appropriations by greedy Soviet officials under the guise of *podsobnoe khoziaistvo* as a pressing problem:

> Soviet and land authorities embezzle public lands through illegal rulings. All kinds of organisations and individuals even seize collective farmland arbitrarily under the guise of establishing on them all sorts of *podsobnoe khoziaistvo* and individual vegetable gardens for workers and employees. At the same time, such plunder of public lands often happens with the connivance of the boards of collective farms [and the] chairmen of village and district councils.[3]

The bulk of appropriation cases that had been reported back to the Council on Collective Farm Affairs from their representatives across the Soviet Union since late 1946 testified to this connection between officials and embezzlement.[4] These illegal appropriations, if recorded as *podsobnoe*

[2] Arutiunian, *Sovetskoe krest'ianstvo*, 329–30; Kessler and Kornilov, eds., *Kolkhoznaia zhizn'*, 18.
[3] Postanovlenie Sovmina i TsK VKP(b) SSSR no. 2157, 'O merakh po likvidatsii narusheniia Ustava sel'skokhoziaistvennoi arteli v kolkhozakh' (19 September 1946).
[4] See numerous items of correspondence to the Central Committee in Moscow on corruption in the agricultural sector in RGASPI f. 17, op. 122, and the following *dela* of the Council on Collective Farm Affairs in DAKO f. 4810, op. 1, dd. 27, 31, 33.

khoziaistvo, were disguised as institutions' or factories' legal land expansions to accommodate new workers, the recovery of institutions or industries' pre-war land-holdings, or part of legitimate urbanisation, which was a much larger process. Officials continued to use these reasons to conduct appropriations after late 1946, when it became much more difficult to do so, given the change in law and its enforcement by the Council.

The problem that the cases of Raska and Bila Tserkva pose to this understanding is that local authorities conducted illegal appropriations of collective farmland for actual *podsobnoe khoziaistvo* but obfuscated them in their records in same way officials commonly did to hide their embezzlement of the land. The Council was concerned more with illegality than with identifying the different motivations of appropriations that may have been part of broader rebuilding practices as opposed to simply local corruption for personal gain. The Council did attempt to make this distinction in some cases and in their investigations generally provided evidence that identified motivations, but distinctions between them were often blurry, as appropriations could be corrupt, illegal and aimed at reconstruction all at same time.

Whereas in our case studies of Raska and Bila Tserkva, these blurry distinctions over corruption were established as a means to different ends in 1948, an analysis of them today helps us clarify them. In both of these cases, the farms were barely populated when authorities appropriated their land from 1945. The areas surrounding Raska and the broader urban periphery of Bila Tserkva were regional and mostly vegetable-growing areas. Raska sat adjacent to light industry, particularly timber, while the farms in Bila Tserkva were only three to six kilometres away from the significant industrial enterprises in the city. All farms supplied surplus vegetables to industrial or city areas before the war, with the farms in Bila Tserkva being major suppliers of the city. In 1945 and 1946, there was no indication that any of the barely operational farms in these areas were capable of resuming their pre-war supply. Local authorities thus considered the land more valuable if transformed into *podsobnoe khoziaistvo* for workers and low-level officials to feed themselves, especially during famine.

These collective farms started to rebuild seriously only when their menfolk returned from war to Raska from late 1945 and to Bila Tserkva from 1946. By this time, the land was already being used by its new owners. When *raion*-level authorities in Borodianka and city authorities in Bila Tserkva (*gorkom* and *gorsovet*) redrew the maps of the areas in which the farms were located at the end of the war, they omitted the farms. This omission reflected both the current realities and especially the aspirations for land usage among its new owners at the time. Urban residents, workers and institutions had appropriated the land in wartime and continued to use it after war's end. It is clear that in both cases authorities sought to expand this usage, by freeing up more collective farmland to feed themselves, as well as to accommodate growing numbers of workers in Bila Tserkva and the sprawling urban population of a rapidly reconstructing city.

In these and other cases of illegal appropriations discussed later in this book, it was the enduring context of disorganisation in the agricultural sector in Kyiv Oblast, particularity of land boundaries, tenure and related farm documentation, that provided possibilities for redefining the geography and use of collective farmland from liberation into the post-war period. Within this context, officials in Kyiv Oblast were able to officially transform sparely populated tracts of pre-war collective farm areas into *podsobnoe khoziaistvo* by rezoning the broader rural areas in which the land was located into industrial or urban areas when redrawing their post-war *raion* maps.[5] When the farms to which the land belonged were omitted from the revised maps of these areas, most *kolkhozniki* who remained on the land seemed to have complied with these changes. Whether they liked it or not, they were resettled on nearby farms or entered the urban workforce. Where people would not comply and leave the now-deleted farms, battle ensued, as in Raska and Bila Tserkva from 1945 and 1946 respectively. In the eyes of the local authorities, in appropriating the land and moving the *kolkhozniki* off it, they were not so much destroying these collective farms as removing 'rotten' squatters in the name of 'reconstruction'.

Making the Farms Invisible

These battles endured for so long and the injustices perpetrated on *kolkhozniki* were so severe because they were played out 'in the dark'. Rezoning these areas and deleting the farms therein made them less visible in the collective farm system and put them beyond the reach of superior republican and certainly central authorities, at least until 1948. This invisibility enabled the *raion*- and oblast-level authorities to act with the greatest scope to enforce the realities of rezoning in these areas. The most severe violence meted out by authorities to the remaining and recalcitrant *kolkhozniki* came when they threatened to thwart the broader rezoning

---

[5] Some Ukrainian scholars see the post-war industrialisation of Ukraine as the second wave, the first being in the 1930s. The character of this second wave, however, was different. See Smolii, *Ekonomichna istoriia Ukraïny*, 361.

project by their continued resistance to leaving the areas and by their supplications to superior authorities for assistance, which might make visible local authorities' illegal conduct.

The process of rezoning was different in Raska and Bila Tserkva, but the outcomes were similar. In Raska, Borodianka *raion* authorities redrew the map of their collective farms in the *raion* without Pershe Travnia in 1946 after they passed a decree liquidating it.[6] Raska and its surroundings thus eluded the approximately 16,000 commissions organised by the Council for Collective Farm Affairs to implement the September 1946 Campaign on Collective Farm Rules. Located ninety kilometres from Kyiv and on the border with Zhytomyr Oblast, Raska was not visited by oblast-level authorities, let alone republic-level ones. In 1946, it was not even a dot on the new map; there was a larger timber industrial complex on one side and a small town on the other. Between these dots on the map, *raion*-level authorities could act with the greatest impunity and protection from their superiors at the oblast level.

On the new map, the *raiispolkom* had reclassified collective farmland within the broader area in which Raska was located as *podsobnoe khoziaistvo*; as later became apparent, this was part of officials' plans to establish a workers' settlement around the large timber factory and other small light industries in the area. These industries sought expanded *podsobnoe khoziaistvo* to facilitate growth in their workforces, which – it was anticipated – would consist of demobilised soldiers returning to the areas from 1945 onwards. The problem for the fourteen industries and institutions that had appropriated Raska's land was that they were unable to transform much of it into fertile *podsobnoe khoziaistvo* to facilitate the expansion of their workforces or, by late 1946, even to sustain their existing ones. Much of the land that they had appropriated was sandy and not very fertile (the closest town to Raska is called Piskivka, from the Ukrainian word for sand – *pisok*). This lack of expansion was less of a problem for those institutions that used the land to generate profit, mostly from hay production.[7] It was more of a problem for the light industries around Raska that used it for food production, especially the timber and glass factories. The industries and institutions failed to attain their expected yields of vegetables from the land in their possession and sought more. By 1947, only 189 of Raska's 585 arable hectares were being used by the 14 appropriators. The institutions and factories could not afford to lose this land in the 1946 campaign. They needed more of it. The extra land was

---

[6] DAKO f. 4819, op. 14, d. 2, ll. 6–7, and f. 4810, op. 1, d. 3, ll. 5–6.

[7] DAKO f. 4810, op. 1, d. 3, l. 26.

supposed to come from the few hundred hectares of fertile land worked by most of the 287 or so inhabitants of Raska, but these inhabitants refused to evacuate despite the *raiispolkom* decree and enforcement of it.[8]

In Bila Tserkva, farms were deleted by the urban expansion of the city's peripheries in 1946 when city authorities successfully petitioned to elevate Bila Tserkva to a main administrative city in the oblast (*gorod oblastnogo podchineniia*). These authorities could meet the population requirements for this elevation only by artificially expanding city boundaries into its regional outskirts to claim this rural population as urban. The three collective farms located within this three- to six-kilometre range from the city centre, 'Peremoha' in Rotok, 'Imeni Lenina' in Oleksandriia and 'Tretii Vyrishal'nyi' in Zarichia, were enveloped into the city's new borders and deleted from the new city map. Again, for both the city authorities and the *raiispolkom*, the value of this collective farmland lay not in its collective farming application. This land was valuable in as much as it could support the post-war industrial boom in Bila Tserkva by providing *podsobnoe khoziaistvo* for workers and gardens for urban dwellers.

Industrial appetite for this land matched the intensity of the post-war industrial boom in the city. Having been reduced to rubble during the war and occupation, with an estimated 130 million roubles worth of damage, 1,125 houses and 23 industrial enterprises had been rebuilt by the end of 1944, along with a host of broader industrial infrastructure. Coupled with state investment of 20 million roubles in 1944, industrial output more than doubled by the following year and the city reached its industrial output targets of the 1946 five-year plan in only three and half years. Total industrial output by 1950 was 177 million roubles, about four times the pre-war level. Bila Tserkva was also one of the top four *raiony* in Kyiv Oblast in terms of both total acreage and rapidity of expansion of land used for *podsobnoe khoziaistvo*, for which the town was lauded by oblast-level authorities. Bila Tserkva seemed to have earned its title as a city of oblast-level importance conferred on it in 1946.

This was a serious economic boom, though the figures above must be treated cautiously as they are taken from official Soviet-era works that were published to highlight the phoenix-like rise of the USSR after the war.[9]

---

[8] Of the 287 total *kolkhozniki*, 150 were able-bodied: DAKO f. 4810, op. 1, d. 3, l. 40.
[9] Instytut istoriï NAN Ukraïny, *Istoriia mist i sil URSR. Kyïvs'ka oblast* (Kyiv: Instytut istoriï Ukraïny NAN Ukraïny, 1971), 116–20. See Chapter 3 for an explanation of why these areas were 'struggling'.

These works do not mention any industrial progress that required the appropriation of collective farmland; labour and resources came at the expense of agricultural progress in Bila Tserkva as it did across the Soviet Union.[10] Nor do they mention that rural areas even on the outskirts of big cities could ever hope for the same rate of investment as urban ones. The narrative of the 'phoenix rising' continues in post-Soviet city histories that are popular in Ukraine. In one of these recent multi-volume works on Bila Tserkva, the towns in which the farms are located are mentioned only in passing as struggling rural areas in 1946, with no further explanation as to the reasons why.[11]

On paper at least, the performance of the collective farm sector in Bila Tserkva was no poorer than the median level for Kyiv Oblast. Deliveries of grain to the state began to grow from 1944 onwards, were stunted by the famine, and resumed their upward trajectory afterwards. Bila Tserkva's collective farms delivered about 80 per cent of their grain quota to the state in 1947 and almost 100 per cent the following year.[12] But this overall picture of the *raion*'s agriculture conceals the difference between performing farms that took up the slack from struggling ones that *raion* authorities were keen to amalgamate with stronger farms nearby. The three farms under study here produced little of their food quotas when authorities denied them any support in 1946, and produced hardly any once most *kolkhozniki* had left by 1947.

The eradication of the farms on paper assisted this liquidation in reality. Both city and *raion* authorities issued decrees expanding *podsobnoe khoziaistvo* of numerous institutions and factories already using the farmland.[13] The lack of pre-war farm records documenting land boundaries and tenure arguments enabled the institutions to claim that the land had always been part of their pre-war land-holdings. The farms still remained operational on paper in *raion* documents and were supposed to be supervised by *raion* authorities. But *raion* authorities appropriated land for other purposes as well. In Bila Tserkva they pressured farm chairmen to 'temporarily' lease their farmland to other organisations, citing the incapacity of the farms to cultivate it, or passed false decrees to this effect when the chairmen did not

---

[10] On the broader illogicality of the collective farm system – that its exploitation to fund industrialisation and urban needs depleted the system so much that it produced rolling economic crises which clawed back the very urban progress it facilitated – see Popov, *Rossiiskaia derevnia*, 180.

[11] Oleksii Starodub et al., *Budivel',na istoriia Biloi Tserkvy XI–XXI stolit'*, vol. II (Bila Tserkva, 2017), 366.

[12] See harvest collection figures in DAKO f. r-880, op. 9, d. 29.

[13] DAKO f. 4810, op. 1, d. 31, ll. 12–16, 78–79.

comply.[14] In both areas, authorities encouraged *kolkhozniki* to give up 'useless' collective farm work and take up good employment in the towns. When encouragement was unsuccessful in Raska, authorities sought to remove farmers from the land violently but claimed *kolkhozniki* had given up their land voluntarily because labour and resource shortages meant they could not farm it. Both city and *raion* authorities were chief causes of these shortages and the chief beneficiaries of them.[15]

It should have been harder, however, for authorities in Bila Tserkva, as opposed to Raska, to pursue these policies without detection from superiors. In Bila Tserkva, the affected farms remained part of the collective farm sector despite city authorities' attempts to liquidate them. The farms remained officially operational after the war with set food obligations to the state and were administered at the *raion* level under the supervision, however imperfect, of the central authorities, which would demand explanations for any shortages in food deliveries to the state. How was it possible that the poor functioning of the farms, let alone the malicious policies of local authorities, remained invisible to republican and central authorities until 1948?

As a result of rezoning these rural areas as urban, the *kolkhozniki* and their personal land plots were now included in the city authorities' map and came under their authority, while the farms remained under the control of *raion* authorities. This jurisdictional distribution between *raion* and city authorities for farms and *kolkhozniki* effectively nullified the authorities' responsibilities to both. The city authorities refused to recognise these people as *kolkhozniki*, and not even as rural dwellers, classifying them instead as urban dwellers. As the head of the Bila Tserkva *gorsovet*, the 'old communist' Comrade Malashkevich explained, 'we don't deal with *kolkhozy*. That is not a matter for the city. For us there are no *kolkhozniki*, but only urban dwellers.' But when *kolkhozniki* complained about the city authority's confiscation of their land, its representatives replied: 'Go out onto your collective farmlands in the *raion* and get your land from there.'[16]

Raion authorities refused to meet the pleas of the *kolkhozniki* exactly because they were now classified as urban dwellers and thus not under their jurisdiction. *Kolkhozniki* fell deeper into a jurisdictional synapse of governance between town and country as local *sel'sovet*s (village councils) had

---

[14] See Archive Department of the Bila Tserkva Raion District Administration (Arkhivnyi viddil Bilotserkivs'koi raiderzhadministratsii – AV BRDA) f. 1, op. 1, dd. 63 and 99.
[15] DAKO f. 880, op. 9, d. 17, ll. 170–173.   [16] RGASPI f. 122, op. 122, d. 316, ll. 156–159.

been dissolved, which would have helped administer the farms, and may have provided a vehicle for *kolkhozniki* to pursue their interests, as it had in Raska.[17] In addition to being deleted from the new map, as the farm had been in Raska, those in Bila Tserkva within this jurisdictional synapse also became less visible to republican and central authorities supervising the collective farm system. This invisibility made them more vulnerable to the ambitions of local authorities, who wanted to push them off farms into industrial work and put collective farmland to other uses.

Taking the Farms

Rezoning on maps to reflect the actual realities of land usage on the ground or to expand urban peripheries was not uncommon at this time.[18] What was uncommon was the violent conduct of authorities to enforce the types of realities they anticipated, expanding light industry in Raska or extending urbanisation and industrialisation in Bila Tserkva. Authorities in Borodianka and Bila Tserkva pursued these aims within this context of invisibility that rezoning afforded them in both similar and different ways. The Borodianka *raiispolkom* failed to evict the villagers with its periodic raids on village livestock and food and the destruction of farm property in an attempt to substantiate the false claim of the 1945 decree that the land was uninhabited. The *raiispolkom* denied seed loans to the farms to replace what had been taken from them, but this too was ineffective, as nearby villages supplied Raska with seed to stave off starvation. Even the most pernicious attempt to arrest Raska's *kolkhozniki* for collaborating with anti-Soviet Ukrainian nationalist forces (who were known to operate in the nearby woods) had failed. This accusation was baseless and unconvincing to superior authorities for numerous reasons, not least because of the mass murder of Polish civilians by Ukrainian nationalist forces in the west of the country.[19] But it fit well with the pre-war history of baseless

---

[17] In Raska, Chairman S. I. Kuriata was also a member of the local *sel'sovet*.

[18] See land usage records in DAKO from the oblast-level agricultural department, f. 4819, op. 4, d. 2, and op. 13, d. 2, for 1944–6; and f. 4819, op. 24, d. 2, and op. 25, d. 2, for 1947.

[19] Statiev, *The Soviet Counterinsurgency*, 123; on broader ethnic cleansing and population exchanges between Ukraine and Poland at this time, see Snyder, *Bloodlands*, 313–39. There are some cases of joint operations between anti-communist Polish military formations and Ukrainian nationalists in the immediate aftermath of the war during the territorial and population exchanges between Poland and Ukraine, but these were dwarfed by the general conflict between Ukrainian and Polish groups. See Yaroslav Hrytsak, *Narys istorii Ukraïny. Formuvannia modernoi natsii XIX–XX stolittia* (Kyiv: Heneza, 1996), 201.

discrimination against Poles in Raska,[20] who 'smelled bad' to local authorities even before they became 'rotten' after the war.

By early 1948, *raion*-level officials began to ease their violent conduct
towards the *kolkhozniki*. Accelerating this shift was their growing fear that
representatives of the Council on Collective Farm Affairs in Kyiv Oblast
were aware of their conduct in Raska and elsewhere, and that the veil of
invisibility in which these areas were shrouded would come loose. The
Borodianka *raiispolkom* learnt in mid-1947 of the supplications Raska's
kolkhozniki had sent to Moscow asking for assistance in rebuilding their
farm and the accompanying indictment of *raion*-level authorities for their
behaviour. The *kolkhozniki* sent their supplication to Lazar Kaganovich,
who had now displaced Khrushchev as head of the CP(b)U, but were
informed by his office that it was returned to the head of the Kyiv
obliispolkom as the relevant superior authority (likely without the busy
secretary's knowledge):

> We inform you that your letter addressed to Secretary of the TsK VKP(b)
> Comrade Kaganovich was received on 3 June 1947 (No. LK-13008) and
> passed on for review to the head of the Kyiv Oblast Council of Workers,
> Comrade [Z. F.] Oleinik.[21]

Having received no news from the *obliispolkom* as to the status of their
supplication, the *kolkhozniki* travelled to its office in Kyiv to see Oleinik.
But they were dismissed by *obliispolkom* deputy chairman concerned with
agricultural affairs, Dvornikov, at his office door. He refused to hear their
complaints and told them that 'it had already been decided' that they
would be forcibly resettled and Raska liquidated. Not that seeing Oleinik
would have done much good. Another report to Kaganovich outlining the
successes and failures of the 1946 campaign in Kyiv Oblast identified
Comrade Oleinik as one of the officials who had failed to prosecute low-
level appropriators. It did not implicate him in any broader conspiracy but
intimated it in the following sentence: 'our review shows that while the
low-level appropriators are arrested, those in higher positions who push
them into committing such crimes remain free'.[22] Unable to get
Kaganovich's ear, pleas for assistance from the *kolkhozniki*, like those of
so many other supplicants, thus returned to the secrecy of the circle of
corruption and protection that it sought to uncover.

---

[20] For a history of denunciations among industrial workers in the Soviet Union during the 1930s, see
Wendy Z. Goldman, *Inventing the Enemy: Denunciation and Terror in Stalin's Russia* (Cambridge:
Cambridge University Press, 2011).
[21] RGASPI f. 316, op. 17, d. 122, l. 153.   [22] TsDAHOU f. 1, op. 23, d. 4783, l. 129 (October 1946).

But this was only a temporary setback. Kaganovich might not have read this report implicating Oleinik either, but someone close to him did, and it is an important indication that the republic-level bureaucracy were at least aware of the acute problems in agricultural management in Kyiv Oblast. The chief representative of the Council on Collective Farm Affairs in Kyiv Oblast, M. Gordienko, read this report as well, and he was the first to make the connection between Oleinik at the top and crimes in Raska and Bila Tserkva from late 1947. The supplications of the *kolkhozniki* thus initiated a chain of events that led to Gordienko visiting them in January 1948 and beginning to draw attention to disparate oblast-level abuse that, it is now clear, formed part of a major conspiracy to illegally appropriate land here and elsewhere across the oblast.

By late 1947, oblast-level authorities had become wary of Gordienko and accelerated their efforts to liquidate the farm and village before the invisible farm became more visible. In September 1947, oblast-level authorities pushed through a major decree to reaffirm the post-war *raion* map by officially clearing what remained of the area surrounding Raska and its non-operational farm, fulfilling Dvornikov's promise. Oleinik ensured that the decree was passed by both state (*obliispolkom*) and party (*obkom*) executive bodies. This decree allocated all of Raska's 585 hectares to the Local Anti-Aircraft Defence Organisation (MPVO) as part of the *obliis-polkom*'s 'recovery' of MPVO pre-war land-holdings, a broader process across the oblast.[23] The decree sealed off the village's single road to the nearby town and declared it a forbidden zone which no one other than the MPVO could access – as was the norm in these sorts of areas. The decree stipulated precise instructions for the evacuation of the *kolkhozniki* to the nearby villages and farms.

It is clear that this bogus decree was not intended to be implemented, as the *kolkhozniki* remained on the land and the appropriating institutions continued to use it. Nor was it intended, as the 1946 Sovmin decree imagined, to provide a 'guise' under which officials would use the land for their own profit. This decree was clearly intended to stifle investigations into the area by other authorities. This 'military appropriation' promised to be especially effective to this end because local authorities were expected to help facilitate the expansion of military installations and airport

---

[23] On the recovery of MPVO land-holdings, see DAKO f. r-880, op. 9, d. 3; specifically for land recovered from collective farms, see ll. 51, 52, 74. On central authorities' ill-considered redirection of raw materials and resources designated for local civilian reconstruction to the emerging military-industrial complex in the immediate post-war period, see A. Danilov and A. V. Pyzhikov, *Rozhdenie sverkhderzhavy. SSSR v pervye poslevoennye gody* (Moscow: Rosspen, 2001), ch. 2.

construction around Kyiv as part of the broader post-war military build-up in the Soviet Union.[24] The initial liquidation decree for Raska in 1946 had mentioned that a large chunk of its appropriated land was intended for the Kyiv military *okrug* to feed its hungry soldiers, and Oleinik had received numerous similar requests for such land previously. Given their military nature, many requests were granted without fuss or attracting any attention from superiors.[25] This breathing space from higher authorities would give the *raiispolkom* time to deal with the recalcitrant *kolkhozniki* in Raska before the Council on Collective Farm Affairs could act.

The *raiispolkom* did this, surprisingly, by abandoning their violent methods and offering positive incentives to the *kolkhozniki* to leave the land and cease their supplications. The *raiispolkom* officials now promised the *kolkhozniki* they could remain in their homes and keep the graves of their loved ones if they gave up their remaining farmland to the appropriating industries and took up employment therein. The *kolkhozniki* would be part of a broader transformation of the area into a workers' settlement, where more workers would come and improve the area's economy.[26] Most settlements at this time comprised at least a couple of thousand residents and were, in terms of development, a halfway point between village and town, but with most of its residents engaged in industrial rather than farm work. *Kolkhozniki* would thus be able to take a money wage without having to move to the city – something many other *kolkhozniki* in their position travelled illegally to the cities to acquire, even under threat of prosecution. They would just need to 'sign up' to industrial work and forego their applications for rebuilding the collective farm. The chairman of the Borodianka *raiispolkom*, Comrade Shidaev, visited Raska for the first time in January 1948 to make this offer in person. It was still dangerous for Soviet officials to visit, as Ukrainian nationalist forces were active in the area. Previously, even lower-level officials had travelled to the area under armed guard. Shidaev 'asked' the *kolkhozniki* to reflect on the deeper purpose of their struggle: 'Even if the government gives you 100,000 roubles tomorrow to rebuild your farm, what will that money really buy you?'[27] Shidaev's rhetorical question did not have the desired effect of prompting the *kolkhozniki* to contemplate the hopelessness of their struggle or make his offer more appealing. The *kolkhozniki* rejected not only this

---

[24] DAKO f. r-880, op. 9, d. 50, ll. 2–11.   [25] DAKO f. 4819, op. 14, d. 2, ll. 6–7.
[26] On workers' settlements, see Donald Filtzer, 'Standard of Living versus Quality of Life: Struggling with the Urban Environment in Russia during the Early Years of Post-War Reconstruction', in Fürst, ed., *Late Stalinist Russia*, 85–90.
[27] DAKO f. 4810, op. 1, d. 3, l. 13.

offer, but also his last-ditch 'compromise', delivered on 26 January by his subordinate, Comrade Marchenko. Marchenko's last interaction with Raska's farm chairman, Comrade S. I. Kuriata, had been to warn him against appealing to authorities to rebuild his farm and especially from travelling to Kyiv for this purpose. Marchenko now told the *kolkhozniki* that, if they were not ready to become part of a workers' settlement, they could remain in their homes only if they gave up to the nearby glass factory (which would employ them) another 185 hectares of the fertile land that they occupied and, perhaps in year or so, if the agricultural situation improved, they could resume their efforts at rebuilding the farm.

The *kolkhozniki* rejected these 'good offers', clearly distrustful of promises made by the same people who had been trying to evict them from their homes for three years. They had no indication that officials would keep their promises of employment or, especially, of allowing them to remain in the village. They also probably understood that these promises were mutually exclusive, though neither Shidaev nor Marchenko mentioned it. Both offers required *kolkhozniki* to become workers just like others who would likely come to their area as a result of freeing up the farmland. *Kolkhozniki*, turned into workers, would lose their priority access to the food, albeit meagre, grown on it as well as their legal bond to the farm and land.

Though in a desperate situation, the *kolkhozniki* thus had little reason to take up either offer. It was fortunate that they did not, as the following day, 27 January 1948, Kyiv *obliispolkom* passed a resolution nullifying the previous decree in September 1947 ordering the liquidation of Raska and its farm Pershe Travnia. This resolution instructed that Raska be reconstructed.[28] But nothing happened until May 1948 when the Council on Collective Farm Affairs in Moscow was so incensed at the lack of implementation that it issued its own decree, which it forced Kyiv *obkom* to reissue. This decree demanded the return to the farm of all land appropriated by others, insisted that all officials now aid in its reconstruction, and sought to punish Shidaev and his superiors at the oblast level responsible for destroying Raska (Dvornikov but not Oleinik).[29] It seems Shidaev had made the last-ditch effort to get the *kolkhozniki* on side and sign up to industrial employment to help avoid the necessity of passing of the 27 January 1948 decree in the *obliispolkom* (his superior body) and of his likely punishment. The *kolkhozniki* did not know about this impending

---

[28] RGASPI f. 17, op. 122, d. 316, l. 155. It was passed by Kyiv *obliispolkom* on 27 January 1948 and then by Kyiv *obkom* in March: DAKO f. 4810, op. 1, d. 3, l. 2, and f. r-880, op. 9, d. 30, l. 37.
[29] DAKO f. 4810, op. 1, d. 33, ll. 75–76.

decree. But, as later collective farm meetings (*sobraniia*) indicate, they may have suspected that the pressure from above was beginning to be felt by local authorities. They had communication with Gordienko at the time and, in any case, were suspicious of the 'friendliness' of the same officials who had long sought to destroy their home.[30]

When the Bila Tserkva city and *raion* authorities learnt of the Council on Collective Farm Affairs' growing interest in the farms on the outskirts of the city in late 1947, unlike in Raska, they did not adopt more positive methods to persuade the *kolkhozniki* to give up their fight. Instead, they redoubled their violent methods of moving *kolkhozniki* off the land and inducing them to take up industrial employment. Officials here facilitated the appropriation of more than 1,000 hectares of land from these farms in 1947 alone and encroached on their homesteads, appropriating several of these too. This commitment to appropriations continued despite growing concern among officials that their conduct would be revealed by the Council, partly because their violent conduct on the farms had significantly decreased their populations and hindered them from functioning as collective farms. Officials thus had good cause to argue against advice from the Council to assist the farms in late 1947, claiming that a farm could not be run properly with only a handful of households. In Raska, Gordienko could cite the commitment to the land displayed by the *kolkhozniki* as evidence of the need for farm reconstruction in his appeals to his superiors for assistance. But in Bila Tserkva he could not.

Authorities in Bila Tserkva were also more successful in liquidating the farm populations until late 1947 because they possessed a weapon that the Borodianka *raiispolkom* lacked. As operational collective farms, those in Bila Tserkva remained bound by collective farm rules stipulating the size of their private plots. Authorities had an additional lever to starve the *kolkhozniki* out from their homes by minimising or even entirely confiscating all of the private plots. These plots remained the only source of food for *kolkhozniki*, as they were not paid in money and scarcely in food for days worked as per the law. These 'incentives' to leave the farms worked. The farms lost the majority of their post-war *kolkhoznik* households to out-migration and urban relocation so that, by 1948, they could not function as collective farms without hired labour – especially at sowing and harvest time – a key justification used by authorities to take more land from the farms.

---

[30] For records of farm meetings, see DAKO f. 4819, op. 1, dd. 15, 16, 21, 25.

The reduction of private plots on the farms in Bila Tserkva was severe, but by no means uncommon across Ukraine.[31] The difference was that the outcomes for them were more severe than those farms that continued to operate with state support. The reduction in the private plot size of the *kolkhozniki* in Bila Tserkva began in late 1946 from two directions: from *raion* authorities implementing the 1946 Campaign on Collective Farm Rules and from the city authorities, reducing the size of *kolkhozniki*'s private plots, supposedly to align with the smaller plots permitted to urban dwellers in 1946. In the first case, *raiispolkom* officials found that most *kolkhozniki* had expanded their private plots beyond their allocations during the war and reassigned the land to the collective. They were clearly implementing the 1946 campaign here in the same way as they did in some other places in the *raion*, that is, excessively and often arbitrarily. However, it was even more evident on the farms under study because these officials did not take into account the actual reductions in plot size already made by the city authorities, which also exacerbated the impact of future reductions they would make. In the case of Imeni Lenina, the scale of double land reductions from the *raion* and city authorities had become so absurd that by March 1947 both had to concede that most of its *kolkhozniki* were left with no private plots whatsoever.

Excessive reductions in plot sizes in some areas were imposed by authorities, who were under severe pressure from central authorities to produce results. When authorities implemented the 1946 decree, they not only reduced the size of *kolkhozniki*'s plots, sometimes to below the level set in law, but often took the most fertile land available from these plots to give back to the collective. The 1946 campaign's fundamental purpose is evident here. Reducing plot size was the means by which *kolkhozniki* would be dissuaded from working on their private land, where they spent most of their energy, and forced into engaging in collective farm work for the state.[32] The reduction in size and fertility of private plot land devastated *kolkhozniki* and, along with new and higher taxes on the food that they produced from the smaller plots left to them, threatened their survival in the midst of a mass drought from mid-1946.[33]

[31] For the massive reduction in Kherson Oblast, see TsDAVOU f. r-2, op. 7, ll. 3, 6, 35, 39.

[32] D. V. Milokhin and A. F. Smetanin, *Komi. Kolkhoznaia derevnia v poslevoennye gody, 1946–1958: sotsial'no-ekonomicheskie aspekty razvitiia* (Moscow: Nauka, 2005), 37.

[33] On the scale of private plot reductions across the Soviet Union, see Chapter 3, and Rashit Mukhamedov and Evgeni Nikolaev, 'Priusadebnye khoziaistva kolkhoznikov v poslevoennyi period (1946–1953 gg.)', *Obshchestvo: filosofiia, istoriia, kultura* no. 5 (2017), 89. Thousands of collective farm chairmen and local officials were prosecuted for failing to deliver quotas to the

The barrage of land reductions, new and higher taxes, and the massive purge of collective farm leaderships for their connivance in land expansions brought an already devastated collective farm sector to its knees. These were among the major factors exacerbating the impact of drought on agricultural production that was unable to meet demand from a higher population, which led to famine from late 1946 and early 1947 across the western parts of the USSR, especially in Ukraine. But, as with most Soviet campaigns, the pressure on the sector from above was not sustained. *Kolkhozniki* resumed enlarging their plots or at least using collective farmland for private purposes once the pressure of this campaign receded and when authorities reapplied pressure on the countryside with their anti-theft campaign as famine continued into late 1947.[34] As much of the literature on collective farming attests, central authorities' attempts to squeeze *kolkhozniki* and enforce compliance by more draconian taxes and rules often forced the latter to disobey these rules to survive the growing demands made on them.[35]

The problem in Bila Tserkva was that *kolkhozniki* on the farms under study here were barely able to employ these survival mechanisms in the wake of the Campaign on Collective Farm Rules, at least not for long. No such partnership was possible with authorities there. Not only were the authorities' actions distinguished from those of others across the Soviet Union by their continuing pressure to reduce private plot sizes into 1948. They were also unique in their frequent appropriation of often the most fertile collective farmland for distribution to institutions and factories and other 'urban dwellers' so as to increase their private plot size far beyond what was permitted by law. City authorities appropriated private plots, while *raion* authorities also appropriated the most fertile farmland, reducing the capacity of *kolkhozniki* to recover production losses from their smaller private plots by using collective farmland for private purposes.

---

state. For prosecutions across Ukraine, Yurii Shapoval writes, 'During 1946 and the first quarter of 1947, 1,131 collective farm chairmen were convicted, 513 of them were sentenced to three years' imprisonment, 219 for five years, 112 to 10 years, and two executed': Y. Shapoval, 'Holod 1946–1947 rokiv v Rosii ta v Ukraini. Potreba porivnyal'noho analizu', in V. M. Danylenko, ed., *Ukraïna XX st. Kul'tura, ideolohiia, polityka*, vol. XIII (Kyiv: Instytut istoriï Ukraïny NAN Ukraïny, 2008), 345–6.

[34] O. R. Khasianov, 'Khoziaistvennaia povsednevnost' kolkhoznoi derevni v poslevoennoe desiatiletie (na materialakh Kuibyshevskoi i Ulianovskoi oblastei)', *Istoriia: fakty i simvoli*, no. 3, 2016, 35–43. For the continuation of this problem into the 1950s, see Popov, *Krest'ianstvo i gosudarstvo*, 278–80. On the famine and other survival mechanisms developed by *kolkhozniki* during the famine, i.e. market trade, flight to the cities etc., see Ganson, *Soviet Famine*, ch. 4.

[35] Ganson, *Soviet Famine*; Verbitskaia, *Rossiiskoe krest'ianstvo*; T. D. Nadkin, *Stalinskaia agrarnaia politika i krest'ianstvo Mordovii* (Moscow: Rosspen, 2010); Milokhin, *Komi. Kolkhoznaia derevnia*.

Neither authority was interested in implementing the 1946 campaign for its intended purpose, but more interested in taking land for their own uses.

A *kolkhoznitsa* (female member of a *kolkhoz*) from Peremoha in Rotok, Comrade Dubova, best described this process of land transfer or the fundamental reversal of urban and rural land rights, the accuracy of which was later confirmed by investigations into the activities of the city and *raion* authorities:

> City authorities try to convince us that our farm will not be rebuilt. They liquidated the *sel'sovet* and freed former collective farmers from their agricultural taxes by classifying them as urban dwellers. They don't work anywhere, and the city authorities have permitted them greater private plots than the remaining *kolkhozniki* [who still pay their taxes] but whose plots they have reduced to the size permitted to urban dwellers . . . This is why our farm is on the brink of collapse and twenty-nine more families have already left it in 1948.[36]

Authorities continued to levy taxes on the *kolkhozniki* who remained on the farms, but not on those who left farm work and continued to use the land to produce food for private purposes.[37] This policy made a mockery of city authorities' claims that neither farms nor *kolkhozniki* remained on land that was rezoned from rural to urban and is indicative of their primary motivation of liquidating the farms. When the area was rezoned in 1946, its land was classified as *podsobnoe khoziaistvo* for former *kolkhozniki* and other urban dwellers to produce their own food while also working in the city. There was no tax burden on food produced on this land. But former *kolkhozniki* hardly worked in the city. They used this land mostly to produce food for subsistence and/or sell at market. This food thus should have been taxed as food produced on private plots on collective farms, in fact, even more so (see Chapter 4). Instead, city and authorities' reduction of the size of *kolkhozniki*'s private plots and continual taxation of their produce, while removing these taxes for those who left farm work and enlarged their plots at the expense of those who remained, encouraged more and more *kolkhozniki* to leave farm work until the farms were unviable.

Almost 1,000 hectares of the land belonging to *kolkhoznik* private plots had been taken since 1944 and given to those families who had left the farms or other urban dwellers on Tretii Vyrishal'nyi, with similar amounts on Peremoha and Imeni Lenina. City and *raion* authorities took thousands

---

[36] See both RGASPI f. 17, op. 122, d. 316, ll. 157–158, and TsDAHOU f. 1, op. 51, d. 3648, l. 150.
[37] RGASPI f. 17, op. 122, d. 317, l. 11.

more hectares of fertile land from the collective. They reduced the larger plot size permitted to *kolkhozniki* with the smaller plots permitted to urban dwellers. But this reduction was not, as the authorities claimed, in line with the 'new status', which was intended to align the land-holdings of *kolkhozniki* with their new position as 'urban dwellers'. Authorities transferred the land from these private plots to other real 'urban dwellers', that is, those not engaged in farm work, whose land-holdings grew massively beyond the size legally permitted and certainly beyond the size held by *kolkhozniki*.

The local land surveyor (*zemleustroitel'*), who was charged with measuring plot sizes, and two officials from the *gorsovet* were the key executors of this land transfer across all three farms. The *zemleustroitel'* took land from both 'troublesome' *kolkhozniki* and ordinary ones, limiting their recourse against the land confiscations by imposing sanctions on them or threatening them with arrest. *Kolkhozniki* suffered significant reductions. Some had reductions of their entire plots and others a reduction below the minimum legal allotment (0.25 hectares). Much of the land they were left with was of the poorest quality, which compounded the destitution of the households. Investigations into the state of the farms from 1947 consistently noted this destitution in addition to the general degeneration of collective farmland and crop failure.[38]

The *zemleustroitel'* gave the land taken from these *kolkhozniki* directly to those who had left the farm or farm work to take up industrial work, but still lived in the villages or in the vicinity of the farms. As a side business, the *zemleustroitel'* offered remaining land to other urban dwellers in exchange for bribes, which is a further reminder of how self-enrichment still could still play a role in illegal appropriations intended for *podsobnoe khoziaistvo*. Former *kolkhozniki* also enlarged their plots on their own, usually by cutting into collective farmland. City authorities enabled them to do this without punishment, while continuing, along with *raion* authorities, to punish remaining *kolkhozniki* for the same transgression.[39] When collective farm chairmen sought to push back against this reversal of urban and rural land rights, the *raiispolkom* and city authorities mobilised the local prosecutor to punish them. Chairmen of the three farms in Bila Tserkva were charged with numerous contrived offences during 1947 and 1948, exactly when authorities learnt they were writing supplications to superior authorities outlining the abuses of local officials and the crimes of the *zemleustroitel'*. Farm Chairman Krugliakovskyi on Peremoha (Rotok) was specifically removed not only for complaining, but also for conducting

---

[38] DAKO f. 4810, op. 1, d. 33, ll. 12–13.   [39] AV BRDA f. 1, op. 1, d. 103, l. 17.

his own investigation of the actions of the *zemleustroitel'*.[40] Ironically, the one accurate charge made by authorities against the chairmen was stripping collective farm membership from *kolkhozniki* who had left the farms and/ or farm work and were given more land by authorities.[41]

This reversal of urban and rural land rights and tax regimes along with legal pressure constituted the key method used by city and *raion* authorities to move the *kolkhozniki* from farm work into industrial work in the city. This fed into the broader transformation from collective farm areas to *podsobnoe khoziaistvo* on the city's outskirts to fund urban and industrial expansion. This absurd tax regime further squeezed *kolkhozniki* who were already tempted to flee from rural areas to the town to deal with the food shortages of the famine and thereafter.[42] They left the farms in Bila Tserkva in their droves. In addition to Peremoha, by the end of 1947, on Tretii Vyrishal'nyi only 162 households remained of 560 before the war, and on Imeni Lenina, 70 remained of 170. On this farm, which *gorkom* head Comrade Tkachenko referred to as a 'leader in our *raion*', almost all of the sowing and harvesting had to be completed by hired workers, which plunged the farms into crippling debt.[43]

By the end of 1947, city and *raion* authorities had succeeded in rendering the farms in Bila Tserkva non-operational, with the majority of their pre-war land-holdings controlled by institutions, factories or non-collective farm members. These farms were not officially liquidated as in Raska, but may as well have been. Cognisant of the failures of the farms, authorities still refused to provide them with any further basic implements needed for operation, from pitchforks to seed – and certainly not livestock. The farms failed to produce any meaningful crops in 1947. *Kolkhozniki* who remained committed to the farms struggled to survive from land and resources left to them. By this time *kolkhozniki* in Raska were also struggling and their farm had been officially liquidated. Unlike in Bila Tserkva, most remained on the land and survived the violence meted out to them largely because of their capacity to feed

[40] DAKO f. 4810, op. 1, d. 33, l. 13.   [41] AV BRDA f. 1, op. 1, d. 103, ll. 17–18, and d. 116, l. 202.
[42] Ganson, *Soviet Famine*, ch. 4.
[43] These reductions should be seen within the broader context of the general increase in the number of households per collective farm in spite of the significant reduction in the collective farm population. This was due, in part, to *kolkhozniki* artificially claiming larger households or fake divisions within families to create new households. Both entitled *kolkhozniki* to greater private plot land. This abuse became widespread after the war. On this broad development, see Arutiunian, *Sovetskoe krest'ianstvo*, 331; for the Urals, see R. R. Hisamutdinova, 'Narusheniia kolkhoznogo zemlepolzovaniia na Urale v 1940–1950-e gg.', *Vestnik Leningradskogo gosudarstvennogo universiteta im. A.S. Pushkina* 4, no. 1 (2014), 116–23.

themselves from the sliver of land left to them and help from their neighbours or hired hands.

Until 1948 when the farms were officially reconstructed, *kolkhozniki* had no recourse against the illegal land seizures and broader abuse from the local authorities. In Bila Tserkva, authorities noted serious abuses in authorities' confiscation of the private plot land of *kolkhozniki* as part of a broader Ukraine-wide review commissioned by the Ukrainian government (Sovmin) into overzealous confiscation made during the 1946 campaign. In mid- to late 1947 the oblast-level agriculture department earmarked some land for return to *kolkhozniki* on these farms, especially on Imeni Lenina where all of the private plot land had been confiscated. But there is no evidence that any of recommendations for returning land to these farms were acted upon by oblast-level officials, including Oleinik, who was charged with reporting on the findings of the commission to his superiors.[44] Nor did these officials do much to 'reconstruct' the farms when they were ordered to in 1948. In some ways, conditions on these farms worsened after the decrees, especially in Bila Tserkva. Authorities did not provide much assistance to the farms nor punish those they were supposed to for their crimes. These land abuses and failure to take seriously pressure from Moscow on land usage and punishments, as evidenced below, were symptomatic across the oblast and in some other areas of Ukraine, especially at this time. In the wake of famine and the better 1947 harvest, central pressure on the collective farm sector for resources reduced, as did the power of the Council on Collective Farm Affairs to enforce its recommendations on punishments. Raska and Bila Tserkva were extreme but not isolated cases of a broader problem.

The Broader Problem across Kyiv Oblast and Ukraine

Council on Collective Farm Affairs representatives claimed to their superiors in Moscow that the illegal activity of *raion*-level officials was possible only because of the failure of their oblast-level superiors to monitor them. They provided examples of how the failure of the overworked and under-staffed oblast-level agriculture department to check and formalise changes in land ownership had caused massive problems in the sector. These problems included confusion in agricultural planning, grain losses by letting arable grain-growing land be used inefficiently for private use, land falling into disuse, and incorrectly applying taxes to farms for using

---

[44] TsDAVOU f. r-2, op. 7, d. 5038, l. 118.

land that been appropriated from them by institutions. At the same time, numerous examples in the archival record clearly indicate that oblast-level authorities permitted abuses in land usage and protected those responsible at lower levels of government. These were not 'isolated incidents', and many escaped the attention of Council representatives.[45] It is clear from these examples that Dvornikov was a key player in charge of the agriculture department in his position as *obliispolkom* secretary for agricultural affairs, much more so than the nominal head of the agriculture department.

Chapter 4 calculates the scale of illegal land appropriations in Kyiv Oblast and Ukraine and traces the consequences on post-war agriculture and broader economies of reconstruction. Here it is important to identify oblast-level participation, rather than negligence, in illegal land appropriations to determine how widespread its policy of using land for non-collective farm purposes was, beyond the case studies offered here. Differentiating between negligence and participation in land appropriations can be difficult. It is not a matter of simply listing the many examples of land abuse that may testify to either, as in most examples distinctions between negligence and participation are unclear. The primary way that we can clarify these cases and demonstrate the scale of this secretive policy is to identify the methods used by oblast-level authorities to obfuscate illegal appropriations in the archival record. The authorities' methods were effective in avoiding attention from investigative organs, at least for some time, because they were also used to process daily legal land appropriations and transfers of ownership. By interrogating some of the 'legal' examples where these same methods were used, we can begin to identify how much of the 'legal record' is likely false and thus the scale of the problem.

Raion- and oblast-level authorities often claimed the appropriations of collective farmland were for military use and airport construction. When redesignating it as *podsobnoe khoziaistvo*, they justified the appropriation mainly on the basis that the land was empty and, if it had belonged to collective farms previously, these farms had not been reconstructed or had been amalgamated. Large tracts of collective farm areas were certainly under- or unpopulated at the end of the war, given the massive population losses across Ukraine and the delay in the return of people from abroad, from military service or from bondage. Wartime farm amalgamations had also made some areas uninhabited. But surviving members of the farms were still usually nearby and started rebuilding their farms in anticipation of the return of their

[45] DAKO f. 4810, op. 1, d. 31, ll. 61–86.

families. This was a gradual process, and authorities usually waited for it to play out before making claims about unreconstructed farms, unless the land had already been put to other uses, as it had been in Raska and elsewhere. This claim of 'empty land' often became a justification to continue the wartime usage of the land for non-collective farm purposes into the post-war period once it had become illegal to do so. This happened initially in Raska after the liquidation orders and on four other farms in other *raiony* besides Bila Tserkva that authorities also liquidated 'on paper', despite the fact that in most of them *kolkhozniki* continued to live and work 'in the dark' without help or, indeed, recognition from authorities.

Even after Kyiv *obkom* passed the 1948 decrees reinstating the farms in Raska and Bila Tserkva, officials continued to hold to this false line of 'empty farms' to explain why they had appropriated the farmland in the first place and, at least in Raska, why the farm was still struggling. The secretary of the party organisation (*raikom*) in Borodianka *raion* where Raska is located, Comrade Petrov, lied openly about empty land in Raska to the head of the CP(b)U, Nikita Khrushchev, in front of sixty-four delegates at the May 1949 Kyiv *obkom* CP(b)U Plenum. Petrov was countering criticism from the plenum delegates on live-stock production in his *raion*, boasting that every farm therein possessed sufficient cattle. Petrov conceded that there was one poor struggling farm with only a single cow called Pershe Travnia (or Pervoe Maia in his Russian usage) in Raska. By chance, Petrov mentioned this at the same time as Khrushchev entered the plenum hall to the applause of delegates. Perplexed, Khrushchev interrupted Petrov's speech and interrogated him about this strange 'one-cow farm' in front of the other delegates:

KHRUSHCHEV: Really, you mean to say that from the entire *raion* they gave only one cow to this farm? Surely if they could give one cow in 1948, they could have given them more cows five years ago upon liberation?

PETROV: The farm has only just been reconstructed.

KHRUSHCHEV: Why has it only been reconstructed now?

PETROV: It was burnt to the ground by the Germans.

KHRUSHCHEV: That does not make any sense. We had hundreds of farms burnt to the ground, but they were all reconstructed in the same year that they were liberated.

PETROV: There weren't any people there.

KHRUSHCHEV: I don't know about this specific case, but I think the problem is not with the people, but with the authorities. Clearly, the *kolkhozniki* were hiding somewhere, probably in nearby villages, and were given no help whatsoever by anyone to reconstruct their village upon liberation. Where else would the *kolkhozniki* have come from, Siberia?

PETROV: From other collective farms in other *raiony*.[46]

Khrushchev allowed Petrov just enough rope to hang himself. Khrushchev most likely knew the details of this case from a report outlining the abuses in Raska and Bila Tserkva that had been sent to him in mid-1948 and had had its claims verified by his deputy.[47] The report explains that survivors of the 1943 massacre in Raska did indeed hide in adjacent villages and began rebuilding their village slowly from late 1944 and in earnest when their menfolk returned from war from the following year, but were stopped by *raion* authorities. Not only was Petrov lying about Raska, but, as Khrushchev likely understood, he was also part of the vertical chain of officials responsible for denying the rebuilding efforts of Raska and others in a *raion* that Khrushchev himself had earmarked for the growth of collective farming at a CP(b)U Central Committee Plenum only four months prior.[48]

Petrov survived Khrushchev's interrogation. By mid-1949, Khrushchev was preparing to leave Ukraine for another position in Moscow and had little time and limited capacity to unravel the vertical of which Petrov was part (discussed in the next chapter). Petrov and other officials along this vertical of power conducted many of their appropriations through the oblast-level agriculture department, using the body responsible for enforcing legal land usage to circumvent it. Department officials approved illegal appropriations mostly on the basis that the collective farmland was empty or had never belonged to the farm in the first place. They helped cover up these illegal claims if they were investigated by other bodies. Minutes of a meeting of departmental officials in February 1946 are most revealing of the department's active participation in this illegal activity. This document was not available to representatives from the Council on Collective Farm Affairs when they were indicting this department for its failures, but is available to researchers now. The officials at the meeting claimed that, by the end of 1945, almost all of Kyiv Oblast's 2,378 pre-war collective farms had been reconstructed and their pre-war land boundaries completely re-established. Only thirteen farms had not been reconstructed. These claims were erroneous. The Council's commissions found during their investigations in late 1946 that many farms were reconstructed only on paper and were not operational, and it was clear that most farms had not

---

[46] TsDAHOU f. 1, op. 52, d. 837, ll. 64–72.   [47] DAKO f. 4810, op. 1, d. 3, l. 5.

[48] 16th Plenum of the Central Committee of the Communist Party of Ukraine, January 1949 (Petrov was clearly aware of Khrushchev's instructions here): TsDAHOU f. 1, op. 52, d. 837, l. 66.

been reconstructed to their pre-war land boundaries given the dearth of relevant documentation.

Of the thirteen farms not reconstructed according to the department, ten were due to permanent amalgamations while three because the people who worked there had all been either killed or evacuated completely by the Germans.[49] Raska's farm was listed here, despite the fact that Raska's *kolkhozniki* and first returning soldiers were on site by the end of 1945 and had already submitted an application to Borodianka *raiispolkom* for reconstruction by this time. The author could not locate similar submissions made by *kolkhozniki* from the other listed farms in other *raiony* and the nearby town of Shpola, but found submissions by *kolkhozniki* from other farms later listed as unreconstructed by the department for the same reason of 'emptiness'. These additional farms in the Korsun-Shevchenko *raion* (adjoining Bila Tserkva) were 'liquidated' by the department at the end of the war despite the fact that *kolkhozniki* remained on the land and continued to make submissions for assistance until 1948.[50] Their lands were appropriated for *podsobnoe khoziaistvo* as well. When the department sent one of its senior officials (present at the February 1946 meeting mentioned earlier) Comrade Belous, to investigate queries from the Council about these farms (in 1948), he falsely reported failing to find any people on these farms, writing that the 'facts are not confirmed by the investigation'.

This single phrase, 'facts are not confirmed by the investigation', is the key one to look for in agriculture department documents to spot cover-ups. Comrade Belous and his colleagues applied it widely to complaints that came before the agriculture department concerning land appropriated from collective farms by officials, institutions or factories. They applied it regardless of whether the complaints were accurate or if they actually investigated the complaint or not.[51] They rarely intervened on behalf of collective farms in disputes with appropriating institutions, especially when the farms were small and poor and the institutions large and powerful.[52] This type of conduct was not uncommon of *raion*- and oblast-level state departments that were chronically understaffed and overworked,

---

[49] DAKO f. r-880, op. 11, d. 95. See the minutes of the meeting, ll. 1–8, and the statistical information attendant to it, ll. 9–13.
[50] See the full report in DAKO f. 4810, op. 1, d. 31, ll. 61–86.
[51] This phrase is found in Soviet reports across the Union at this time investigating complaints of illegal activity among Soviet officials, made particularly by civilians in their supplications to superior authorities.
[52] DAKO f. 4819, op. 14, d. 2. See the entire *delo* and, for examples of compensation for land taken, l. 18.

despite the fact that the complaints made to them concerned the very essence of their work. This Union-wide problem was exacerbated in the liberated territories as the rapidity of the repopulation of Soviet state and party structures ensured that many lower-level officials were inexperienced or unfit to deal with the work before them. Many remained unfit and inexperienced because they were consistently moved to new positions during mass purges of the bureaucracy, launched by superior authorities frustrated with the incompetence of their subordinates. These purges, in turn, denied their subordinates the necessary on-the-job experience needed to improve and reinforced the incompetence that superior authorities derided.[53] In this case, however, Comrade Belous and some of his colleagues were senior cadres with pre-war experience and, as will become evident, conspired to conceal the scale of illegal land appropriations by using this phrase.

Again, Comrade Belous' investigations into Bila Tserkva are most revealing of this active concealment. Representatives from the Council on Collective Farm Affairs throughout 1948 repeatedly asked the agriculture department why complaints made by *kolkhozniki* in Bila Tserkva about the mass appropriation of their farmland had not been investigated, until the department finally sent Comrade Belous to the area. Unsatisfied with Belous' initial claim that facts of illegal appropriations were 'not confirmed by the investigation', Council representatives continued to hound the department for further explanations until they received one. According to Belous, the fish enterprise that had allegedly appropriated 1,000 hectares from farms in Bila Tserkva, including Peremoha, had not forcibly appropriated the land, as the *kolkhozniki* claimed, but simply recovered land that had belonged to it before the war and was being used illegally by collective farms. Council representatives were clearly taken aback at the gall of Belous' inversion of facts:

> Instead of bringing the fish enterprise managers to justice for seizing public lands of the collective farms, [Belous], contrary to any common sense, sought to prove that this land had always belonged to the fish enterprise and ratify this theft by decree ... He has chosen to protect the plunderers of public lands.[54]

The *obliispolkom* passed a decree to this effect, ratifying the pre-war land-holdings of the fish enterprise, much like numerous other cases in the oblast

---

[53] Lieberman, 'The Re-Sovietisation of Formerly Occupied Territories'; Lewin, *The Soviet Century*, 47–8.

[54] DAKO f. 4810, op. 1, d. 31, l. 64, and f. 4819, op. 14, d. 2, ll. 21–22.

when officials and enterprise managers worked together to legitimate land appropriations. They did this by claiming that the land had always been theirs or was being appropriated for special purposes, such as for the MPVO. Luckily, after seven months of hounding the agriculture department, the Council finally secured the return of this particular tract of land to Peremoha, although thousands more hectares remained in illegal hands.

Council representatives claimed to their superiors in Moscow that such cases remained widespread across the oblast by 1949. They had identified several others concerning numerous farms across the oblast amounting to thousands more hectares of illegally appropriated farmland that remained in the wrong hands in addition to the 36,000 specified in late 1946. This finding casts doubt on the veracity of hundreds of other claims made by *raion-* and oblast-level authorities of 'legitimate reasons' for transferring land from collective farms to institutions and factories.[55] Instead of listing these newfound examples of illegal transfers in their report or, indeed, investigating every land transfer (which was unfeasible then and especially now), Council representatives explained that they would rather discuss how these examples testified to a deeper problem in post-war Soviet governance, which encouraged mass illegal appropriations. The key problem they identified was that both oblast- and *raion*-level officials, especially in Kyiv Oblast, had misunderstood the September 1946 and further decrees on improving agriculture as a temporary exertion of central power over the countryside, ironically, as just a campaign, rather than as the reconstruction of the pre-war agricultural sector. Oblast-level officials also investigating agriculture came to a similar conclusion when reporting to their republican superiors, again only with regard to the misinterpretations of their *raion*-level subordinates, not their own.[56]

To get a sense of the scale of this retention or recovery of illegally appropriated farmland by officials, institutions and factories, this chronology is vital. As evident from Table 1, Kyiv Oblast was among the leading areas for the total amount of land appropriated from collective farms by institutions by the beginning of 1947.

But there is little difference in this lead group, which includes oblasts such as Dnipropetrovsk (now Dnipro), where the great industrial reconstruction booms freely swallowed similar tracts of farmland in the post-liberation period to feed a rapidly growing workforce. The real measures of the scale of illegal

[55] DAKO f. 4819, op. 14, d. 2; for further examples of 1946 land transfers away from collective farms, see op. 7, d. 2.
[56] TsDAHOU f. 1, op. 23, d. 4783, l. 254.

Table 1 *Lands Returned to Ukrainian Collective Farms, 1946–1947*

No.	Oblast	Number of organisations that temporarily used collective farm lands	Number of collective farms that received the returned land	Area of land returned to collective farms in thousands of hectares
1	Kyiv	2980	1019	35.5
2	Vinnytsya	1223	902	24.1
3	Kamianets-Podilskyi	585	376	3.2
4	Kharkiv	3137	1108	48.6
5	Poltava	3421	1191	36.6
6	Kirovograd	1908	570	15.1
7	Odesa	1782	633	18.7
8	Mykolaiv	940	250	11.6
9	Kherson	1163	387	11.1
10	Zaporizhzhia	970	747	35.9
11	Dnipropetrovsk	2596	712	39.6
12	Stalino	2858	647	37.1
13	Voroshilovgrad	971	325	11.2
14	Zhytomyr	1892	835	22.2
15	Chernihiv	2418	740	24.3
16	Sumy	1975	816	24.8
	Total in eastern oblasts	30829	11218	398.6

Note: The title of this table in the original document is 'Statement on the Amount of Collective Farm Lands Returned to Farms of the Ukrainian SSR That Were Temporarily Used by Various Subsidiary Farms of Enterprises and Institutions'. The rows in this table are presented in their original order; western oblasts are omitted as in the original.
Source: TsDAVOU f. r-2, op. 7, d. 5032, l. 67.

appropriations are the amount of land that remained in illegal hands outside the collective farm sector after the 1946 campaign specifically sought its return, and the incidence of officials' continuing appropriations thereafter.

In terms of this resistance to the reassertion of central control over local agricultural sectors, Kyiv Oblast was the worst offender in all of Ukraine. By this time, Council representatives were reporting in detail less about the negligence of officials in allowing land abuses here, and more about how local authorities had intentionally used the lack of tenure as cover to continue illegal appropriations.[57] Much of the rest of Ukraine had

---

[57] TsDAVOU f. r-2, op. 7, d. 7024, l. 88, and TsDAHOU f. 1, op. 23, d. 4805, ll. 10–11. On the amount of land not returned to farms in Kyiv Oblast for 1948–9, see DAKO f. 4810, op. 1, d. 31, l. 86.

completed conferring land tenure by April 1947, and even the famine-affected oblasts of Mykolaiv and Odesa had done so quicker than Kyiv later that year. Land abuses were still widely reported in these and other oblasts at this time and until 1949, but not as widely as in Kyiv. Something was clearly still 'wrong' with Kyiv, as noted in 1948 by the minister of agriculture in Ukraine, Hryhorii Butenko,[58] though it was difficult at the time for officials to explain exactly why Kyiv Oblast was so problematic and to assess properly the scale of illegality there. In January, the Ukrainian republican government, Sovmin, ordered the Kyiv *obliispolkom* to find out why and to punish the guilty officials.[59] Not surprisingly, there was little explanation given of the crimes. This was clearly because the officials charged with explaining them were the ones committing and concealing the crimes in the archival record.

This chapter has explained Kyiv Oblast's seemingly exceptional and enduring problem with illegal appropriations and broader land abuses by undoing this concealment. To achieve a better sense of the scale of this problem we need to compare it with what appear to be similar cases after 1946. In most other areas of Ukraine, the Campaign on Collective Farm Rules was more effective in reducing illegal appropriations after 1946. Most of the cases of illegal appropriations that endured here concern more modest amounts of land, not thousands of hectares as in Kyiv. They were usually conducted by small groups of *raion*-level officials working directly with factory owners without much indication of the involvement at the higher oblast level.[60]

The enduring devastation of the agricultural sector in Ukraine encouraged illegal appropriations of collective farmland more so here than in other areas of the Soviet Union, but different forms of illegal appropriations were evident elsewhere in better-performing agricultural sectors. The common element in these abuses was the large conspiratorial networks that drove them, co-operating vertically from *raion* to oblast level and horizontally across *raiony* as well. It was primarily outside Ukraine, in Vologda Oblast in the Russian Republic, where such networks were most active in land abuses. Along with that in Kyiv Oblast, this network conducted the largest-scale illegal appropriations of collective farmland

---

[58] TsDAVOU f. r-2, op. 7, d. 7024, l. 80; for his subordinates' conclusion on tenure, see l. 88.

[59] TsDAVOU f. r-2, op. 7, d. 7024, l. 154. Kyiv Oblast eventually caught up in conferring tenure, but by that time, 1949, local authorities had reduced their illegal appropriations; they had mostly stopped them by 1950 (see next chapter).

[60] See comparisons of illegal land appropriations and broader agricultural issues in Ukraine in 1948 in TsDAVOU f. r-2, op. 7, dd. 5032, 7024, and TsDAHOU f. 1, op. 23, d. 4805.

in all of the Soviet Union after 1946. The key difference between them was that in Kyiv Oblast the enduring devastation of the agricultural sector in Ukraine encouraged illegal appropriations of collective farmland as part of a shift from collective farming to *podsobnoe khoziaistvo*, which sometimes liquidated the farms. In Vologda, the good agricultural conditions encouraged these networks to target farms that were performing well for illegal appropriations of land and labour, but to keep them running in order to exploit them best for personal profit.

This distinction in the motivations and conduct of illegal appropriations requires short elucidation. It emerged from the different historical geography of Kyiv and Vologda Oblasts: in the latter, the wartime disruption to the collective farm sector was far less severe. There was no mass occupation and collapse of the Soviet administration and farms in Vologda, but significant continuities from the pre-war to the post-war period. Food crises were less severe in Vologda than in Kyiv Oblast in 1946 and 1947.[61] Though Vologda was not a food-producing region like Kyiv Oblast, general rates of civilian food consumption in the countryside were higher than in the latter, and the collective farm sector was more stable at this time. These factors encouraged officials to appropriate collective farmland less as *podsobnoe khoziaistvo* to deal with food shortages and more to grow cash crops to sell on the black market to generate revenue. In 1947 alone, *raion*-level authorities in Vologda Oblast approved the illegal appropriation of 5,817 hectares of collective farmland after the 1946 Campaign on Collective Farm Rules.[62] This was a similar amount to Kyiv Oblast in 1947, though these appropriations seemed to fit the description of illegal appropriations of collective farmland made 'under the guise' of *podsobnoe khoziaistvo* to the letter, as investigators sent from Moscow explained:

> The distribution of land to *raion* and village organisations for the purposes of allotment farming is a ruse, a sham. In reality, the land has been distributed to specific individuals who use it only for their own profit. For

---

[61] The historical geography of the areas generated different motives for and types of appropriations. Industrial production by 1945 was at almost 81 per cent of the 1940 level; total sown area in agriculture was at 101 per cent. Although these indicators only indicate rather than describe economic realities, they are representative of broader economic progress inclusive of rising civilian consumption in Vologda Oblast. See K. I. Efremov, 'Ekonomika Vologodskoi oblasti v gody Velikoi Otechestvennoi voiny', *Istoriia narodnogo khoziaistva* 2, no. 10 (2010), 138.

[62] The total sown area for 1947 in Vologda Oblast was 770,000 hectares. This was down considerably from 1945 at 911,000 hectares and 1946 at 836,000. This reduction in 1947 was due primarily to drought and famine from mid-1946 onwards, though, as usual, Soviet officials blamed appropriations and other 'human factors' more than the weather. See RGASPI f. 17, op. 122, d. 316, ll. 95–96.

example, the Vologda *raiispolkom* gave twelve officials of the food procurement ministry seven hectares of hayfield each.[63]

The farms had remained mostly operational during the war in non-
occupied Vologda, and their continued operation was essential to the
corrupt scheme, whereas in Kyiv the farms' liquidation was key to make
use of the land on which they were located. These twelve procurement
officials compelled collective farm members to work the appropriated
hayfields without remuneration and then sold the hay they had produced
back to their collective farms at exorbitant prices. That the farms had no
money to pay for the hay that they produced did not prevent the scheme
from being carried out, as the farms could pay officials (on whose land they
worked) in credit and continue to rack up huge debts.[64]

Exploiting collective farm labour for hay production was a common
problem. Authorities could legally mobilise collective farm labour for
a range of purposes other than farm work, and this often gave rise to
collusion among authorities, institutions and farm leaderships that encouraged these labour abuses. But such abuses rarely occurred on the land that
these institutions had stolen from the farms, let alone having the products
of the exploitation forcibly sold back to them. This was an especially
egregious offence against collective farmland and labour evident, as far as
the author can see, only in the mass scale abuses recorded in areas such as
Vologda and Kyiv at this time. Officials from the institutions that had
appropriated Raska's hayfields also hired its desperate *kolkhozniki* to work
them and sold the bulk of it to other organisations at a handsome profit.
Unlike in Vologda, they could not sell the hay back to the collective farm
via credit because they had already liquidated it officially it to make use of
its land as *podsobnoe khoziaistvo*. At least in this case, one abuse cancelled
out the other.

Officials in Kyiv Oblast thus may have been unique in their motivations
to continue to engage in illegal appropriations after 1946 and had a unique
capacity to liquidate farms, given the collapse of land tenure records in

---

[63] RGASPI f. 17, op. 122, d. 316, l. 96.

[64] RGASPI f. 17, op. 122, d. 316, l. 87. Nor was the *kolkhozniki*'s hayfield work counted as labour days,
the set number of days *kolkhozniki* were required by law to work each year. This implicated them in
the continuation of the corruption schemes, as collective farm chairmen often threatened to
prosecute them for failing to meet their quotas if they ever complained. Some chairmen even
provided 'opportunities' for at least women and girls to make up days lost. They could do additional
work as domestic servants to the chairmen's wives and have their servitude counted as collective
farm work and thus labour days – an equally egregious, though not uncommon, abuse of collective
farm labour. See RGASPI f. 17, op. 122, d. 316, l. 101. On punishment for failing to meet labour-day
quotas, see Danylenko, *Povoienna Ukraïna*, 11.

Ukraine. But the most important element enabling this illegal activity on a mass scale here and in Vologda was that it could only be conducted by conspiratorial networks from *raion* to oblast level, and horizontally across different *raiony*. These networks were so difficult to unravel because the officials responsible for enforcing the legality of land abuse were commonly also responsible for circumventing it. Like officials from the Kyiv Oblast agriculture department, who could cover up their crimes by lodging false reports, it was the procurement officials in charge of collecting the produce of the farms they were abusing who could hide food production and/or collection losses in their corrupt schemes. The 12 corrupt officials and their 100 associates counted by investigators in Vologda, including the head of the *obkom*, and the 40 to 50 counted by the author in Kyiv, including the head of the *obliispolkom*, were tied in knots of mutual responsibility, profit and risk in different ways but with similar outcomes.

It is these networks that caused most damage to specific collective farms and their localities, and we need to understand how they operated to begin to assess properly the scale of this damage. The following chapters do this mainly in Kyiv Oblast, but also in Vologda and elsewhere. They address specifically the question of how the confluence of local activism as in Raska and Bila Tserkva with central authorities' pressure, though resulting in the return of some land to the farms, ultimately failed to unravel these networks and reverse the damage they caused. These case studies, much like shedding light on the broader problem of illegal appropriations, help explain the wider issue of how such networks were not an aberration in post-war Stalinism, but formed its fundamental building and, indeed, stumbling blocks.

CHAPTER 3

Taking Land Back: The People and Central Authorities' Recovery of Land and Prosecution of Local Party and State Officials

COMRADE SEREBNIAK, BILA TSERKVA GORKOM: The collective farm [Tretii Vyrishal'nyi] has made massive transgressions against the rules, particularly the *kolkhozniki*'s theft of state farmland. The collective farm is on the brink of collapse, yet the farm leadership does nothing to bring the farm back from the brink and does not even appeal to the *gorkom* for help.

E. P. NESTERENKO, CHAIRMAN, TRETII VYRISHAL'NYI: Our collective farm is on the brink of collapse because you [city authorities] have given us no help whatsoever. It is you who take our farmland from us without our consent. The farm has no resources ... not even scythes, sickles, pitchforks, nor enough labour to cope with our workload. You could have provided this to us, but you have not.[1]

Comrade Nesterenko was not an ordinary collective farm chairman. Chairmen rarely spoke so frankly to leading officials in Stalin's Soviet Union, let alone in front of other leaders and, in this case, another 103 people at a farm meeting (*sobranie*) in June 1948. Nesterenko had more to lose than the others who remained silent. He was facing criminal charges for abusing his position as chairman. He was speaking out during the 1948 Exile Campaign, a massive government-led operation designed to 'cleanse' the countryside of people leading an 'anti-social way of life'.[2] Meetings such as these were called across Ukraine and the Soviet Union during 1948, where *kolkhozniki* were asked to nominate a list of people whom they could then vote to exile to far-flung regions of the Soviet Union. Officials not uncommonly presented to the vote their own lists of troublesome

---

[1] AV BRDA f. 280, op. 1, d. 15, ll. 31–34 ob. (*oborot*: the reverse side of the page).
[2] Ukaz Prezidiuma Verkhovnogo Soveta SSSR 'O vyselenii iz Ukrainskoi SSR lits, zlostno uklo-niaiushchikhsia ot trudovoi deiatel'nosti v sel'skom khoziaistve i vedushchikh antiobshchestvennyi, paraziticheskii obraz zhizni' (21 February 1948).

kolkhozniki they did not like, such as Nesterenko, and manipulated the results they desired. 'No one dared' openly oppose the wishes of Soviet officials when they had made their mind up in these cases.[3]

Serebniak's claim that the farm had never appealed to city authorities for assistance was false. Nesterenko and chairmen of other farms on the outskirts of Bila Tserkva had spent the immediate post-war years pleading with the city and *raion* authorities to help rebuild their farms. Serebniak's audacious claim was likely targeted at his superior seated nearby, the *obkom* secretary, rather than the *kolkhozniki*. Less than two weeks before this meeting, the Council on Collective Farm Affairs in Moscow and republican authorities in Ukraine had forced Kyiv *obkom* to pass the June 1948 decree reinstating the farms. As discussed in the previous chapter, this decree punished subordinate officials for their destructive behaviour towards Tretii Vyrishal'nyi and two other collective farms in Bila Tserkva. It demanded all authorities now help the farms rebuild and reversed the rezoning of the area back from urban to rural. Unlike their state colleagues in the *obliispolkom*, *obkom* officials, as party representatives, were less involved in the daily abuses in Bila Tserkva, but nonetheless remained responsible to their own republic-level superiors for the decree's implementation (under the watchful eye of Council representatives).

Serebniak had clearly not followed the *obkom* decree to assist the *kolkhozniki*, which was his job as head of agricultural affairs in the *gorkom*. His false claim that he had received no appeal from the *kolkhozniki* was likely intended as defence against charges of non-compliance with the decree and based on his sense that the *kolkhozniki* would not speak up to expose him in a public forum. After all, Serebniak and others implicated in abusing farms had survived in the leadership of the city authorities despite the June 1948 *obkom* decree, and the *kolkhozniki* remained under their

---

[3] Jean Lévesque, 'Exile and Discipline: The June 1948 Campaign against Collective Farm Shirkers', *Carl Beck Papers in Russian and East European Studies*, no. 1708 (January 2006), 27. *Kolkhozniki* were usually only encouraged by superior authorities to publicly denounce local ones in this fashion during purges of officials in the 1930s. See Sheila Fitzpatrick, 'How the Mice Buried the Cat: Scenes from the Great Purges of 1937 in the Russian Provinces', *Russian Review* 52, no. 3 (1993), 299–320. For other forms of peasant resistance to collectivisation, see Lynne Viola, *Peasant Rebels under Stalin: Collectivization and the Culture of Peasant Resistance* (Oxford: Oxford University Press, 1999). There is some indication that during early 1947 farmers were encouraged to criticise farm leaderships as well as local political leaders for the lack of 'democracy' on collective farms as part of a broader 'revitalisation' of agriculture in line with the well-publicised (all-Union) Central Committee Plenum on Agriculture in February 1947. For example, see Weiner, *Making Sense of War*, 318.

control. Whether it was the temerity of Serebniak's claim, years of growing destitution, or the sense of Moscow's long and, in this case at least, benevolent hand into central Ukraine, Nesterenko fearlessly spoke 'truth to power'.

And what great truth he did speak. His criticisms of the local authorities pinpointed the key cyclical problem of land and labour that beset poor collective farms suffering abuse and neglect. In short, authorities' pernicious or poor management of farms exacerbated the post-war destitution in the collective farm sector, particularly as a result of reduced labour and resources required to operate them. This destitution in turn allowed authorities to justify first their appropriation of collective farmland and then, in some cases, the eventual liquidation or amalgamation of 'struggling' farms. These policies in Bila Tserkva punished *kolkhozniki* committed to collective farming and further empowered those who used collective farmland only for private and not collective purposes at a time when a broader Exile Campaign in 1948 was trying to 'cleanse' the sector of the latter, referred to as 'sham [*mnimye*] *kolkhozniki*', among other derogatory names.

Bila Tserkva city authorities continued to pursue their policies aimed at liquidating Tretii Vyrishal'nyi and other farms on the outskirts of the city even after the June 1948 *obkom* decree. The *gorsovet* chairman, Comrade Malashkevich, even removed Nesterenko and other collective farm chairmen from their positions after the decree as punishment for making the supplications to superior authorities that resulted in the decree being passed.[4] Though *gorkom* officials did not exile the chairmen at the June meeting in Tretii Vyrishal'nyi, Serebniak was sure to remind Nesterenko and others present of what was at stake when demoting him:

SEREBNIAK: Nesterenko is not being exiled from the farm but will now serve as
            a secretary to the [new] chairman and answer for the farm's grain collections.[5]

Removing Nesterenko as farm chairman but maintaining his personal responsibility (liability) for collections was a smart move and typical of the sophisticatedly destructive policies officials pursued towards farms in Bila Tserkva. The continuation of these policies made recovering farmlands and rebuilding the farms difficult for the *kolkhozniki*, even with the weight of Moscow behind them. Eighteen months after the decrees were issued forcing the return of stolen land and resources to the farms and punishing the offending officials, the city and *raion* authorities in Bila

---

[4] DAKO f. 4810, op. 1, d. 33, ll. 12–16.   [5] AV BRDA f. 280, op. 1, d. 15, ll. 31–34 ob.

Tserkva had done neither.[6] From 1950 onwards, the farms here, as in Raska, would be amalgamated with larger ones.

The Borodianka *raiispolkom* had also failed to return stolen resources and give assistance to Raska's *kolkhozniki*, many months after the January 1948 decree reinstating the farm. It also succeeded in protecting its offenders from prosecution indefinitely. Raska's *kolkhozniki*, however, behaved more diplomatically towards senior officials than did their ethnic Ukrainian counterparts in Bila Tserkva at farm meetings. In response to similar criticism of their farm's performance from these officials at farm meetings, the *kolkhozniki* politely pointed out that the reason why their harvest was a failure was because they had received no additional seeds to sow from the authorities, but they accepted that the ultimate responsibility for the failure was theirs and promised to do better.[7] This approach kept them safe from criminal charges in 1948. It helped to ensure, at least, that *raion* authorities would stop trying to liquidate them. The long history of dangerous ethnic discrimination against Raska's *kolkhozniki* by these authorities, the same ones who had been punished but remained in their positions, encouraged the former to maintain this diplomatic posture to best achieve their aims – at least when facing authorities in person. The aim of the 1948 decree, beyond punishing the guilty, was the return of all appropriated land, stolen goods, livestock, and housing, and providing seed, machinery and money to officially rebuild the farm. These too were the likely aims for those other liquidated farms or the many more whose resources and land were stolen, but whose supplications failed to result in such decrees.

This chapter answers two questions that emerge from the case studies of Raska and Bila Tserkva. First, why were supplications for assistance to central authorities successful in Raska and Bila Tserkva when numerous other supplications to recover illegally appropriated land and resources were not? Second, how could local authorities and the broader conspiratorial networks of which they were part successfully resist implementing major parts of these decrees – especially regarding the punishment of officials – for so long after they were passed, and survive? In answering both questions this chapter offers insights into much wider-ranging issues – the relationship between the success or failure of supplications with central policy campaigns and how conspiratorial networks manipulated these

---

[6] DAKO f. 4810, op. 1, d. 33, l. 79.
[7] See records of farm meetings from 1948–50 in DAKO f. 4974, op. 1, dd. 15, 16, 18, 21, 25, 27.

campaigns to their advantage to strengthen their foothold in rural governance in late Stalinism.

On the first question, supplications in Raska and Bila Tserkva got a good hearing in Moscow because they were so compelling in their claims of criminality by officials and supposed virtue of victims. But thousands of others were compelling too. Central authorities acted to meet *kolkhoznik* demands here and elsewhere only because of their rhetorical consonance with the broader campaigns they were pursuing in the countryside at the time. Timing was everything, but until now we have not been aware of the consonance between redressing land abuses and the 1948 Exile Campaign.

On the second question, conspiratorial networks under central pressure to assist *kolkhozniki* and punish abusive officials during these campaigns resisted it successfully through various methods that are only now becoming clear via research in the archives. These methods included lying openly to superior authorities and silencing and intimidating officials whose job it was to monitor them. In Kyiv Oblast, oblast-level leaders threatened Gordienko and sabotaged the work of the Council on Collective Farm Affairs across the oblast in response to the 1948 decrees in Raska and Bila Tserkva. This network then moved its members who were named for punishment in these decrees and those suspected of crimes around the oblast to other posts to avoid prosecution. These methods helped such networks here and, as we will see, across the Soviet Union avoid implementing the decrees they did not like and survive recriminations for doing so. While we know much about these types of conspiratorial networks forming a central building block of Soviet power from the literature, this analysis sheds new light on what their conduct meant for the capacity of the Stalinist regime to manage the Ukrainian countryside.

Successful Supplications and 'Timing'

Thousands of supplications from *kolkhozniki* complaining about abuses by their farm leaderships and local officials fill the archives. Most of these supplications went unmet, driving these *kolkhozniki* to join others engaging in traditional passive resistance to the extremities of the 1946 campaign and following famine, particularly flight to the cities or other rural areas.[8] In Raska, Bila Tserkva and other areas, however, a core group of *kolkhozniki* continued to stay and fight for their land and to make

---

[8] On resistance by *kolkhozniki*, see Ganson, *Soviet Famine*, ch. 4. On soldiers' population movements from city to village and vice versa, see Edele, 'Veterans and the Village'.

numerous supplications to superior authorities, despite them being unmet for years.

To have any chance of success, any supplicants at the very least needed to appear to be 'good citizens' wronged by corrupt officials, ones who were breaking the law and hurting the interests of the state.[9] The problem was that the 'rotten' *kolkhozniki* in both Raska and Bila Tserkva struggled to appear to be 'good citizens' in their supplications for different reasons. The *kolkhozniki* in Raska suffered from the remaining stigma of pre-war Soviet anti-Polish repressions, which gave local authorities scope to demonise them as allies of anti-Soviet forces in the post-war period. City authorities in Bila Tserkva denigrated *kolkhozniki* as criminals and habitual transgressors against collective farm rules (and thus suitable candidates for exile in 1948). In both cases *kolkhozniki* were able to successfully disentangle themselves from these associations, but it took time. They achieved this disentanglement in their written supplications to superior authorities and in their personal interviews with representatives of investigative organs who met them on their farms from the beginning of 1948 to assess the 'quality' of the supplicants and accuracy of their complaints.

Even once investigators were satisfied on both counts, it did not follow that their superiors would act for the supplicants. The archives are full of 'good' unmet supplications as well as those that had been investigated but not further acted upon for a range of reasons. In the Ukrainian countryside after the war, 'good' supplications were often serendipitously successful: that is, when the complaints *kolkhozniki* made were identified and remedies to them made more feasible by broader policy settings at the time. In Raska and Bila Tserkva, *kolkhozniki* made continued supplications to superior authorities from 1945 onwards but were successful only in 1948. Remedies often took time, but success in 1948 in Raska was partly due to a new republic-level policy in Ukraine that promoted the expansion of collective farming in the very region where it was being denied. In Bila Tserkva, the supplication was successful in 1948 because of the Exile Campaign, launched by Khrushchev in Ukraine at the beginning of the year, to exile from the collective farm sector 'sham *kolkhozniki*', like those the supplicants had been complaining about since 1946. In both cases, *kolkhozniki* and their supporters on the Council for Collective Farm

---

[9] On the success and failure of different supplications to superior authorities for assistance in the immediate post-war period, especially among veterans, see Dale, *Demobilized Veterans*; Edele, *Soviet Veterans of World War II*. For earlier periods, see A. I. Livshin, I. B. Orlov and O. V. Khlevniuk, *Pis'ma vo vlast', 1928–1939. Zaiavleniia, zhaloby, donosy, pis'ma v gosudarstvennye struktury i sovetskim vozhdiam* (Moscow: ROSSPEN, 2002).

Affairs, particularly Gordienko, inverted the language of new state policies and campaigns usually used by local officials against *kolkhozniki* to attack them and to convince superior authorities to assist.

Raska's *kolkhozniki* had to work hardest to make this inversion. Unlike their fellow collective farmers in Bila Tserkva, they 'smelled bad' to authorities even before they became 'rotten' after the war. Villages like Raska, ethnically homogeneous and relatively wealthy, were prime targets for Soviet authorities in their dekulakisation and massive anti-Polish campaigns during the 1930s. It was on Raska's fertile ground that the accusations levelled against the *kolkhozniki* by other locals and their friends in authority fell after the war, even absurd ones like the *kolkhozniki*'s supposed links with Ukrainian nationalist forces operating in the area. Somehow, local authorities were able to mould two mutually exclusive suspicions of being both pro-Polish and pro-Ukrainian nationalists into one anti-Soviet conspiracy. In this endeavour authorities were assisted by some locals who libelled the *kolkhozniki* as 'Banderites', the Soviet term for Ukrainian nationalist forces.[10] This local clique of informants and officials mobilised the language of the broader anti-insurgency campaign to stifle the progress of Raska's supplications for assistance even before they left the village, and certainly before the *kolkhozniki* travelled personally to the capital to seek assistance from oblast-level authorities.

This is exactly what Raska's *kolkhozniki* intended to do after failing to persuade the *raiispolkom* to reverse its decision to liquidate Raska in 1946.[11] Before the *kolkhozniki* could arrive at the eventual disappointment at Dvornikov's office in Kyiv during the middle of 1947, they needed to overcome the threats of authorities who learned of their plans to travel to the capital.[12] Still in the midst of famine in March 1947, the hungry villagers held a meeting at which they agreed to send their collective farm chairman to Kyiv to present to the *obliispolkom* a signed statement declaring the village's commitment to rebuilding and the district authority's refusal to assist. More than anything else, they hoped to secure seed loans for sowing the year's harvest; otherwise, they would continue to go hungry into the following season. The farm chairman, decorated Red Army veteran Comrade Kuriata, collected at least ten roubles from every household to pay for food, transport and perhaps lodgings in Kyiv – difficult to come by but often necessary, as it could take days to be seen by the relevant

---

[10] Stepan Bandera (1909–59) was one of the leaders of the Organisation of Ukrainian Nationalists (OUN), which fought against, among others, Soviet forces in western Ukraine during and after World War II. See Chapter 5.

[11] See Chapter 2.   [12] RGASPI f. 17, op. 122, d. 316, l. 152, and DAKO f. 4810, op. 1, d. 3, l. 22.

officials. Soon after this meeting, however, Kuriata was called to the office of Comrade Marchenko, the secretary of the *sel'sovet* in whose jurisdiction Raska was located and of which Kuriata was a member. Marchenko gave Kuriata an official warning for calling an unauthorised farm meeting and collecting money illegally to rebuild a farm and village that had already been liquidated by *raiispolkom* decree. Marchenko forbade him from sending further supplications to superior authorities and from leaving the village boundaries.[13]

There was deeper menace inherent in Marchenko's official warning, which is perhaps why it was effective in convincing Kuriata not to travel to Kyiv at least in this instance. Marchenko was a long-time party member and former chairman of the collective farm that the *raiispolkom* decree directed Raska's *kolkhozniki* to join after the formal liquidation of their farm, Pershe Travnia. Kuriata's family were among the fourteen villagers who had been arrested and deported in the 1937 anti-Polish purge. His relative was the only one to return home.[14] Kuriata's tainted past could have made his supplications null and void. Families of the repressed often lacked the credibility to petition superior authorities to help them combat the greater levels of abuse they suffered at the hands of local ones, who, in any case, were only acting in the spirit of discrimination sanctioned from above.[15] Both men clearly understood that Kuriata's 'enemy status' could quash his supplications and lead to his arrest should he continue them.

However, Marchenko's threats, actual and implied, were not successful in dissuading Kuriata from appealing to superior authorities for long. Kuriata understood much better than Marchenko that central authorities might view the successful wartime service of former repressed citizens as a counterweight to their tainted pre-war past. The Soviet press printed stories to this effect at the time, and a representative of the Ukrainian government (Sovmin) visited the village in 1946 and suggested the *kolkhozniki* write to a Sovmin secretary for assistance in dealing with local officials.[16] As a member of a front-line generation of victorious soldiers, Kuriata chanced that he, writing in the new language of 'Soviet patriotism',

[13] RGASPI f. 17, op. 122, d. 316, l. 154, and DAKO f. 4810, op. 1, d. 3, ll. 5–8.

[14] See http://piskivska-gromada.gov.ua/s-raska-23-25-00-23-06-2016/.

[15] On difficulties encountered by 'enemies of the people' and others with tainted or criminal pasts under Soviet rule, see Golfo Alexopolous, *Stalin's Outcasts: Aliens, Citizens and the Soviet State, 1926–1936* (Ithaca: Cornell University Press, 2003). For broader histories of 'marginal' and mostly impoverished people in Soviet society in the post-war period, see E. I. Zubkova and T. I. Zhukova, eds., *Na 'kraiu' sovetskogo obshchestva. Marginal'nye gruppy kak ob'ekt gosudarstvennoi politiki. 1945–1960-e gg.* (Moscow: Rosspen, 2010).

[16] DAKO f. 4810, op. 1, d. 3, l. 23.

could apply to someone like Kaganovich to secure the entitlements the state had promised him in the din of war.[17] The most basic entitlement was being able to return home.

Kuriata addressed a supplication to Kaganovich in May but soon received the disappointing response telling him that it had been returned to the *obliispolkom* for review. Having heard no response by the following month from the *obliispolkom*, he called another unauthorised farm meeting, fearing the forced evacuation of the village was imminent. Kuriata updated the supplication to Kaganovich, had it signed by all the *kolkhozniki*, and took it personally to the *obliispolkom* office in Kyiv to present to its head. It read:

> Because of the Borodianka *raiispolkom*'s inexplicable behaviour towards law-abiding Soviet people wishing to reconstruct their collective farm on their home soil [*rodnoi kolkhoz*] destroyed by German occupiers, we, together with our loved ones murdered under occupation, petition the *obliispolkom* and, in the event of another rejection, will petition the highest levels of Soviet government for the reconstruction of collective farm Pershe Travnia in Raska village with the following statement:
>
> *Raion*-level organisations do not reckon with the patriotic feeling of *kolkhozniki* towards their homeland and collective farm, nor with the immeasurable suffering wrought on the citizens of Raska on their home soil under German occupation. We report that the Borodianka *raiispolkom* has sold off and continues to rent out collective farmland from Pershe Travnia to various organisations. The *raiispolkom* considers this land's value only in terms of its own personal profit. We authorise Comrades Kuriata and Somov to enforce this resolution.[18]

As mentioned in the previous chapter, Kuriata and his deputy were blocked at Dvornikov's office before they deliver their supplication to the head of the *obliispolkom*, Comrade Oleinik – not that seeing him would have made any difference given his role in illegal appropriations. Nevertheless, this supplication became important in spite of its not being delivered to the *obliispolkom* and Kaganovich likely not reading it. Once it became official correspondence and was dealt with by Kaganovich's office as a collective farm complaint, it became visible to Council on Collective Farm Affairs representatives in Kyiv Oblast, who investigated it and made it known quickly to their superiors in Moscow.

---

[17] On the development of 'Soviet patriotism' in Ukraine and the role of the war in forging a Soviet identity in rural Ukraine, see Weiner, *Making Sense of War*, ch. 6. On soldiers' supplications to authorities citing the war as 'cleansing' them of their tainted pasts under Soviet authority, see ibid., 323–5.

[18] DAKO f. 4810, op. 1, d. 3, ll. 27–28.

This supplication drew attention from Council representatives, in part, because it was so compelling in its claims of illegal actions by officials and in the supposed virtue of their victims. Its collective nature indicated an internal solidarity among the *kolkhozniki*, and its skilful use of language and format as a *postanovlenie* (resolution) differentiated it from others at the time.[19] Kuriata and his fellow *kolkhozniki* clearly understood how to speak to the state, aligning themselves with it against its officials.[20] The *kolkhozniki* did not present themselves as merely veterans seeking their legal entitlement to housing, pay or state loans for rebuilding, as thousands of others who wrote supplications for assistance did; nor were they simply complaining about abuses and theft from by local authorities, as did thousands more. These two types of supplications were most numerous at the time and rarely found success.[21] *Kolkhozniki* in Raska presented themselves as a collective of war-hardened, patriotic *kolkhozniki*, led by a decorated veteran (Kuriata) and seeking to honour Soviet martyrs by rebuilding a basic element of the Stalinist economy – the collective farm.

This narrative was compelling also because of its skilful application of terms popular in Soviet wartime propaganda and the 1946 campaign in the countryside. *Rodnoi kolkhoz* was a Soviet term prominent in soldiers' vernacular describing the destination of their return from service. The term had a special meaning for ethnic Poles, especially ones discriminated against on this basis by local officials. The *kolkhozniki* in Raska were not Poles who found themselves within Ukraine because of territorial or population exchanges, but ethnically Polish Ukrainians rooted to this soil for generations. Now they were drenched in the blood of Soviet martyrs and equally rooted to the Soviet farm that stood on top of it. They could not move to another farm, as the *raiispolkom* ordered, without uprooting themselves from their homeland (*rodina*).

The mass murder of ethnic Poles in Raska by German occupiers did not automatically turn them into Soviet martyrs, but for the narrative of

[19] There were other group supplications from *kolkhozniki*, but most came from working collectives in industry. These were more akin to signed petitions for increased pay, rations and so forth, or calling out failures of local managers.

[20] See the 'speaking Bolshevik' debate in Stephen Kotkin, *Magnetic Mountain: Stalinism as a Civilization* (Berkeley: University of California Press, 1995), ch. 4.

[21] Edele, *Soviet Veterans of World War II*, chs. 2, 3 and 8; Dale, *Demobilized Veterans*. For letters to authorities by *kolkhozniki*, see Kessler and Kornilov, eds., *Kolkhoznaia zhizn'*, 655–67, and the dedicated *fond* for these letters to authorities in RGAE f. 9476. For ordinary citizens' supplications, see Zubkova, *Sovetskaia zhizn'*.

'rooted *kolkhozniki*' to be successful, they had to be seen as such.[22] Soviet citizens who were killed on occupied territory may have been referred to as 'martyrs' in the press,[23] but Soviet authorities were generally cautious in assessing supplications from people, especially ethnic minorities, in areas long under German occupation. Authorities wanted to find out whether the dead and the survivors had at some stage been allied to the German occupiers, shown or failed to show any resistance to them, or rendered assistance to Soviet partisans and the Red Army.

The *kolkhozniki* understood this and had long established in previous supplications that their loved ones had died as retaliation for partisan activity in the village.[24] These claims are now verified by other Soviet archival sources and, importantly at the time, were accepted by Council representatives who passed them on to Moscow as factual accounts.[25] Partisans, including ethnic Poles from Raska, operating in the wooded areas mostly along the banks of the Teteriv River than runs along the western side of Raska, killed three German soldiers in an ambush near there at some stage in early 1943. The partisans' military successes, as was often the case, spelt doom for the civilian population, in this case mostly the wives, children and elderly relatives of men serving in the Red Army or working in factories in the nearby towns. On Sunday 10 April, the villagers and guests from nearby were celebrating a holiday in the lead-up to (Catholic) Easter. German forces alongside local collaborators encircled the village in the early hours of the following morning. They drove the people into a large ditch on the southern entry into village, shot them, and burnt people hiding in their homes and then the entire village. They killed almost all of the 421 people assembled (by the state's account) or 613 (by the *kolkhozniki*'s), including 120 children. Male relatives working in factories in the nearby towns were alerted to the massacre by the thick plumes of smoke emanating from the village visible by dawn's light. They rushed to the scene but found hardly any survivors.[26]

This scene was common across Ukraine, Belarus and western Russia, especially from 1943 onwards as the German 'anti-partisan' war intensified.[27] Raska's *kolkhozniki* and their supporters on the Council on

---

[22] For the failure of Soviet authorities to recognise victims as Jewish as opposed to Soviet citizens, see I. A. Altman, 'Memorializatsiia Kholokosta v Rossii. Istoriia, sovremennost', perspektivy', *Neprikosnovennyi zapas*, no. 2 (2005).
[23] See daily government casualty reports on liberated territory in *Pravda* and *Izvestiia* from 1944–5.
[24] See various texts in DAKO f. 4810, op. 1, d. 3.   [25] RGASPI f. 17, op. 122, d. 316, ll. 150–160.
[26] Horlach and Pal'chik, *Dzvony pam'iati*, 188.
[27] Hamburger Institut für Sozialforschung, ed., *Verbrechen der Wehrmacht*, 387–9.

Collective Farm Affairs stressed this shared experience (without reference to the Polish or Catholic elements) to underscore Raska's suffering as a Soviet one. This was key both to framing the death of Raska's inhabitants as a martyrdom for the Soviet cause without complications of ethnicity and religion, and to using their martyrdom to support the rebuilding of the Soviet collective farm on which they perished.[28] And if death under these circumstances alone was not enough to 'cleanse' massacre victims of the stigma of their Polish ethnicity, then it was their surviving relatives' commitment to the Soviet cause via rebuilding a collective farm that completed the victims' transformation into martyrs and the survivors into 'good citizens' deserving of assistance.

In speaking to central authorities in this language of the Soviet present, *kolkhozniki* in Raska were drawing on a much older tradition in peasant–ruler relations, one that reached far back into tsarist times. Peasants of the Russian Empire had long understood how to speak to the tsar to establish their allegiance to him when seeking to enlist his support against local officials, even if the tsar never listened to them. Knowing how to speak in this way could nonetheless be useful for peasants to justify their revolt against corrupt local officials who broke the tsar's laws, as a way of doing the tsar's good work and, hopefully, avoiding punishment.[29] There is an enduring debate in the literature about whether or not peasants' allegiances were sincere, instrumental or both. Concerning the Soviet period, this debate is really over how 'Bolshevised' the population were, that is, the degree of their political and social indoctrination, which is addressed in detail in Chapter 5.[30] What is important to note here is that the supplication in Raska was so successful because its narrative drew on a tradition well learnt by *kolkhozniki* whose families had lived here at least since the nineteenth century and aligned so well with the contemporary political and cultural mores in the post-war Ukrainian countryside.

Specifically, the narrative aligned well with the broader cultural celebration of Soviet veterans and the 1946 Campaign on Collective Farm Rules. Soviet press and literature at the time celebrated the return of veterans to the countryside as a moral force bringing new energy into post-war reconstruction. Veterans were lauded not only for inspiring other

---

[28] Gordienko relayed this passionately to his superiors on the Council: DAKO f. 4810, op. 1, d. 33, ll. 75–76.
[29] See Dan Field, *Rebels in the Name of the Tsar* (Boston, MA: Houghton Mifflin Co., 1976).
[30] See the discussion of Stephen Kotkin's work in Igal Halfin and Jochen Hellbeck, 'Rethinking the Stalinist Subject: Stephen Kotkin's "Magnetic Mountain" and the State of Soviet Historical Studies', *Jahrbücher für Geschichte Osteuropas* 44 (1996), 456–63.

kolkhozniki to work harder but also for occupying leadership positions on the farm and local officialdom, replacing 'lazy' and 'corrupt' officials who had sat out the war in the rear.[31] Kuriata suited this narrative well – a decorated veteran who took up the role of farm chairman and a position in the local *sel'sovet* fighting hard against corrupt officials, including his immediate superior Marchenko. The supplication's reference to selling and renting land referred to the September 1946 Sovmin decree on collective farm rules that chided officials for embezzlement in the collective farm sector.

After Council representatives investigated these complaints on site and verified their authenticity in January 1948, the decree re-establishing Raska and its farm was passed by the Kyiv *obliispolkom* by the end of the month. But nothing happened. The *obliispolkom* officials ignored Gordienko and the Council's requests to discuss the matter further.[32] Raska's supplication was solid enough in its original form for Council representatives to adopt exactly the same terms and language when writing their reports to their superiors in Moscow for assistance to break this deadlock. This choice was not due to laziness. Council representatives reported the *kolkhozniki*'s version of events as factual to their superiors as well as their sincere 'pro-Soviet' attitudes in contrast to claims made by local officials. Central authorities – specifically Kuznetsov's office in the Central Committee – accepted the veracity of both claims, deciding not to pursue the usual process of sending higher-level investigators to the area to substantiate them.[33] Instead, they accelerated their usually slow response to Council representatives' requests on the ground to pressure republican-level authorities to order their subordinates on the oblast level to issue the relevant decree by the end of January 1948. They did so again in May when progress on implementing the January decree was slow.

As scholars of Soviet supplications remind us, though central authorities were often interested in citizens reporting on the corruption and criminality of local authorities, it was their privilege to 'decide which supplications to meet and which to ignore'.[34] If the content of the supplication from Raska sufficiently aligned with Moscow's concerns at this time to enact this privilege quickly by decree, then the specific policy setting in central Ukraine suggested the decree should be implemented quickly on the ground. Republican authorities understood this case as further evidence

[31] Weiner, *Making Sense of War*, 314–19.   [32] RGASPI f. 17, op. 122, d. 316, l. 159.
[33] RGASPI f. 17, op. 122, d. 316, l. 160.
[34] Livshin, Orlov and Khlevniuk, eds., *Pis'ma vo vlast'*, 11.

of the problematic vertical hierarchy of power in Kyiv Oblast from *raion* to oblast level that fostered the illegality, and of the broader *bezdushnost'* of the Kyiv *obliispolkom* towards *kolkhozniki* reported to them in early 1947.[35] The case of Raska was clearly the worsening of an existing problem that republican authorities had not properly addressed but now quickly took action to resolve.

At the same time, Khrushchev had been signalling to his colleagues probably since the beginning of 1948 the need to expand collective farming in the Ukrainian part of Polissia, in which Borodianka *raion* is located. Polissia is the historical region of mostly wooded lowlands between the Bug and Desna Rivers, incorporating parts of Ukraine, Belarus, Russia and Poland. Though not an administrative territorial region in Ukraine (it was in Belarus), it retained its historical geographical importance for its inhab- itants and its Ukrainian officials. At the January 1949 Central Committee Plenum of the CP(b)U, Khrushchev demanded the 'liquidation' of 'Polissia *raiony*' such as Borodianka. It seems that by 'liquidation' Khrushchev meant the transformation of remaining individual farms into collectives and clearing of suitable wooded areas to accommodate the expansion of collective farm sown area. This was certainly the case with regard to 'Polissia *raiony*' in western Ukraine, where farms had been forcibly collectivised only starting the previous year. With regard to his own *raion* in central Ukraine, the secretary of the Borodianka *raikom*, Petrov, clearly understood Khrushchev's call not as a liquidation of his *raion* as a territorial unit. It was a call to expand both the sown area and livestock operations in line with a major push across the Soviet Union in 1948 to improve livestock breeding in the collective farm sector. It was under these expectations that Petrov was reporting at the May 1949 Kyiv *obkom* Plenum, where his boasting of collective farm and livestock suc- cesses was cut short by Khrushchev's interrogation of him about the 'one- cow farm' in Raska in Chapter 2. For Khrushchev, clearly, Petrov was preventing the rebuilding of a farm in the areas exactly where it should be happening. Moreover, he was obstructing the expansion of livestock by denying the operation of mostly a vegetable-producing and livestock- breeding farm in Raska with a long history of successful livestock production.

Khrushchev had been informed that Raska's farm had 100 cows on the eve of the war, 50 horses, sheep, pigs and bird-breeding facilities.[36] At the beginning of the war all of the livestock and facilities were evacuated

---

[35] TsDAHOU f. 1, op. 23, d. 4805, ll. 10–11, and d. 4783, l. 254. [36] DAKO f. 4810, op. 1, d. 3, l. 5.

eastwards and, as was often the case, not all had been returned to Raska after the war.[37] Unusually here, though, nothing was returned even years after the war, and the *raiispolkom* confiscated most of the livestock the *kolkhozniki* did manage to acquire. For these reasons, by 1949 the farm had only one cow but *kolkhozniki* hoped that they would receive more cows for breeding with the farm's official reconstruction. They had even built a 'beautiful' cowshed in 1948 to house the hundred cows they imagined would be returned to them. Not surprisingly, these officials were on record as deriding Raska's *kolkhozniki* for their commitment to livestock rather than food production.[38] The timing for Raska's reconstruction was thus right on many counts by 1948.

Khrushchev's specific concerns in expanding vegetable farming in post-war Ukraine dated back to early 1945, when he was pressured by central authorities in Moscow to root out localism in agriculture in Ukraine to free up vegetables to deliver to the Russian capital.[39] At the onset of the famne in 1946, Khrushchev convened a meeting of the Central Committee of the CP(b)U with key allies to develop 'vegetable zones' in the regional peripheries of city and industrial areas. This was a pre-war policy from the 1930s, but Khrushchev resumed it with gusto now. Khrushchev identified areas around Kyiv and other cities such as Bila Tserkva as prime locations to expand collective farm operations to include greater vegetable production. There was also more land available to turn to vegetable farming, given the return of illegally appropriated farmland from the 1946 Campaign on Collective Farm Rules. However, Khrushchev reiterated that vegetable growing should not interfere with grain growing but form an additional task for collective farms. Though this policy was not implemented as widely or quickly as Khrushchev had planned, boosting vegetable production remained a pressing concern for him.[40]

His erratic intervention to 'save' a vegetable farm was part of a broader policy concern, but also was symptomatic of his personal attempts to assist 'good *kolkhozniki*'. He had lobbied Stalin directly to relieve Ukrainian farms from excessive central grain collections during the famine, intervened in other cases of egregious crimes committed by local officials against them and, broadly, was attracted to the 'idea' of supporting *kolkhozniki* with whom he clearly identified.[41] He shared this sentiment with

---

[37] RGASPI f. 17, op. 122, d. 316, l. 150.   [38] DAKO f. 4810, op. 1, d. 3, ll. 21–25.
[39] TsDAVOU f. r-2, op. 7, d. 1748, l. 125.   [40] TsDAVOU f. r-2, op. 7, d. 3151, ll. 20–31.
[41] See Khrushchev's correspondence with Stalin and others requesting assistance for *kolkhozniki* on the onset of famine in 1946 in TsDAVOU f. r-2, op. 7, d. 3057 (especially l. 12).

representatives of the Council for Collective Farm Affairs and, unlike some leading officials, was attentive to their concerns before and between the spikes in campaign energy in late 1946 or early to mid-1948. Gordienko would send his reports directly to Khrushchev when no one else listened to him and could count on Khrushchev's support, though even his support, at times, was not enough to get things done (discussed later).[42] Khrushchev rejected desperate pleas from institutions to keep land appropriated from collective farms as *podsobnoe khoziaistvo* after the 1946 campaign and ordered its return to farms.[43] In response to these reports or other signals about crimes against 'good *kolkhozniki*' Khrushchev sometimes sent direct messages to *obkom* secretaries to deal with the crimes committed by their *raion*-level subordinates, lest he personally visit the areas in question and deal with the criminals and, by implication, with the secretaries himself.[44]

This type of 'support' for *kolkhozniki*, however, was not sustained nor was it capable of seriously improving their lot at the hands of corrupt officials in Ukraine. In fact, Khrushchev's own policies in the countryside would be injurious to most of them. As will become evident below, the 1948 Exile Campaign spearheaded by Khrushchev provided opportunities for some of Ukraine's most vulnerable farms to survive, but punished innocent people. His 1950 campaign to amalgamate small farms into larger ones swallowed up the farms that had been saved during the campaign or by his intervention, including those in Raska and Bila Tserkva.

Raska's official reconstruction boded well for other farms suffering from local abuse in 1948. Raska's case was taken on by Gordienko, who worked tirelessly to assist the *kolkhozniki* by pressuring the *obliispolkom* and then his superiors to intervene on their behalf. His investigation in Raska revealed the large role played by oblast-level authorities in denying Raska's rebuilding. He began investigating the oblast agriculture department more closely, which led him to uncover numerous other unmet supplications from farms about officials preventing them from rebuilding or operating properly and about mass illegal land appropriations. The first and most severe case he uncovered after Raska was in Bila Tserkva. From early 1948, Gordienko was beginning to unravel the broader conspiratorial networks through which these illegal appropriations had been made.

[42] DAKO f. 4810, op. 1, d. 33, l. 83.   [43] TsDAVOU f. r-2, op. 7, d. 5050, ll. 36–37, 51, 68.
[44] TsDAVOU f. r-2, op. 7, d. 1748, l. 173.

Bila Tserkva and the 1948 Exile Campaign

If the Borodianka *raiispolkom* had prevented the reconstruction of Raska's farm, in Bila Tserkva city and *raion* authorities were intentionally driving the three farms on the city's outskirts into 'self-liquidation', as Gordienko called it.[45] These *kolkhozniki* were not carrying the torch of Soviet martyrs as in Raska but were equally 'good citizens'. Gordienko presented them as *kolkhozniki* committed to their farms surrounded by a sea of 'sham *kolkhozniki*' supported by corrupt local officials. This was, as it turned out, a narrative that was also convincing to Gordienko's superiors in Moscow and republican authorities in Ukraine, perhaps more so than in Raska, with authorities in the midst of the 1948 Exile Campaign to root out 'sham *kolkhozniki*' from the collective farm sector.

Khrushchev launched the campaign at the end of February 1948 in Ukraine as a test case. Seemingly satisfied with its results, Stalin then approved the campaign to be implemented by corresponding governments in other Soviet republics in June.[46] Khrushchev's brain child, this campaign organised meetings on selected farms in each oblast where *kolkhozniki* were forced to vote for candidates put forward as 'sham *kolkhozniki*' living in an 'anti-social manner [*antiobshchestvennyi obraz zhizni*]' to be exiled from the farms.[47] This campaign was supposed to target those *kolkhozniki* (or peasants who were not *kolkhoz* members) whom the state deemed to be exploiting collective farmland, using the resources for their profit but not contributing to farm work. A two-thirds majority was required to exile these people to the far-flung regions of the Soviet Union, mostly to the far northern tip of the Soviet Union from Ukraine, and to the Far East from elsewhere. Almost 40 per cent of all Ukrainian farms held these meetings, exiling 12,367 people in total, with many thousands more 'warned' that if they did not improve their collective farm work, they would follow the others.[48]

The impact of the campaign was felt far beyond the farms chosen to hold these meetings and beyond the relatively small number of people exiled or

[45] He used this term throughout his correspondence with Moscow: see DAKO f. 4810, op. 1, dd. 31, 33.
[46] Ukaz Prezidiuma Verkhovnogo Soveta SSSR 'O vyselenii v otdalennye raiony lits, zlostno uklo-niaiushchikhsia ot trudovoi deiatel'nosti i vedushchikh antiobshchestvennyi, paraziticheskii obraz zhizni' (2 June 1948).
[47] Authorities also used other derogatory terms to refer to some people, such as *lzhekolkhozniki* (false *kolkhozniki*).
[48] Most of the meetings had been held by mid-1948, but the total number of those exiled is given for 1948–52. Most of those exiled, however, were sentenced in 1948. See Lévesque, 'Exile and Discipline', 386.

more officially warned. The campaign was a warning to all *kolkhozniki* to follow collective farm rules and commit more of their time to collective rather than individual farm work. This 'educational character' of the campaign was Khrushchev's primary aim.[49] The campaign failed to improve discipline among *kolkhozniki* in the longer term, but it was most successful in instilling the fear into them that they might be exiled any time in 1948. Word of mouth spread that decisions to exile were not necessarily taken by a democratic process as envisaged by Khrushchev and laid out in the decree that launched the campaign. Some meetings were simply for show, with neither *kolkhozniki* nor officials willing to exile anyone, while some local officials manufactured lists of candidates for exile instead of procuring them from *kolkhozniki* and then manufactured the two-thirds majority required to exile them.[50] Central authorities derided local officials for exiling in this way either the wrong *kolkhozniki* or those they simply disliked, such as those who had made supplications against them to superior authorities, rather than the real 'sham *kolkhozniki*' who were destroying the collective farm sector. They sent revised instructions to republican governments on how to improve the 'democratic character' of the campaign and tried to put in more checks and balances on local officials, but with little effect.[51]

The campaign's purpose of improving discipline in the sector by intimidation and central officials' frustration with arbitrary rule at the local level are key elements of the broader context in which Bila Tserkva made successful supplications. Within this context, Bila Tserkva's 'good *kolkhozniki*' were calling on central authorities to help them rid their areas of 'sham peasants' protected from justice by the corrupt local officials who harboured them. *Kolkhozniki* in Bila Tserkva took great risks to succeed within this context, challenging local officials at a time when these officials were charged with extraordinary powers to (further) destroy the *kolkhozniki*'s lives; some had the proclivity to use these powers tyrannically, even if exile meetings had not been called at specific farms.

Gordienko's assistance to the *kolkhozniki* was key to their success. He took the content of their complaints, translated it into the language of the campaign in his reports, and broadly mobilised the campaign's energy to resolve the long-standing complaints of *kolkhozniki* in Bila Tserkva. He did this in both his written and his oral reporting in party fora, such as the May 1948 Kyiv *obkom* CP(b)U Plenum, where he publicly indicted the officials responsible for abuses in Bila Tserkva (who were mostly present) as

[49] Ibid., 16.　[50] Ibid., 25–8.　[51] RGASPI f. 17, op. 122, d. 314, ll. 142–144.

acting against the law and spirit of the campaign. Gordienko's direct pressure on oblast-level authorities in this way converged with pressure from the Council on Collective Farm Affairs in Moscow on Ukrainian republican authorities to force the *obkom* to pass the decree some two weeks after the plenum was held, ordering the reconstruction of the farms and punishing the guilty officials. The same power vertical was thus at play here as in Raska, but (as will become evident) *obkom* officials were more vocal in their support for the Bila Tserkva case.

In his speech before the plenum, Gordienko gave a short history of the city and *raion* authorities' abuses against the farms. He quoted more from Comrade Dubova on the absurd reversal of *kolkhozniki*'s and urban dwellers' land rights and tax regimes that empowered the 'sham *kolkhozniki*' and led to the mass exodus of *kolkhozniki* from the farms cited in the previous chapter. He claimed that the overall conduct of *raion* and city authorities had perverted party and government policy and

> *either intentionally or not* fostered the growth of the non-working population in the city ... and fostered among them an anti-social lifestyle [*antiobshchestvennyi obraz zhizni*] of engaging in speculation ... all of which has brought the farms to the point of liquidation.[52]

Gordienko lamented the fact that none of the guilty officials had been punished, despite his reports to oblast-level authorities over the previous months, and stressed the broader consequences to the locality and collective farm sector of the officials' illegality and their superiors' refusal to address it. The most important consequence was further accelerating the mass exodus of the farm population, reduced from thousands in the immediate post-war period to only a handful by 1948.

Comrade Tkachenko, the head of the Bila Tserkva *raikom*, was in the plenum hall and responded to Gordienko's accusations in the same way that Bila Tserkva's *raion* officials had responded to them, by blaming the city authorities, who, in turn, blamed the *raion*-level authorities for the mess. Tkachenko and others sought to define this situation as one of dual authority (*dvoevlastie*), where each authority was rendered a passive agent by the other, incapable of taking action within the other's jurisdiction. Tkachenko's false characterisation drew frustration from the plenum hall:

TKACHENKO: Comrade Gordienko says we must eliminate transgressions against collective farm rules. How is the *raikom* supposed to do this on farms made

---

[52] TsDAHOU f. 1, op. 51, d. 3648, l. 151 (my emphasis).

up of urban dwellers? The farmland is under the *raion* jurisdiction, but the *kolkhozniki* are under the city's ... We have dual authority [*dvoevlastie*] here.

SHOUTS FROM THE PLENUM HALL: Rebuild the farms!

TKACHENKO: How can we rebuild them with only thirty *kolkhozniki*? How can we hold farm meetings and exile the sham *kolkhozniki* from this number?[53]

Part of the frustration in the plenum hall can be explained by Tkachenko avoiding responsibility for not rebuilding the farms by referring to *dvoevlastie*, but also clearly misrepresenting the basic point that Gordienko was making. The *kolkhozniki* who remained on the farms were the real *kolkhozniki*; as Gordienko had stressed in his speech, he did not count the sham *kolkhozniki* who had left the farm or at least farm work in this number. Tkachenko said nothing about how his and the city authorities' policies had led to this mass exodus of *kolkhozniki*, but was using this consequence of his policies to justify their refusal to reconstruct the farms. This duplicitous narrative was no longer a tenable position in the midst of the 1948 Exile Campaign as it had been earlier. Gordienko was now able to paint the *kolkhozniki* who remained on the farms as 'good *kolkhozniki*' surrounded by those who had been empowered by the authorities to leave the farms or farm work, but who retained their privileges of farm membership to exploit its land and resources. These were exactly the type of people officials were supposed to remove from the sector and exile according to the campaign.

Gordienko's rejection of Tkachenko's arguments was effective at the plenum, with the head of the Kyiv *obkom*, Z. T. Serdiuk, demanding that action be taken in Bila Tserkva and that the *obliispolkom* agricultural department stop its 'apolitical' stance towards enforcing collective farm rules. He called on the entire state organisation to commit to enforcing these rules to align with the spirit of the broader Exile Campaign. Serdiuk was clearly reinforcing the importance of keeping this campaign at the forefront of officials' thinking. This was common for the head of a party organisation (*obkom*) to do when at this time responding to criticism of their state colleagues (*obliispolkom*) publicly. And, broadly, it was the job of *obkom* heads to pressure publicly the oblast machinery to devote all of its energies to the fulfilment of whichever central campaign was in motion at the time.

This pressure was often bluster with regard to this type of campaign, aimed at improving social behaviours. *Obkom* heads were rarely punished or removed for performing poorly in such campaigns, in contrast

---

[53] TsDAHOU f. 1, op. 51, d. 3648, ll. 161–162.

to grain collections or purges. But Serdiuk was likely genuine in his sentiments, as he was also a longtime and close ally of Khrushchev, sharing the latter's concern about *kolkhozniki* suffering abuse from bad officials in the collective farm sector. Serdiuk seemed convinced of Gordienko's claim, made at the plenum and in the weeks prior in his background briefings to the *obkom*, that *raion* and city authorities' policies were targeting good *kolkhozniki* and empowering bad ones.[54] Gordienko showed in his reports to the *obkom*, cited in the previous chapter, that Tkachenko and his colleagues were not passive in the face of supposed *dvoevlastie*, but had actively pursued policies to destroy the farms by fostering the growth of the very criminal elements that the Exile Campaign was designed to eliminate. The decree reinstating the farms was passed two weeks later and signed by Serdiuk, with Tkachenko the primary official punished from Bila Tserkva with a 'strong party punishment' (*strogoe vzyskanie*) and his counterparts in the *gorsovet*, Comrade Malashkevich and *gorkom* secretary Comrade Yarygin, punished with reprimands (*vygovory*). Though not severe punishments, they were nonetheless a rejection of the *dvoevlastie* argument and, with Dvornikov also given a *vygovor*, an indictment of the oblast-level agricultural department for its 'apolitical' stance.[55]

In the second and third quarters of 1948, in the midst of the Exile Campaign, the *obkom* made a slew of similar decrees and decisions to satisfy supplications for the return of illegally appropriated land and stolen resources to collective farms.[56] The three other farms that had been 'liquidated' illegally in the same way as in Raska in 1946 were reinstated by August 1948 by decree and the offending *raion*- and oblast-level officials punished as in Bila Tserkva (by *vygovory* or *vzyskaniia*). In 1948 alone, another 101 cases of illegal appropriations of collective farmland by institutions or officials for *podsobnoe khoziaistvo* were settled, with almost 3,000 hectares returned along with stolen money, houses, livestock and hay by the end of the year.[57] Comrade Belous, the land surveyor at the oblast-level agriculture department responsible for the sham investigations and cover-up in Bila Tserkva, ran out of luck, losing his job as punishment for a long

[54] Serdiuk had worked with Khrushchev from 1937 in Moscow and had gone with him to Kyiv, becoming Second Secretary of Kyiv *obkom* in 1939–41 and 1943–7, before becoming First Secretary from 1947 to February 1949.
[55] RGASPI f. 17, op. 122, d. 317, l. 12.
[56] See DAKO f. 4810, op. 1, d. 27, for the general progress of land returns to collective farms and l. 30 for a summary of returns for the fourth quarter of 1948.
[57] DAKO f. 4810, op. 1, d. 27, l. 39.

string of offences.[58] Many more supplications remained unaddressed, especially those with more common complaints of abuse and theft by officials. But this was a season of heightened enforcement of collective farm rules by the Council on Collective Farm Affairs not seen since the beginning of the campaign in late 1946.

After the two bursts of campaign energy, in late 1946 and early to mid-1948, there was a reduction in the scope of Council representatives' responsibilities and punitive actions they could facilitate.[59] Though the Exile Campaign was not aimed at discovering or punishing abuses by officials, it is clear that central authorities' refocusing of attention on collective farm rules in general encouraged officials in Kyiv to do the same. Council representatives reminded these officials of their new responsibilities in any case, and framed officials' abuses against farms as specifically against the letter of the new law and spirit of the broader campaign. Oblast-level officials now began paying attention to Council representatives again, whom they had been ignoring since early 1947, when the energy of the campaign had receded and representatives complained about the unresponsiveness of officials to their requests.[60] Action on behalf of *kolkhozniki* seemed most feasible at the crests of these waves of attention.

This 1948 campaign was the last significant wave in which Council representatives were able to exert considerable influence to achieve remedies, at least on paper, on behalf of *kolkhozniki* in Kyiv Oblast and across Ukraine. Their focus shifted from investigating new abuses by officials to ensuring that the 1948 decrees passed to remedy them were enforced. Council representatives in Kyiv Oblast in 1949 and 1950 reported a reduction in illegal land appropriations by officials. A reduction in land abuses by officials was also reported across Ukraine, though decrees on land returns and their enforcement were less widespread there, given that illegal land appropriations lessened in other oblasts after the 1946 campaign and officials there did not resist the return of this land for as long a time.[61] In some of these other oblasts, Council representatives, together with republican authorities, declared the implementation of the 1946 decree to be complete by 1948, and the

---

[58] DAKO f. 4810, op. 1, d. 27, l. 27. For comparative trends on the removal of officials in agriculture in 1947 on charges of corruption or incompetence, see TsDAVOU f. r-2, op. 7, d. 7024, ll. 19–31.

[59] By the third quarter of 1947, collective farm chairmen had been replaced for abuses of collective farm rules in only 452 of the 14,703 farms in 9 oblasts of Ukraine surveyed by investigators (3.1 per cent), compared to replacements in 4,316 farms (29.4 per cent) at the beginning of the year. See TsDAVOU f. r-2, op. 7, d. 7024, l. 67.

[60] DAKO f. 4810, op. 1, dd. 31, 33.

[61] See Council reports from 1949–50 in DAKO f. 4810, op. 1, dd. 36, 40.

types of abuses listed in the decree were no longer tolerated, at least by farm chairs, even if they continued to a lesser degree.[62]

This optimistic claim born of the excitement of the Exile Campaign glosses over the reality that illegal private plot expansion by *kolkhozniki* and pilfering of resources resumed after the energy of the 1946 and 1948 campaigns subsided and remained endemic to the collective farm system. In Kyiv Oblast there was certainly more work to do to eradicate these abuses, but here too representatives' punitive work eased in line with general pressure on the countryside from central authorities, in both the enforcement of collective farm rules and the collection of foodstuffs into 1950.[63] Representatives' claims of a reduction in illegal appropriations during this period were probably accurate, but these claims likely also reflected the reduced scope of their activity, which limited their ability to discover and certainly prosecute these cases. This reduction in scope reflected the clearly discernible relaxation of signals from central authorities on rooting out corruption among officials across the Union.

The greater capacity to achieve remedies, at least by paper decree, for *kolkhozniki* against officials in the 1948 campaign is not addressed in the literature about it, which is not wide. Much of it focuses on the failures of the campaign to achieve its primary aims of improving work discipline among *kolkhozniki* at the cost of uprooting them from their ancestral homes, breaking apart families and sending a not insignificant number to their deaths en route or in exile: in short, another government failure to improve an inherently unworkable collective farm system at great human cost.[64] But the above analysis shows how, at least in some cases, *kolkhozniki* used the campaign to their advantage in perhaps the same way that historians note they used it to rid their villages of unpopular *kolkhozniki*.[65] Even more, it shows how local authorities

---

[62] Report from Zaporizhia Oblast submitted to republican authorities in TsDAVOU f. r-2, op. 7, d. 7024, l. 21.

[63] The 1947 harvest saw a massive increase in grain production over the previous year's famine-affected harvest of 1946, by as much as 40 per cent by some calculations. Grain production continued to improve considerably in 1948, though the amount collected by the state remained more static, leaving significant grain surpluses in the countryside for *kolkhozniki*'s consumption and trade on collective farm markets or in agreements with factories and institutions. For grain production figures across the USSR and Ukraine from 1945 to 1950, see RGAE f. 1562, op. 324, dd. 5295–5301. For making sense of conflicting production figures and the rate of increasing grain stocks held by *kolkhozniki* into the late 1940s, see Wheatcroft, 'The Soviet Famine of 1946–1947', 993, 999.

[64] Lévesque, 'Exile and Discipline', contains a significant critique of earlier accounts of the campaign in Zima, *Golod v SSSR*, 180–93; Weiner, *Making Sense of War*, 319–23; E. I. Zubkova, 'Mir mnenii sovetskogo cheloveka, 1945–1948 gg. Po materialam TsK VKP(b)', *Otechestvennaia istoriia*, no. 3 (1998).

[65] Weiner, *Making Sense of War*, 322–3.

reacted to pressure from above during mass campaigns in the country-side and then to the easing of this pressure and central oversight over their activities once the energy of the campaigns had receded. Officials in Kyiv Oblast made all the right noises to their superiors when passing the decrees during the campaign in 1948 but did little if anything to enforce them months or even years afterwards. They did so cognisant of the greater opportunities for independent conduct that was now afforded to them. The task of the following section is to examine how the post-campaign context of easing pressure encouraged this behaviour.

Enforcing and/or Avoiding the Decrees

Raion and city authorities in Kyiv Oblast were not alone in avoiding implementing some decrees issued by their oblast-level superiors. This was common across the Soviet Union and made possible by the broader problems that beset the entire party and state structure under Stalin, which have long been addressed by historians.[66] Overworked oblast-level authorities issued general decrees to their *raion*-level subordinates in response to pressure from above, with limited capacity to oversee their implementation. Many oblast-level officials generally knew and cared little about the practical difficulties of implementing decrees in the conditions of the relevant *raion* and lower localities. Party conferences called across the Soviet Union in the first half of 1948 allowed for the public airing of grievances of *raion*-level officials towards their oblast-level superiors on this and other points. These are colourful and under-utilised sources in the literature. A *raion* secretary in Penza, Comrade Kunitsin, spoke for most of his colleagues across the Union when he criticised his *obkom* for trying to control the agricultural sector just by issuing paper decrees (*kantseliarsko-biurokraticheskie metody*) rather than actually doing any work to manage it:

> We receive whole packets of decrees from the *obkom* during the harvest. If
> we actually tried to implement any of these decrees or operated in the same

---

[66] This perennially problematic relationship between these levels of Soviet governance was exacerbated by the chaos of the post-war period when millions of lower-rung officials were replaced due to wartime losses (see Chapter 1). As many historians have noted, the high turnover of officials compounded the failures in party and state work. In addition to Lewin, *The Soviet Century*, for a Ukraine-specific discussion on cadres, see Lieberman, 'The Re-Sovietisation of Formerly Occupied Territories', and T. V. Motrenko and V. A. Smolii, eds., *Istoriia derzhavnoi sluzhby v Ukraïni*, v. II, *Holovne upravlinnia derzhavnoi sluzhby Ukraïny* (Kyiv: Nika-Tsentr, 2009), 376–402.

way as the *obkom*, the *kolkhozniki* would think that we had gone insane and stop listening to us.[67]

Central authorities encouraged these criticisms 'from below' within broadly accepted ideological guidelines and language among party members, especially in 1948 with the broader push for officials to engage in public self-criticism (*samokritika*). In public party fora, by 1948 at least, this push amounted to officials having to admit their personal shortcomings as key factors in policy failures.[68] Many oblast-level officials were forced to suffer this type of criticism 'from below' and promise to improve on their shortcomings, though only a handful lost their positions. Replacing leaders was not really the point of this public spectacle, which offered little practical chance to improve party work. As one *obkom* secretary told his *raion*-level subordinate in Riazan: 'You can criticise me at the conference all you like and I will accept it. But when we get home, when I say jump, you say how high!'[69]

This exchange remains an accurate characterisation of the conferences as public spectacle that resulted in little change in party structures. But an analysis of the spectacle still provides insight into the common dysfunction between levels of Soviet governance, even if little was done to fix it.[70] The conferences throw into sharp relief the relationship between *raion*- and oblast-level authorities in Kyiv Oblast. Here, it is less oblast-level ignorance in local affairs that explains the non-fulfilment, and more their conspiracy to do so. Again, this was not immediately apparent to Council on Collective Farm Affairs representatives. It was common for oblast-level agriculture departments across the Soviet Union not to investigate complaints made to them. In such cases, the Council expected oblast leaders with whom they were in contact to rectify the situation and usually wrote to them from Moscow.[71] Given the workload of Council representatives, this was usually the end of the matter, and follow-up investigations on the ground were unlikely unless Council representatives received notice of continuing abuse.

However, the extreme nature of illegality in Raska and Bila Tserkva and the lying of oblast-level officials about conducting false investigations encouraged follow-up investigations months later. This resulted in new

---

[67] RGASPI f. 17, op. 122, d. 295, l. 159.

[68] On the multifarious use of *samokritika* by Communist Party officials to pursue their own ends in the pre-war period, see J. Arch Getty, '*Samokritika* Rituals in the Stalinist Central Committee, 1933–1938', *Russian Review* 58, no. 1 (1999), 49–70.

[69] Denisov et al., eds., *TsK VKP(b) i regional'nye partiinye komitety*, 176.

[70] As was often the case in these fora, intelligent officials at these conferences spoke of this problem and others, but only as symptoms of deeper ones in party structures that they dared not address publicly.

[71] On the failure of oblast-level agricultural departments to investigate complaints passed on to them by Council representatives in Tambov Oblast, see RGAE f. 9476, op. 2, d. 24, ll. 29–30.

pressure from Moscow on republican authorities in Ukraine to bring their oblast-level subordinates into line. These investigations revealed not ignorance, but a conspiracy between oblast-level officials and their subordinates to engage in illegal appropriations and prevent investigations into them. Council representatives may have suspected this conspiracy from the beginning but did not report it to their superiors until they had this proof.

This finding had the immediate effect of further souring of relations between the Council representatives and oblast-level officials in Kyiv Oblast, which helps explain why the latter refused to implement the decrees forcing the reinstatement of the liquidated farms in 1948. The Council operated at the oblast level of Soviet government in each oblast across the Soviet Union with subordinate branches concerned with enforcing collective farm rules on the ground. One intention of the Council's structure was to enable its representatives to work with oblast-level officials, specifically in the *obliispolkom*, to address abuses against the farms, which, they assumed, were committed by lower-level officials. Sitting on this horizontal axis of power at the oblast level would allow for swift action to correct violations downward to the *raion* and lower levels, and swift access to central power upward to the Council in Moscow to break through any gridlock encountered in their work. This structure afforded Council representatives considerable power and reflected the importance that central authorities placed on the Council as the executive body of the 1946 campaign.

Council representatives and oblast-level officials were at times characterised by the same tension between agents from investigative organs and the state and party officials they monitored. But this operational structure and the joint work of Council representatives and officials in monitoring the abuses of the collective farm system by their subordinates distinguished this relationship from others. It could work reasonably well, at least during the height of the campaigns in 1946 and 1948. But in the wake of the 1948 campaign, Gordienko's finding of oblast-level conspiracy crashed their entire operational structure. As soon as Gordienko and other Council representatives made allegations of the illegal conduct public in party fora from 1948 – and certainly after the decrees were passed to punish these officials and reinstate the liquidated farms – oblast-level officials would hardly speak to them.[72] By 1949, *obliispolkom* secretaries even began publicly discrediting Council representatives.

---

[72] There was a similar breakdown of relations among competing Soviet occupation forces in Germany, when they complained about one another's conduct to superior authorities as part of the battle to realise their competing occupation aims. See Slaveski, *The Soviet Occupation*, ch. 4.

These public discreditings began in earnest from April 1949 when the new leadership of Kyiv *obkom* were deeply offended by Gordienko's public accusations of corruption and wrongdoing of their subordinates at the *raion* level. Gordienko spoke at an *obkom* meeting accusing numerous *raion* authorities of engaging in a corrupt scheme whereby they permitted building enterprises to organise 'construction projects' on collective farms without the farms' knowledge. The farms were forced to pay for building works that were never commenced or completed, or were completed to such a poor, unsafe standard that they were unusable. This assessment of poor housing construction was particularly shocking given the desperate housing shortage that saw millions of *kolkhozniki* living in ramshackle dirt hovels (*zemlianki*). Also, given that in some cases *raion* authorities provided loans to the farms to pay for building works and refused to try and recover the money on behalf of the farms, Gordienko was implicitly accusing them of being party to this corruption. In his speech at the meeting, the Second Secretary of Kyiv *obkom*, K. F. Moskalets, denied these allegations and refused to accede to Gordienko's request for a further investigation into them.[73]

As was his wont, when confronted with such intransigence, Gordienko wrote directly to Khrushchev for assistance. These sorts of corrupt schemes were not uncommon in the collective farm sector, and Khrushchev quickly issued a resolution calling for an investigation into the matter to the new head of the Kyiv *obkom*, A. A. Gryza, who had replaced Serdiuk in February that year. Upon taking over from Serdiuk, Gryza had tried to placate Gordienko with assurances that he would look into the corruption scheme described above as well as the failure of *raion* and city authorities in Raska and Bila Tserkva to implement the 1948 reconstruction decrees. But, by the time of the April meeting, Gryza had done nothing.[74] Khrushchev's resolution put him on notice, and he was clearly embarrassed by Gordienko going over his head to his new direct boss. Gryza now showed none of the respect that his predecessor had for Gordienko, the Council and its work. Barely three months after Khrushchev issued the resolution, Gryza told those assembled at the next Kyiv *obkom* plenum, including Gordienko, in July that:

> We have a certain representative from the Council on Collective Farm Affairs with us here, Gordienko. Once we organised for him to travel into

[73] DAKO f. 4810, op. 1, d. 33, l. 83.
[74] For Gordienko's pressure on Gryza in February 1949, see DAKO f. 4810, op. 1, d. 33, l. 16.

the *raion*, but he declined to go, and so we decided not to entrust him with any more work.[75]

This was a clear signal to all officials present that the decrees Gordienko was trying to enforce were meaningless and, broadly, that he should continue to be ignored.[76] Gryza also took practical measures against Gordienko, reducing the power of his small office by reassigning his subordinates to other duties.[77]

Discrediting and reducing the power of Council representatives further impeded the implementation of the 1948 decrees, none of which had been successfully implemented anyway. Raska received little assistance from *raion* authorities, who returned little of the fertile land they had illegally appropriated, but at least they stopped trying to liquidate the farm and village. In Bila Tserkva, city and *raion* authorities were not so kind, sacking the farm chairmen and continuing to abuse and illegally appropriate land from the farm into 1949. Until 1949, Council representatives would have addressed this problem by petitioning Khrushchev directly for support, or indirectly via their superiors in Moscow. These superiors would usually write to republican authorities (not so much Khrushchev but the relevant Ukrainian Central Committee secretaries) about a matter, expecting them to pressure their subordinates at the oblast level to address it. *Obkom* secretaries would usually comply. But the situation had changed by 1949. Serdiuk had shown some sympathy to the Council and Gordienko's work, even if he was not terribly effective in assisting it. Gryza had no sympathy. He was smart enough to make a formal recognition of the resolution issued by Khrushchev, but kept stalling the investigation it called for until Khrushchev departed for his promotion to Moscow in late 1949, taking his long-time ally Serdiuk with him. No one was even charged over the corrupt housing scheme. Nor would they be, because with Khrushchev and Serdiuk gone Council representatives lost their direct line to sympathetic

[75] DAKO f. 4810, op. 1, d. 33, l. 84. See Cadiot and Angell, 'Equal before the Law?', 253, on similar threats to members of the judiciary who were investigating the crimes of party members.
[76] This false accusation of Gordienko's complacency on agricultural matters is telling of how personal denunciations worked among officials in the Soviet system. By criticising Gordienko for the same shortcoming he noted among oblast-level officials – never going out to the *raiony* – Gryza impugned his enemy with his own crimes. This was a more common practice among officials. See Slaveski, *The Soviet Occupation*, 51. Gordienko actually spent much of his time travelling around Kyiv Oblast taking supplications from *kolkhozniki* and investigating their veracity.
[77] DAKO f. 4810, op. 1, d. 33, l. 85. On the rising of the 'regional elite', especially *obkom* heads such as Gryza, into a powerful class of long-serving officials and the broader centre–local problems in late Stalinism, see Oleg Khlevniuk, 'Sistema tsentr–regiony v 1930–1950-e gody' *Cahiers du monde russe* 44, nos. 2–3 (2003), 253–68.

ears. The indirect line was also weakening. Council representatives still wrote to Moscow, but not much was returned to the republican level in Kyiv. The head of the Council in Moscow, Andreev, had been seriously ill since late 1947 and took several periods of sick leave thereafter, engaging less and less with his work on the Council as well as the other anti-corruption bodies which he chaired.[78] His secretary on the Council, Andrianov, lacked the gravitas of his boss and struggled to meet the demands from his subordinates in the field for action.

There were broader reasons for this reduction of Council power beyond personnel. The agricultural crisis of 1946–7 was over. The importance of agriculture in the day-to-day business of the central leadership had moved sideways, and central authorities' pressure on the sector for grain collections had eased with improved harvests. There was a discernible relaxation in central authorities' prosecution of corruption among officials from the heights of the anti-corruption campaigns in 1946–7, particularly in agriculture.[79] A roughly commensurate reduction in the power of the internal party and state organs responsible for it, including the Council, followed. Historians have traced this relaxation in different ways with slightly different periodisations, though most agree that the relaxation was a recognition of the party's disengagement from its role in overseeing the moral and legal conduct of its members and its acceleration towards embracing corruption in the late Stalin era.[80] This embrace was supposedly mutually beneficial, with officials paying back with their political loyalty the central authorities who put them 'above the law', thus 'strengthening' the overall Stalinist regime.[81]

One signal of this relaxation of central authorities was made in April 1948, when the all-Union Politburo issued a decree on party officials stealing state resources by trying them in 'honour courts', as opposed to judicial ones. This decree clearly sought to discourage mostly senior officials from stealing and from tolerating it among their subordinates rather than prosecuting them for these acts, as had been the case in the anti-corruption drive of 1946–7.[82] Similar signals of relaxation followed, especially in Stalin's dealing with corruption claims against Central Asian party

---

[78] Andreev was also chairman of the Party Control Commission (KPK), but by late 1947 he was again very ill and soon away from all of his posts on sick leave. On his health, see Simon Sebag Montefiore, *Stalin: The Court of the Red Tsar* (London: Weidenfeld & Nicolson, 2003), 552.

[79] Heinzen, *The Art of the Bribe*, ch. 5.

[80] See Edward D. Cohn, 'Policing the Party: Conflicts between Local Prosecutors and Party Leaders under Late Stalinism', *Europe-Asia Studies* 65, no. 10 (2013), 1912–30; Cadiot and Angell, 'Equal before the Law?'

[81] Denisov et al., eds., *TsK VKP(b) i regional'nye partiinye komitety*, 5–12.   [82] Ibid., 6.

officials and putting clear restraints on judicial officials' capacity to prosecute them in early 1949.[83] It is clear that senior officials not only in Central
Asia but also in the European parts of the Union discerned this change in
practice quite quickly, in Kyiv from at least early 1949. It is also clear that
central authorities were aware that officials were emboldened in their
corrupt behaviour by this relaxation as well as by its impact on managing
the countryside. Reports of senior-level officials ignoring senior Council
representatives and investigators from party and state investigative organs
began to appear more throughout 1949, much like the Gryza case in Kyiv.
In one report to Central Committee Secretary Georgii Malenkov in
June 1949, a senior investigator complained that the head of the party's
investigative body in Riazan was in cahoots with the *obkom* head, rubber-
stamping his illegal decisions and ignoring his failure to address serious
abuses in the collective farm sector. This was not only a problem of
corruption, the report's writer complained, but also one of bad governance,
which was encouraging sabotage in the collective farm sector and limiting
food supply.[84]

A year earlier, similar reports had sparked an investigation into the
Riazan *obkom* by central authorities.[85] The Central Committee (all-
Union) passed a resolution in April 1948 in anticipation of the Exile
Campaign (it was implemented in June outside Ukraine) to reduce the
number of *kolkhozniki* failing to report to work by punishing them as well
as collective farm chairmen and officials tolerating high absentee rates.
These were not especially high in Riazan, but there was considerable
reporting from investigative organs on the *obkom*'s failure to enforce
collective farm rules and broader mismanagement of agricultural
affairs.[86] By July the resolution seemed to have worked, reducing absentee
rates (temporarily) from 54,696 *kolkhozniki* to 13,000.[87]

A year later, however, reports such as those sent to Malenkov above,
explaining that collective farming had reverted to its previous parlous state,
could spark nothing but apathy from the central authorities in the context
of relaxed food collections and the prosecution of corruption. Their
apathetic attitude was clear to officials on the ground. In Kyiv Oblast,
for instance, oblast-level officials understood that by 1949 that the recent
pressure brought to bear on them to clean up the sector had subsided and
their superiors' interest in this matter had waned – there remained little

[83] Ibid., 9.   [84] Ibid., 123.
[85] For the Riazan resolution and investigation results, see RGASPI f. 17, op. 122, d. 313, ll. 126–142.
[86] Denisov et al., eds., *TsK VKP(b) i regional' nye partiinye komitety*, 170–8.
[87] RGASPI f. 17, op. 122, d. 313, l. 134.

incentive to implement the decrees and properly punish their comrades. They could now ignore Council and other representatives from investigative bodies with few, if any, consequences.

Until this relaxation became clear to leaders in Kyiv Oblast, they had protected their subordinates from prosecution, real or anticipated, by issuing 'paper punishments' or dispersing their members along a horizontal axis of governance. After the pressure from above had subsided, officials returned to their posts. None of the officials punished in the 1948 decrees to reinstate the farms in Raska and Bila Tserkva actually served their sentences, and those who were supposed to be removed from their positions did not lose their jobs. Officials continued to engage in the illegal abuse of the collective farm sector for which they were meant to be punished, although there was less illegal appropriation of land, which seems to have reduced considerably by 1950. Malashkevich remained head of the Bila Tserkva *gorsovet* and, unmoved by a warning from the party, immediately fired Nesterenko and other farm chairmen for their part in these events.[88]

Oblast-level officials still punished others named in the decrees, but this was done primarily for show, to establish a paper trail of fulfilling the decree if they were ever questioned by their superiors. They removed from their positions those officials required by the decree, but did so by moving them into positions along the horizontal level of governance. The head of the Borodianka *raiispolkom*, Comrade Shidaev, took up the same position in the adjacent *raion*, while his deputy, equally responsible for the crimes in Raska, was promoted to Shidaev's former post. Other deputies not identified by the decree for punishment also moved positions, partly due to their association with the guilty but also to avoid any further investigation and possible punishments. The other officials who received party warnings for their crimes, including Dvornikov and Tkachenko, went on leave after the decrees were passed and were thus 'unable' to attend the meetings called to discuss their punishments. In early 1949 both were re-elected to their posts, though Dvornikov, at least, was clearly active during his leave and most certainly played a hand in the dispersion of his acolytes from Borodianka.[89]

It was more common for central authorities to disperse guilty officials into other positions within the state/party hierarchy to break apart their conspiratorial networks.[90] The case studies in Kyiv Oblast, however, indicate how these circles dispersed themselves to cope with punishments

[88] DAKO f. 4810, op. 1, d. 33, l. 13.   [89] TsDAHOU f. 1, op. 52, d. 829, ll. 1–6.
[90] Denisov et al., eds., *TsK VKP(b) i regional'nye partiinye komitety*, 6.

from above and, more problematically, employed this strategy prophylactically: that is, oblast-level officials dispersed their subordinates in anticipation of sanctions. This was happening in Kyiv Oblast in mid- to late 1948, at a time when the signals about the relaxation of pressure on corruption from the centre were only first being seen and punishments were still widely feared.

Dispersions of officials also happened elsewhere. As discussed in the previous chapter, in Vologda Oblast, 112 officials were named by party investigative organs as part of a large-scale programme of illegally appropriating farmland 'under the guise of *podsobnoe khoziaistvo*' to fund a massive corrupt scheme making millions of roubles. They kept their money despite the investigation from central authorities, as the *obkom* head dispersed them all into other state and party positions across the *raiony* of Vologda Oblast as soon as he became aware of its progress. When members of the investigative organs pleaded with their superiors in Moscow months later to seek out those officials who had been dispersed, in order to bring them to justice, it was already too late.[91] The logistical difficulties of locating these officials and resuming a broken investigation were too much for their superiors to pursue when their broader appetite for prosecuting corruption had clearly waned. By 1949 these vast dispersions became less necessary in this more relaxed atmosphere. If the powers of central party leadership had always been strong in replacing and appointing officials and thus being able to disperse networks, but weak in terms of controlling what they did, horizontal dispersion now weakened both.

The wide literature on corruption in the Stalinist system in the immediate post-war period, and that specifically on the methods by which local circles of corruption avoided prosecution for it, does not mention this prophylactic measure. Much of this literature focuses on the relationship between state judicial organs and the party, particularly the difficulties encountered by state prosecutors seeking to bring party members to justice.[92] In Kyiv and Vologda Oblasts, where this prophylactic strategy was widely employed, these cases never made it to the judicial organs because judicial officials were part of the same circles of corruption they were supposed to investigate. These cases were dealt with by investigative organs from Moscow, whose capacity to investigate and bring officials to justice was considerably weakened by late 1948. We have little sense of how

---

[91] RGASPI f. 17, op. 122, d. 316, ll. 94–104.
[92] Heinzen, *The Art of the Bribe*; Cadiot and Angell, 'Equal before the Law?'; Cohn, 'Policing the Party'; and Hooper, 'A Darker "Big Deal"'.

widespread this prophylactic measure was or its impact on the capacity of central authorities to enforce their policies in the countryside at this time outside Kyiv and Vologda Oblasts. It is clear that this measure had already reduced the effectiveness of central authorities' prosecution of corruption before their relaxation of it.

The bigger issue that these case studies help us to understand is how central authorities' exertion or relaxation of pressure on local authorities and rural populations in the countryside influenced the willingness of officials to enforce decrees on behalf of the centre and that of *kolkhozniki* to follow them. Essentially, the case studies help us make sense of the difference between the centre's 'power' and 'control' over the countryside in post-war Stalinism, if we take power to mean the authority to tell people to do something and 'control' the capacity to make them do it. The concurrent relaxation of central pressure on collections and prosecution of corruption among officials had contradictory impacts on collective farm abuses committed by *kolkhozniki* and officials.

The reduction in central pressure for grain collections did leave more food in the countryside, but not in the hands of *kolkhozniki*. The impetus for *kolkhozniki* to keep breaking collective farm rules in expanding and working harder on their private plots to survive continued, with their food consumption levels and living standards rising much more slowly than those of rural workers and urban dwellers after the famine, reaching pre-war levels probably only in the middle of the 1950s.[93] In the immediate wake of the 1946 and 1948 campaigns, Council representatives and other officials were reporting that most *kolkhozniki* had resumed appropriating collective farmland to expand their private plots and, worse, that local authorities were doing little to stop this.[94] This was often the case with Soviet campaigns – once they were over, people usually resumed the behaviour the campaigns were designed to stop, especially any behaviour they needed to do to survive. Neither relaxation nor the punitive policies aimed at forcing them into collective farm work could be ever successful in the long term as long as *kolkhozniki* were hungry.

It was not the campaign designed to tackle land abuses launched in 1946 that eventually worked to reduce this problem among officials in Kyiv and Vologda, but the relaxation of pressure on collections and prosecution for corruption. This is because, unlike with regard to *kolkhozniki*, it removed

---

[93] See *kolkhoz* budgets in RGAE f. 582, op. 24, d. 430, l. 47, for a comparison of pre- and post-war *kolkhoznik* food levels in Kyiv Oblast.

[94] TsDAVOU f. r-2, op. 7, d. 7024, l. 83; TsDAHOU f. 1, op. 23, d. 4783, ll. 117–130.

the impetus for officials to conduct them. Workers needed less farmland to feed themselves as food surpluses became available to them through collective farm markets and supply agreements between farms and their institutions. These types of market exchange were difficult to resume upon liberation and were diminished in 1946, but were now made possible from the time of the 1947 harvest and fostered by the relaxation of subsequent food collections. Significant illegal appropriations continued in Kyiv Oblast, Vologda and other places for different reasons until the turn of the decade, but Council representatives reported a reduction, albeit delayed, in illegal land appropriations by officials, institutions and factories here in line with those seen in other areas of Ukraine after the 1946 campaign.[95]

There is a clear connection here between central authorities exercising restraint to achieve their aims compared to their usual pressure on local authorities, which, as we have seen, was often counterproductive. Nonetheless, this achievement caused more problems, with 'relaxation' encouraging officials to steal the greater amount of food and resources that remained in the countryside and commit a wide array of other abuses towards collective farms. These abuses continued for decades, conducted with even greater impunity, evident in their open antagonism towards officials from investigative agencies. The old problem remained of central authorities ruling the countryside by appointing people to positions of power but having little control over how they exercised it. But by the late 1940s, at least, central authorities seemed at least to better understand other ways to close the gap between power and control in terms of self-supply.

One result of this finding is to give the problem of illegal appropriations some finite chronological boundaries: they were prominent from 1944 to 1947 in most of Ukraine and until the end of the decade in the areas under study here. As the following chapters demonstrate, however, the problem was that the damage done by illegal appropriations to rural economies, to local communities and to people's lives endured long beyond these boundaries, into the post-war decades and, indeed, into the present. These chapters count the costs of this damage.

---

[95] DAKO f. 4810, op. 1, d. 33, ll. 50–51.

PART II

The Cost of the Battle for Land to People and the State

The Cost of Taking Land: The Damage Caused by Illegal Appropriations of Collective Farmland to Kolkhozniki, Communities and the State

The rural outskirts of Bila Tserkva have sufficient population and 5,000 hectares of wonderfully fertile land. Instead of mobilising these resources to rebuild the large and successful farms in this area, as well as the broader healthy communities of which they were part, city and *raion* authorities have perverted state policy and done the opposite ... To make matters worse, all of this has been going on for numerous years, robbing the state of thousands of tonnes of foodstuffs from collective farms whose lands have been misappropriated for use by small organisations and by non-working elements in the city for their own use.

M. Gordienko, 1948 Kyiv *obkom* CP(b)U Plenum[1]

Gordienko, his fellow representatives on the Council on Collective Farm Affairs and, broadly, members of the most powerful Soviet party investigative organs like the Party Control Commission (KPK)[2] all fought hard to recover losses to the state's budget and its broader 'moral authority' wrought by the corruption of its officials. For Gordienko and his allies, the interests of the state as represented by central authorities and those of its most vulnerable citizens were the same. The realisation of these interests was denied only by the corrupt officials who stood between the state and its citizens in the convoluted bureaucracies through which they wielded power.

---

[1] TsDAHOU f. 1, op. 51, d. 3648, l. 151.

[2] The KPK was based within the Central Committee of the Communist Party, relevant here as it was under the control of Secretary Andreev in 1946, who was also minister of agriculture and head of the Council. At this time, it formed part of the revamped Upravlenie po proverke partiinykh organov TsK VKP(b) (Department for the Inspection of Party Organs of the Central Committee of the VKP (b)). It was thus positioned at the centre of the new anti-corruption/anti-theft campaigns of 1946–7 under the operational control of Stalin's long-time supporter Matvei Shkiriatov. For the KPK in the 1930s, see J. Arch Getty, 'Pragmatists and Puritans: The Rise and Fall of the Party Control Commission', *Carl Beck Papers in Russian and East European Studies* no. 1208 (1997); for its postwar operations, see RGASPI f. 17, op. 122.

To students of the Soviet period, Gordienko is easily recognisable as a true believer: in this case, someone who fought hard to eradicate 'aberrations' in the political system – like corruption – without realising or at least admitting that these were not aberrations at all. Corruption and broader criminality were both fostered by and central to the functioning of Stalinism.[3] Historians have long demonstrated that this was especially true in the collective farm sector.[4] Central authorities' primary concern in this sector, after taking as much as they could from the countryside to supply the central economy, was to stop *kolkhozniki* and local officials from extracting too many resources to feed or enrich themselves, but the sector only functioned at all, however poorly, because there was a capacity for *kolkhozniki* and officials to do so.

In the absence of paying sufficient wages to *kolkhozniki* in money or foodstuffs, in order to survive, *kolkhozniki* needed to spend less time working on the collective farm and more time cultivating food on their private plots as well expanding the size of these plots. Local officials compounded this problem. They could usually remain in power only if they balanced the competing needs of delivering foodstuffs to the state and keeping enough to feed locals and supply their networks. There was never 'enough' food, so this meant stealing it and other resources from its producers (*kolkhozniki*) first and feeding them last. This encouraged *kolkhozniki* to avoid working on the collective to produce food on their own private plots for survival, at the expense of overall food production, thus compounding the shortages that drove this system of cyclical abuse. Central authorities bemoaned abuses by *kolkhozniki* and officials alike, but generated the conditions in which they flourished – something no campaign could ever resolve.[5]

The cost to the state's coffers of this system of cyclical abuse, though inevitable, was immense. Gordienko measured one aspect of it, illegal appropriations, specifically in tonnes of food lost and broadly in the loss of the regime's prestige in the countryside. The previous chapters have

---

[3] We have little sense of whether Gordienko and some of his peers understood this irony at the time. Even if they did, they could hardly say anything about it. On the necessity of party/state officials and then industrial managers engaging in illegal activity to survive under Stalinism and, indeed, make the system work, see Gill, 'The Communist Party and the Weakness of Bureaucratic Norms', 123 and Filtzer's 'psychology of circumvention' thesis in *Soviet Workers*, 250.

[4] Popov, *Rossiiskaia derevnia*; Verbitskaia, *Rossiiskoe krest'ianstvo*.

[5] Heinzen, *The Art of the Bribe*, 1. The ability of people we might call 'local power brokers' to distribute benefits providing a key element in their power, and legitimising their authority, is evident across political systems in different times and places. For a broader and more contemporary perspective of the role of power-brokers in regional/border conflict areas with similarities with those under study here, see Jonathan Goodhand, *Bandits, Borderlands and Opium Wars: Afghan State-Building Viewed from the Margins* (Copenhagen: Danish Institute for International Studies, 2009).

given some indication of the broader cost of illegal appropriations to the state and the livelihoods of *kolkhozniki* before 1948 when the farms were being liquidated and sitting outside or at the edges of the collective farm system. This chapter continues this calculation but focuses on the period when farms were reinstated in 1948, becoming part of the collective farm system and more subject to the cyclical abuse described.

Following these farms' unique trajectories into this system of abuse reveals new and broader insights into its operation that unsettle dominant orthodoxies in the literature on land abuse. First, the cost of illegal appropriations was much wider in scope and longer in duration than Gordienko imagined, not merely for the state, but primarily for *kolkhozniki*. Second, local authorities struck the balance between delivering foodstuffs to the state and feeding locals in different ways at different times. In the crisis periods immediately after the war and during famine, local authorities in Kyiv Oblast abrogated balance in favour of feeding localities via self-supply, but after the famine – once agriculture recovered – they found this balance reasonably well. They met their foodstuff delivery quotas to the state from 1948 onwards and slowly improved food supply to their favoured population (rural workers and urban dwellers) and even marginally, to most *kolkhozniki*.

But not to all of them. We now know from following the paper trail of illegal appropriations among oblast-level authorities across Kyiv Oblast that local officials struck this balance only by supporting well-performing farms at the expense of struggling ones. After the farms in Raska and Bila Tserkva were reconstructed, local authorities began treating them more like other small and poor but still operational farms within the collective farm system they derided as *besperspektivnye*: that is, unpromising, without prospects for improvement and thus not suitable for assistance. The farms in Raska and Bila Tserkva joined the 232 (approximately 10 per cent of the 2,368 farms in Kyiv Oblast) classified as such. Not only were they poor, but they also remained so for years because local authorities consistently diverted scarce resources meant for them to supply better-performing farms. Officials did this because they thought they could grow much more food on the better-performing farms than in the poorer ones, therefore boosting overall foodstuff production in the *raion* to meet state and local food demands, and striking the balance between them. The collective farm system in Kyiv Oblast not only operated on the back of all *kolkhozniki*, but also weighed most heavily on the backs of the poorest among them, their farms and their localities. In striking this balance, local authorities laid the groundwork for the imbalance in economic post-war recovery across

Kyiv Oblast for decades to come, in ways that Gordienko and his peers could not have foreseen.

*

The 1946 Campaign on Collective Farm Rules in Ukraine recovered a total of 998,000 hectares of collective farmland, which, by the end of April 1947, was returned or in the process of being returned to the collective farm sector. This total amounted to just over 5 per cent of the approximately 18.5 million hectares of sown area in Ukraine in 1946.[6] This percentage of land recovery in Ukraine was only slightly higher than the all-Union average of 4 per cent of land recovered in relation to total area under cultivation in 1946 (4.7 million of 117.5 million hectares). Of these 4.7 million hectares of farmland recovered USSR-wide, *kolkhozniki* returned 521,000 hectares, 'other unspecified persons another 177,000 hectares and the large remainder recovered from industrial organizations that had encroached on most of the land'.[7]

Historians differ in their assessments of the impact of the recovery of this land from *kolkhozniki* to the collective farm sector. For many, the forcible reduction in late 1946 of the size of private *kolkhozniki*'s plots, their only real food source, at the same time the state was extracting as much grain as it could from the countryside during a mass drought accelerated the famine and exacerbated mortality.[8] For others, the amount of land recovered by the state was minimal, which indicates the reluctance of some *kolkhozniki* to expand their private plots illegally for fear of punishment. In this view, the collective farm sector enjoyed a higher degree of post-war stability.[9] Some argue that even the relatively small amount of illegal land expansion committed by *kolkhozniki* was inflated by authorities keen to demonstrate to their superiors their effectiveness in identifying breaches of collective farm rules during the campaign.[10] Other historians have gone a step further to assess the impact of the return of illegally appropriated farmland from all sources to the sector as a result of the campaign. These historians agree the impact was mostly negative for collective farms. Most of them lacked sufficient labour, machinery and livestock and so were unable to properly

---

[6] TsDAVOU f. r-2, op. 7, d. 5032, ll. 219–220. For sown area statistics in Ukraine and other republics for 1945–50, see RGAE f. 1562, op. 324, dd. 5295–5301.
[7] Weiner, *Making Sense of War*, 304.
[8] Ganson, *Soviet Famine*, 22, offers a critique of earlier interpretations of famine causation that place significant weight on the rate of food procurements in the countryside and the state's callous disregard for life there, to include more analysis of weather, poor governance and the broader international situation.
[9] Weiner, *Making Sense of War*, 304.   [10] Nadkin, *Stalinskaia agrarnaia politika*, 55.

cultivate the returned land and meet the increased foodstuff quotas that were attached to it. The farms fell further into debt and destitution; the returned land went to waste.[11]

An analysis of land recovered by the state and returned to farms in Kyiv Oblast – both those under review in Raska and Bila Tserkva and more broadly – reveals significant weakness in each of these viewpoints. The key factor ignored or not sufficiently taken into account by historians is the extent of enduring disorganisation of land usage records in Ukraine and especially Kyiv Oblast.[12] As discussed in Chapter 1, this disorganisation emerged from the war but was fostered by local officials afterwards. This disorganisation made it impossible to calculate how much land had actually been illegally appropriated from individual farms and broader localities, and thus to calculate how much needed to be returned. Council on Collective Farm Affairs representatives bemoaned the fact that, as a result, the 1946 Campaign on Collective Farm Rules failed to recover large tracts of farmland.[13] With regard to illegal expansion of private plots, amounting to just over 10 per cent of the total of land illegally appropriated in Ukraine, in some areas local officials and farm leaderships did not make or record the initial reductions in plot size made in the 1946 campaign. After the campaign was over, then, many *kolkhozniki* were able to recover the private plot land they had lost. This problem was Ukraine-wide, including the generally more economically successful eastern oblasts, in this case Dnipropetrovsk:

> There is no record on the reduction in the size of private plots in numerous collective farms in the autumn of 1946 and spring of 1947. These reductions in plots [if they were made] have been recovered by *kolkhozniki* with the assistance of collective farm leaderships and local officials in the interest of increasing private farming.[14]

In these areas the campaign was 'only for show', whereas in others the lack of documentation and record keeping of *kolkhozniki*'s land expansions and reductions encouraged more zealous local officials to remove all of the private plot land or reduce it below the legal minimum. Some of these reductions remained in place at the height of the famine in early 1947.

[11] Kessler and Kornilov, eds., *Kolkhoznaia zhizn'*, 18; Motrevich, 'Vosstanovlenie sel'skogo khoziaistva na Urale', 24; Ganson, *Soviet Famine*, 22.

[12] Disorganisation is noted as a problem in the sector in some works, though its impact on reconstruction is not investigated. See Smolii, *Ekonomichna istoriia Ukraïny*, 350.

[13] TsDAVOU f. r-2, op. 7, d. 5032, ll. 46–47.   [14] TsDAVOU f. r-2, op. 7, d. 7024, ll. 83, 86.

These developments clearly indicate that the scale of land illegally appropriated from the collective farm sector was greater than the official figures attest. The percentage of illegally appropriated land in relation to sown area was not 'probably lower when taking the entire *kolkhoz* land into account', as one historian puts it,[15] but probably much higher. The sector in Ukraine was not stable nor were its *kolkhozniki* cowed into following collective farm rules. There were both overzealous and lax recoveries of land from *kolkhozniki*'s plots by officials in different parts of Ukraine. For *kolkhozniki* in some regions, the 1946 campaign left more private plot land in their hands, while in other areas it left them less or none at all. If this land provided subsistence food, as much as possible during drought and famine, then the campaign's impact on the acceleration of famine and its mortality in regions where *kolkhozniki* kept their expanded plots was surely less severe than in those regions where *kolkhozniki* lost everything. It is not a coincidence that some of the most vociferous complaints about overzealous land recovery, at times leaving active members of collective farms with no private plot land at all, came from Kherson Oblast, which was one of the worst-hit regions in Ukraine during the famine.[16] *Kolkhozniki*'s livelihoods in this instance depended greatly on where they lived in Ukraine; but this point of regional differentiation is not always fully appreciated by some historians writing on the 1946 campaign.[17]

Regional differentiation is key to assessing the impacts of the return of illegally appropriated land to the collective farm sector in Kyiv Oblast. Shortages in mechanisation and labour clearly limited the capacity to cultivate the lands returned to the sector as a result of the 1946 campaign across Ukraine, especially for grain-growing. The anticipated benefits of increased food production from a greater sown area were offset by resources such as grain seed and labour wasted to sow land that was poorly prepared for it, yielding much less food than anticipated. These lands probably would have been more productive if left as subsistence plots to grow root crops for *kolkhozniki* or as *podsobnoe khoziaistvo* for workers.[18]

---

[15] Weiner, *Making Sense of War*, 304.

[16] There were broader reasons for this oblast and its neighbours suffering greatly during the famine, especially due to the severity of the drought here. See TsDAVOU f. r-2, op. 7, ll. 3, 6, 35, 39.

[17] Nadkin, of course, appreciates this point of regional differentiation in his local history of Mordovia in *Stalinskaia agrarnaia politika*, although he generalises about all-Union tendencies in the campaign on p. 55.

[18] Two common agricultural procedures – leaving land fallow to regenerate its nutrients and early tilling of the soil in preparation for sowing – were not conducted widely because of the war and various shortages in labour and machinery. Even within the central leadership, there was some discussion about the difficulties of cultivating land returned to the sector due to mechanisation and

This assessment is applicable to many areas of Ukraine and is one factor explaining the enduring poor performance of hundreds of farms across Kyiv Oblast well into 1948.[19]

This assessment is not applicable to those areas in Kyiv Oblast and elsewhere under review in this book. Especially in Raska, Bila Tserkva and some other poor farms, the illegal appropriation of collective farmland and farm property went hand in hand with reductions, sometimes to zero, of the size of *kolkhozniki*'s private plots. Most of the land illegally appropriated by officials, institutions and individuals was not returned to the farms by the campaign nor to the *kolkhozniki* who had lost their private share. Even when some land was returned after the 1948 reconstruction decrees, it was rarely the most fertile. Unlike in most areas of Ukraine, it was not the return of land that plunged farms into further destitution, but the failure of authorities to return the most fertile of it along with farm equipment and livestock they had stolen, that inhibited *kolkhozniki* from properly cultivating the land that remained in their possession. As will be evident below, it was this failure that limited food production for both collective and private use and that plunged farms into further destitution, as they could neither meet their existing food delivery obligations to the state and other taxes, nor provide enough food for *kolkhozniki*.

Bila Tserkva

Local officials in Bila Tserkva did even less than in Raska to reconstruct the farms in line with the June 1948 decree reinstating them. Officials continued to appropriate land and offered no meaningful assistance to the farms, leading to a worsening, not an improvement, of conditions therein. At the same time, *kolkhozniki*'s livelihoods and food production on adjacent farms in Bila Tserkva *raion* were improving.[20] By 1949, many of its forty-seven farms were performing well.[21] But the earliest records of sowing and harvest figures from 1946 reveal that all three farms around Bila Tserkva faced the

---

labour shortages at the Central Committee Plenum of the all-Union Communist Party on Agriculture in February 1947. See Ganson, *Soviet Famine*, 7–8.

[19] DAKO f. 4810, op. 1, d. 33, l. 138.

[20] See accounts of Bila Tserkva's agricultural performance given in public fora in 1948, particularly in successive Kyiv *obkom* CP(b)U Plenums by different officials throughout 1948 in TsDAHOU f. 1, op. 51, dd. 3634, 3646, 3648, 3650. Note, however, that parts of Tkachenko's report on agriculture to the Kyiv *obkom* Plenum in June 1948 were false, as discussed in the Introduction and Chapter 3. These accounts can be verified by grain procurement data, which in 1948 indicate that Bila Tserkva delivered 100 per cent of its quota to the state: DAKO f. r-880, op. 9, d. 29, l. 34.

[21] DAKO f. 4810, op. 1, d. 1, l. 25; TsDAHOU f. 1, op. 51, d. 3648, ll. 159–164.

same problems as others in the *raion* and with similar severity. That is, shortages of seed, machinery and livestock limited sowing areas, whose yield was much lower than expected due to the 1946 drought. These shortages were improving on most other farms for the 1947 spring sowing season as was the weather, which produced a successful summer grain harvest that year in Ukraine.

It is at this point in 1947 that the trajectory of the three farms around Bila Tserkva and in the rest of the *raion* begin to diverge sharply. Shortages in seed, labour and machinery continued on the three Bila Tserkva farms into 1947, as local authorities refused to try to alleviate them here as they did in others.[22] The three farms managed to sow a reasonable amount of crops with what little of these resources remained to them or that they could borrow from other farms. But labour shortages were exacerbated by the harvest period, which was more labour-intensive than sowing, further limiting the capacity of the farms to collect the harvest awaiting them in the fields. The 1947 harvest was a failure for these farms not only because of low yield, but also because of poor collection, which left some 500 hectares of grain in Tretii Vyrishal'nyi to rot in the fields.[23] There was also less incentive to gather the entire harvest in Peremoha, because the city authorities – as part of their broader theft of farm housing and infrastructure – had commandeered the farm's grain warehouse for other purposes, so the grain could not be stored.[24]

The sowing and harvesting of grain and vegetable crops were further compromised in 1948, and livestock production plummeted. Hundreds of *kolkhozniki* left the farms or at least gave up farm work before the spring sowing period. They took livestock with them at the same time as a new livestock campaign was launched across the Soviet Union that demanded increases in animal breeding and higher deliveries of meat from collective farms. In May 1948, a month before the official reconstruction decree for the farms in Bila Tserkva was issued, a *raion* food procurement official reviewed the state of Tretii Vyrishal'nyi and chided its *kolkhozniki* for their livestock production failures:

> Your collective farm is the worst in the *raion* . . . To date, you should have delivered 1,200 kilograms of meat to the state and 2,281 eggs, but you have delivered nothing. You have only fulfilled the milk delivery plans by

---

[22] On broader assistance, such as cash loans, given by oblast-level authorities to poor farms, see DAKO f. r-880, op. 9, d. 17, ll. 14–20. It is important to note, however, that *raion*-level authorities could distribute these loans in unintended ways.
[23] RGASPI f. 17, op. 122, d. 316, l. 157.   [24] AV BRDA f. 1, op. 1, d. 114, ll. 35–36.

7 per cent, but you have all your cattle grazing the fields. We have to talk seriously about this now, because you must fulfil at least the minimum foodstuff delivery plans this year.[25]

As with many problems in agricultural production, those of the previous years snowballed into the next. The sowing of crops was similarly cut short by labour shortages and the limited availability of seed. There was no 'early sowing' of vegetables,[26] which were in high demand by workers in the city, and the spring sowing of grains suffered significantly from the poor preparation of the soil in the previous year, with little tilling due to draught power shortages.[27] In March 1949, Council representatives replied to the deputy head of Council on Collective Farm Affairs in Moscow, Andrianov, who had asked about the condition of all three farms in Bila Tserkva now, almost a year after their official reconstruction:

> The situation on the three farms has considerably worsened throughout 1948 . . . farm infrastructure is decaying, and harvests have been lost. Of the planned cultivation of 2,366 hectares of sowing area, only 1,344 hectares have been ploughed, or 56[.8] per cent. The collective farm Peremoha even lacks 430 kilograms of seed to sow in this reduced amount for the spring sowing.[28]

Even this limited sowing produced a harvest too large for the farms to collect. As noted in the previous chapter, on the eve of the 1948 harvest collection and just after the farm's official reconstruction, city authorities still refused to provide the farms with the additional basic implements required for harvesting, from sickles and pitchforks to wagons, not to mention more livestock. City authorities failed even to provide these implements in sufficient quantity to the city population they had mobilised to help gather the harvest from the farms – the single form of 'assistance' offered.[29]

This mobilisation also failed to improve harvest collection and not only because of shortages of farm implements. The amount of labour was

---

[25] AV BRDA f. 280, op. 1, d. 16, l. 54 ob.
[26] The report writer may have been referring to broader grain-sowing as well, that is, the 'winter' sowing of grain in the autumn before the normal spring sowing in the following year. This practice had been historically difficult for peasants, in that was supposed to take place in the wake of harvest collection when they were exhausted and many of their resources depleted. The earlier sowing was intended to strengthen the crop, allowing the seeds to lie dormant over the winter and germinate quickly upon the arrival of the spring sowing period. Thus, although the sowing periods are different, the grains are harvested at about the same time. For a more detailed explanation, see Stephen Wheatcroft, 'The Turn away from Economic Explanations for Soviet Famines', *Contemporary European History* 27, no. 3 (2018), 467–8.
[27] DAKO f. 4810, op. 1, d. 31, l. 74.   [28] DAKO f. 4810, op. 1, d. 33, ll. 12–13.
[29] Mobilising urban dwellers for harvest collection was a more general phenomenon across the Soviet Union.

insufficient and, as former *kolkhozniki* were exempt from the mobilisation, those recruited were unskilled in agricultural work.[30] Farms were forced to hire labour to assist them in both the sowing and the harvest seasons; they paid for this in credit, but were then punished for running up unstainable debts. Debt was a more general problem in the sector but the levels here were astronomical.[31] Again, as in 1947, hundreds of hectares of grain thus remained uncollected and hundreds more rotted because of poor storage and failure to mill on time. At the same time, soil from (already small) private plots had been exhausted from over-cultivation by hungry *kolkhozniki*, while continual policing by *raion* authorities of private plot size and usage inhibited *kolkhozniki* from expanding their plots to make up shortfalls in food. Their homes and other farm infrastructure (that which had not been taken away from them) were falling apart, and most *kolkhozniki* continued to live in *zemlianki* while others fled.[32] By 1949, only 91 *kolkhozniki* remained at Imeni Lenina and 168 at Peremoha.[33]

Conditions on these farms continued to worsen in 1949, as the enduring shortages in labour, fertile land and equipment were exacerbated by the authorities' continuing illegal conduct towards the farms, for which they had already been punished – moving *kolkhozniki* off the land and appropriating it.[34] Particularly galling was authorities' refusal to punish those who left the farms or farm work for selling the food they had cultivated for profit on legal or illegal markets. The June 1948 decree specifically stipulated these people should return to the farms or be prosecuted. There is no evidence authorities did either.[35] In fact, when questioned by their superiors on their failure to do this, city authorities cited official statistics from

---

[30] AV BRDA f. 280, op. 1, d. 15, ll. 31–34 ob.

[31] The Council had been charged in the 1946 campaign with helping to bring debt down by establishing control over collective farm expenditures, although 'collective farm debt' remained a major problem and concern for central authorities. 'Collective farm debt', for instance, remained one of the major subheadings in reports on the implementation of the 1946 campaign in reporting by all officials into 1948. See a sample of these reports in their dedicated *dela*: TsDAVOU f. r-2, op. 7, dd. 5032, 5034, 5035, 5036, 5037, 5050, 5052, 5059, 5064.

[32] RGASPI f. 17, op. 122, d. 316, l. 157.   [33] DAKO f. 4810, op. 1, d. 1, l. 24.

[34] Throughout 1949, large institutions in the city appropriated more fertile land from the farms of their own accord, which compounded the failed harvests and destitution in *kolkhozniki*'s households into 1950. City authorities supported this practice by institutions that were clearly seeking to expand their area of *podsobnoe khoziaistvo* towards a water source, in this case on the banks of the river Ros where the farmland was located. *Raion* authorities adopted a similar approach to a large timber enterprise that illegally appropriated collective farmland in other areas of Bila Tserkva to expand their operations. Though large, these were not all-Union enterprises with significant backing from central authorities to conduct this sort of land grab and expand their workforce. They were local industries or institutions that relied on support from local authorities. See AV BRDA f. 1, op. 1, d. 114, ll. 30–33.

[35] RGASPI f. 17, op. 122, d. 317, l. 11.

the three towns in which the farms were located to demonstrate that most of the population was employed in urban work.[36] But these figures simply counted those former *kolkhozniki* who had signed up for work at factories in the city, not those who actually did it. These figures failed to take this difference into account and thus indicate an artificially low unemployment rate. Council on Collective Farm Affairs representatives who visited the area made note of the 'free population' – anathema to the purpose of the 1948 Exile Campaign – a problem that requires further explanation.[37]

Bila Tserkva and the 'Cost' of the 1948 Exile Campaign

This permissive or 'lax' attitude of oblast-level authorities to both the initiatives and the negligence of their subordinates towards the farms is logical, even if it was risky. When transformed into *podsobnoe khoziaistvo*, farmland was being used for some useful purpose other than collective farming, with the profits likely to remain in the locality. Less straightforward is the reason why oblast-level authorities allowed their subordinates to protect the 'free population', which brought little apparent gain to the locality.[38] In the Council on Collective Farm Affairs' estimation this 'free population' surrounding the farms, which they labelled derogatorily as *okolokolkhoznyi element* or *okolonaselenie* (in this case loosely or formerly collectivised people)[39] was leeching a living off the collective farm sector but contributing nothing to it. In contrast to the official employment statistics, this population was many times greater than the *kolkhoznik* population committed to collective farm work. These people were costing the sector and the locality thousands of tonnes of produce, not to mention the 'moral cost' of their 'anti-social' lifestyle.

In one sense, the Bila Tserkva population problem was not unique. For the state, the *okolokolkhoznyi element* posed a major problem to the proper functioning of the collective farm sector generally. There were many cases across Ukraine of large populations surrounding towns and cities, but not

---

[36] These figures are derived from city and *raion* authorities, which it seems Council representatives too operated from, estimating that 3,674 people living in 3 towns where the farms were located were employed in urban/factory work, while 620 remained on the farms. Total unemployment, not including housewives, invalids etc., was 654 by late 1949: DAKO f. 4810, op. 1, d. 1, l. 24. More generally, labour truancy was a major issue across Ukraine at this time, though it is found primarily in the industrial regions where work conditions in some industries were notoriously harsh and much of the labour had been conscripted to work there. Filtzer discusses this problem throughout *Soviet Workers*.

[37] DAKO f. 4810, op. 1, d. 31, l. 13. [38] DAKO f. 4810, op. 1, d. 31, l. 13.

[39] Lévesque, 'Exile and Discipline', 3.

working in the industries to which they were assigned or on their farms. Although there was much overlap, authorities viewed these people differently from the majority of *kolkhozniki*, who worked legally in industries seasonally, leaving their families on the farm and returning for the sowing and harvest periods. On especially poor farms in other areas of Kyiv Oblast many *kolkhozniki* could not survive on the food wages paid to them for collective farm work, nor could they supplement them sufficiently by food cultivated from private plots. Many found work in nearby industries or hired themselves out as labour, often returning to farm work on the farms where most of their families remained caring for private plots only for the sowing and harvest periods. Central authorities sought, at times, to minimise this practice, or at least to exert control over how and where *kolkhozniki* moved for work, through their labour recruitment bodies, which conscripted *kolkhozniki* for work in all-Union enterprises, usually on short-term contracts.[40] However, local authorities generally understood that this type of seasonal and usually local labour movement was necessary for the survival of both *kolkhozniki* and the farm, sometimes encouraging co-operation among farm leaderships, local industries and law enforcement to permit *kolkhozniki* to work in this way.[41]

The *okolokolkhoznyi element*, central and most local authorities lamented, worked nowhere. They either bought food directly from collective farmers and sold it at city markets for a profit, or sold the food grown on their private plots (which they kept, despite not working on the farms) in the city as well. When the 1948 Exile Campaign was launched, there was initially some confusion among local officials about to whom it applied. Authorities sometimes wrongly conflated non-collective farm members with *kolkhozniki* who worked outside the farm seasonally but retained access to private plots and farm resources, sending them into exile unfairly. But, in most cases, local authorities probably took advice from farm leaders on the difference between 'their people' who were temporarily away and the *okolokolkhoznyi element*.

What was unique about Bila Tserkva was that city and *raion* authorities, under the auspices of their superiors at the oblast level, encouraged *kolkhozniki* to become part of the *okolokolkhoznyi element* as the same time as officials in other oblasts chomped at the bit to return this population to the farms from which they had come. If they would not go back, officials

---

[40] Filtzer, *Soviet Workers*.
[41] These people were not leeching a living off the farms, but making one outside of them which still contributed to farm work, unlike in Bila Tserkva. Ukrainian officials sought clarification from Moscow about the Exile Campaign and whether such people were subject to exile. See their letters in RGASPI f. 17, op. 122, d. 314, ll. 80–81.

wanted to prosecute them or, by 1948, to apply the new Exile Campaign to them to throw out these 'parasites' from their localities. Oblast-level authorities in Crimea were especially keen to exile thousands of former *kolkhozniki* who made up the majority of the *okolokolkhoznyi element* living in workers' settlements around their major towns. Of the 9,000 people classified as such in Belogirsk, almost half were unemployed, with a similar ratio for Bakhchysarai. Nearly all of the unemployed retained private plots on farms although they did not work there either. Unlike in Bila Tserkva and Raska, authorities here tried to reduce the size of workers' settlements, which turned former collective farmland into *podsobnoe khoziaistvo*. Former *kolkhozniki* would work in nearby factories or projects and be allocated private plots to grow subsistence food, getting the best of both the urban and the rural worlds. Authorities soon realised, however, that settlements were unsuccessful because *kolkhozniki* did not show up to work, instead cultivating only the land given to them.[42] They were living as free peasants. The *obkom* secretary in Crimea, N. V. Solov′ev, wrote to Central Committee Secretaries Zhdanov and Malenkov in Moscow in June 1948:

> How do we force this population back into working on the collective and state farms? I don't know? Could we take the same measures against these people that we take against the parasites on the collective farms and exile them? We are certain that this measure would be approved by workers, officials, the intelligentsia and [real] *kolkhozniki* alike.[43]

The subtext of Solov′ev's complaint was that these 'lazy' elements comprised in part Crimean Tatars, who remained in the area after the forcible deportation of most others in 1944.[44] For Solov′ev, the 1948 Exile Campaign may have presented a chance to deport both labour and ethnic 'parasites'. Neither Zhdanov, Malenkov, nor the central government, however, was moved by the sub- or main text of Solov′ev's request and denied it. The next month, the Soviet government (Sovmin) assessed the viability of applying the exile law beyond collective farmers and concluded, 'it is not possible at this time to apply the law to workers' settlements and *sovkhozy*, as these cases of labour truancy attract only administrative [not

---

[42] Although officials did note that economic slowdown was also a factor in the growth of the *okolokolkhoznyi element* and unemployment among its members. See RGASPI f. 17, op. 122, d. 314, ll. 80–81.

[43] RGASPI f. 17, op. 122, d. 314, l. 81.

[44] Almost 200,000 Tatars were deported by Stalin in 1944 from the Crimean peninsula as a common punishment for the military collaboration of some elements with the German occupiers: O. Subtelny, *Ukraine: A History*, 3rd ed. (Toronto: University of Toronto Press, 2000), 483.

criminal] sanctions'.[45] Unlucky *kolkhozniki* were thus exiled, sometimes to their deaths, for same crimes for which workers and, indeed, former *kolkhozniki* who claimed to be still on the farms were merely fined (though many were not punished at all).[46]

The general reluctance of central authorities to apply the Exile Campaign or criminal sanctions against *okolokolkhoznyi element* throws into sharper relief these authorities' stipulation to do so in the 1948 reconstruction decree in Bila Tserkva. Though it had been issued by Kyiv *obkom*, everyone understood that this decree was coming from Moscow.[47] The greatest cost to *kolkhozniki* and farming localities around Bila Tserkva was not wrought simply by the authorities' failure to comply with this decree in permitting this population to live tax-free on collective farmland without working for the state. Food produced from this land, labelled inaccurately as *podsobnoe khoziastvo*, was not subject to tax. It was authorities' active facilitation of these former *kolkhozniki* into 'free' peasants even after the decree was issued that imposed the greatest cost on *kolkhozniki* who remained on the farms, because it came directly at their expense. These *kolkhozniki* lost land to those who left the farms, who were free from the policing of the size of their private plots, while *raion* authorities punished remaining *kolkhozniki* for any expansion they made to recover their losses in land. *Kolkhozniki* paid double tax on the food they produced to cover that not paid by those who left and paid none.

Kolkhozniki were already fleeing the collective farm sector in their millions by 1949 across the Soviet Union, with significant consequences for agriculture.[48] But rarely did authorities give them such impetus to do so as in Bila Tserkva, and rarely were the consequences on the farms so direct and massive as they were here. By 1949 the farms could not produce food to

---

[45] RGASPI f. 17, op. 122, d. 314, l. 82.

[46] It seems that some authorities did not receive notification of or pay attention to the Sovmin clarification. More than 15 per cent of those exiled to Kazakhstan were classified as *okolokolkhoznyi element*, though this may have made more sense here given the more fluid farming population categories in Kazakhstan compared to Ukraine. This broad application of the law was probably more feasible in Kazakhstan too, given the general leeway in the application of central policy in Central Asia, which was further from central oversight. Lévesque, 'Exile and Discipline', 35, explains that the application of the 1948 exile order beyond active members of the collectives who were 'lazy' or 'truant' into the *okolokolkhoznyi element* was a loose application of the law.

[47] RGASPI f. 17, op. 122, d. 317, ll. 9–13.

[48] Lévesque, 'Exile and Discipline', 9, notes the soundness of the argument on the lack of enforcement of labour laws for *kolkhozniki*-cum-workers by local officials and farm leaderships, but argues that evidence is lacking. Blackwell has since provided some evidence in *Kyiv as Regime City*, 48. On the migratory process, see Zima, *Golod v SSSR*, ch. 8.

even approximate their obligations to the state and, by 1950, they were hardly functioning at all.

Transforming this locality from a commercial food production zone to a subsistence one and facilitating the growth of *okolokolkhoznyi element* brought broader consequences beyond the farms. This transformation discouraged investment in the reconstruction of those areas in any way beyond achieving this transformation. The lack of investment was visible in the infrastructure that had been destroyed by war, such as bridges over the Ros River that connected the area to the city and basic irrigation and transport systems. This wartime damage remained unrepaired for years and contributed to the growing destitution in these areas relative to others, which were successfully reconstructed, especially the city itself. This lack of investment hindered further attempts to rejuvenate collective farming in the following decade. These three small farms were amalgamated into larger ones beginning in the 1950s due to their unsustainability: that is, their lands were mostly acquired by larger farms in the *raion*. Some of these amalgamated farms also struggled to operate well in comparison to others in the *raion* and some were eventually swallowed up into the larger farms or *sovkhozy* in the area in the 1960s – a broader process that accelerated under Khrushchev. It was only then, it seems, that living conditions improved in the areas and employment increased, with infrastructure and better housing built to form a more urban landscape, much of which remains today.[49]

For the first post-war decade, this periphery was thus caught between the rural and urban worlds both figuratively and geographically. The multi-volume history of Bila Tserkva from the eighteenth to the twentieth centuries cited earlier lauds the successes of post-World War II reconstruction, expanding on previous Soviet-era accounts of the city's economic boom. This work mentions in passing that in only three areas on the rural periphery of the city did capital reconstruction stall from 1946: Rotok, Zarichia and Oleksandria – the three towns where the farms were located. There is no mention of the reasons why it was only here that capital reconstruction stalled.[50] We can explain this: it did not stall at all, because no such reconstruction was planned by the authorities at the time, given their aims in this periphery.

Even after their official reconstruction in 1948, local authorities were able to obfuscate from their superiors up to the republican level the food

---

[49] The economic viability of poor farming areas tended to improve once *sovkhozy* were established with farmers being generally better paid with greater access to mechanisation.

[50] Starodub, *Budivel'na istoriia Biloi Tserkvy XI–XXI stolit'*, 366.

production on these farms as well as the broader losses caused in the locality by black market activity and unemployment of the *okolonaselenie*. Obfuscation remained key to allowing the growing destitution to continue in these areas when investment was alleviating it in others. Officials could do this only because the *raion*'s overall agricultural performance was good by 1948. The losses incurred at the farms were made up by *raion* authorities taking greater collections of food from better-performing farms. The state reporting system for grain collections encouraged this practice, whereby only *raion* collection averages were supplied to the oblast level and then to the republican, rather than details of individual collections. In most cases across the Soviet Union, both oblast- and certainly republican-level authorities might not have known or indeed cared if poor farms or even *raiony* were failing, as long as the overall total of grain supplied at the oblast level met the food delivery quotas. Oblast-level authorities in Kyiv knew of failing *raiony*, but clearly did not care.

This collection and reporting system had been 'permitted' by central authorities in the 1946 harvest to afford flexibility to authorities to requisition more grain from better-performing farms than from poorer-performing ones. They tried to refocus attention on improving the performance of poor farms for the 1947 harvest, but the earlier practice remained prevalent after 1946:

> Striving to present a normal level of production in the oblast, the [Kyiv Oblast] agriculture department does not mention the failing *raiony* and collective farms in their assessments and refuses to provide them the required assistance. As a result, numerous farms in the oblast work without supervision; a few have not still been reconstructed and remain on the brink of collapse.[51]

So the areas in which the farms were located remained 'on the brink of collapse', while the *raiony* delivered 100 per cent of their food obligation to the state in 1948, and the city of Bila Tserkva's economic boom allowed it to continue its urban expansion in areas which were not in such trouble. In this way, rural areas could be run down over numerous years as long as the city and the rest of the *raion* were operating well, helping us to understand why some areas remained destitute for years in comparison to others

The pertinent question that arises from this analysis is why local officials continued to purposefully run down some areas into destitution after they had been punished for doing so and, broadly, once the food crisis – the impetus for continuing illegal appropriations of farmland and

---

[51] See Gordienko on this in his yearly review for Kyiv Oblast in 1949: DAKO f. 4810, op. 1, d. 31, l. 83.

thus self-supply – had diminished. The answer is most forthcoming from introducing into this analysis Raska's fate after it rejoined the collective farm system in 1948.

Raska and Kyiv Oblast

Like Bila Tserkva *raion*, Borodianka *raion* delivered 100 per cent of its grain obligations to the state in 1948.[52] *Raion*-level authorities here also made up this total from over-collections from farms that were performing well to conceal losses from ones that were struggling. The trajectory of Raska's failed 'recovery', in particular, after its reconstruction shares many elements with Bila Tserkva, but also with other poor farms in the oblast. According to some estimates, of the 2,368 collective farms in the oblast by 1949, 232 were exceedingly 'poor' and 'struggling'. They were defined by their year-by-year failure to even approximate their foodstuff deliveries to the state, astronomical debt, and failure to pay money wages to *kolkhozniki*. They offered as little as 100 to 300 grams of bread as replacement wages for one work-day, which meant that hardly any *kolkhozniki* worked for this paltry wage, instead spending most of their time on private plots.

Many of these farms were located in 'struggling' areas largely within a circle of adjoining *raiony* in the north-west of the oblast: Borodianka, Kyiv-Sviatoshin and Makariv. *Raion*-level officials hardly mentioned these farms in their reports on the collective farm sector or, if they did so, derided them as *besperspektivnye* and certainly did not allocate funds or resources to support what they considered a lost cause. Land abuses towards the farms by officials, institutions and factories endured especially in these *raiony* into the late 1940s.[53] The dismissive attitude towards the farms was shared at the oblast level, where, despite protestations from Council representatives, authorities also refused to discuss the '*otstaiushchie kolkhozy i raiony*', the 'farms and *raiony* that were lagging behind' or to improve the performance of these farms and broader economic development of their localities.[54]

The motivations of *raion*- and oblast-level officials to treat a chunk of their collective farm sector in this way are now clear. Their job was to balance meeting foodstuff deliveries to the state with feeding locals and supplying their networks. After the famine, they were getting better at it.

---

[52] DAKO f. r-880, op. 9, d. 29, ll. 34–35. Borodianka *raion*'s grain procurement quota was much lower than Bila Tserkva's.

[53] DAKO f. 4810, op. 1, d. 33, l. 128. This report includes number of other illegal appropriations of collective farmland in Borodianka *raion*.

[54] DAKO f. 4810, op. 1, d. 33, l. 138.

The level of pressure from central authorities for foodstuff collections reduced in line with the greater amount of food produced by 1948, and local officials were supporting existing and legal methods of improving food supply more effectively. For urban dwellers and even inhabitants of big rural towns this was through allocating land and supplies for *ogorodnichestvo* – garden growing of fruit and vegetables for personal consumption, and through *kolkhoz* markets, where surplus produce from performing collective farms could be purchased. All levels of government encouraged their growth into the post-war period as an acknowledgement of the necessity of private sources and markets for food exchange to compensate for the limitations of the collective farm sector to feed the country. By 1948 this push was bearing much fruit, sometimes literally. Allocating land to urban dwellers to grow food for consumption while scaling it back for *kolkhozniki* and confiscating it from rural workers in the countryside mostly by the 1946 campaign, though, is one stark reminder of the inherent bias of central authorities against rural food producers/consumers and in favour of urban recipients.[55]

This is also a reminder that even rural bias had layers. Local officials could meet their full foodstuff quotas to the state and provide a baseline of *kolkhoz* produce to supply local needs only by diverting scarce resources such as seed, livestock, fodder, machinery and even expertise away from poorer farms to more productive ones. As mentioned above, in Kyiv Oblast these poorer farms amounted to about 10 per cent of the total sector. Given the scarcity of resources officials had to allocate, it made sense for them to 'wager on the strong' farms in their management of the collective farm sector. They would not have used this term, which was employed by the tsarist prime minister Petr Stolypin for the state helping good, entrepreneurial peasants drive reform at the beginning of the twentieth century in the Russian Empire's archaic agricultural sector.[56] But the term is entirely fitting to describe their attitude and behaviour.

---

[55] Lovell, *Summerfolk*, 156; Hessler, 'A Postwar Perestroika?', 524. This bias operated even beyond official policy in officials' everyday practice towards *kolkhozniki*, even when central authorities sought to reverse it. Famine relief provided specifically to starving *kolkhozniki* in Moldova in late 1946 was redirected en route by local authorities to their urban dwellers to meet ration demands: RGASPI f. 17, op. 122, d. 220, l. 62.

[56] Justifying his agrarian reforms, Stolypin wrote that they 'wagered not on the wretched and drunken, but on the sturdy [*krepkie*] and strong [peasants]'. To be fair to Stolypin, some scholars think he probably imagined the majority of the empire's peasants to be strong, and maintained the state's welfare responsibilities to the 'wretched'. He certainly maintained greater levels of welfare to the wretched than did local Soviet officials to the 'rotten' in Kyiv Oblast. See Abraham Ascher, *P. A. Stolypin: The Search for Stability in Late Imperial Russia* (Stanford: Stanford University Press, 2002), 157.

Central authorities did not share this attitude towards poor farms. They could hardly be aware of the specific conditions on poor farms and in their localities across the Union, and the concealment by local officials did not help. Nonetheless, central authorities remained concerned about this type of attitude among local authorities and the capacity to conceal losses via their reporting on grain collections. Improving *otstaiushchie kolkhozy i raiony*, if only to improve their capacity to deliver grain to the state, became a greater concern for the leadership in the wake of the failed 1946 harvest. Especially in Ukraine, republican authorities responded to pressure from Moscow to issue specific instructions in early 1948 aimed at offering more assistance or at least supervision of the operation of especially struggling farms.[57] This supervision came in the form of sending more and more party members and agricultural specialists into the sector at sowing and harvest time to whip up enthusiasm. *Raion* and oblast authorities reported on the 'successful' implementation of the decrees, evident in harvest collection, and the amount of support they had given to some struggling farms. But they said little or nothing about the poorest regions.[58] They implemented the policy, thus, in much the same way as they allocated resources.

The impact of this enduring *raion*- and oblast-level attitude of 'wagering on the strong' on the post-war development of poor farms and their localities was significant in the late 1940s and beyond. On the poor farms, bread wages increased only slowly, and money was hardly ever paid to *kolkhozniki* for work-days, even by 1950. Not surprisingly, more than half of the *kolkhozniki* on these farms did not meet their minimum work-day requirements for such paltry wages even at sowing and harvest times. This last point further differentiated them from other struggling farms in the oblast at this time. Even subsistence farming from private plots was difficult, evident in the destitution of *kolkhoznik* households on these farms. More and more *kolkhozniki* left them, exacerbating labour shortages. Some of these farms simply never recovered from the war in terms of lost resources, labour and damage to infrastructure. Other farms continued their pre-war trajectories of economic destitution into the post-war period. But numerous farms, like those in Raska and Bila Tserkva, had been successful in the pre-war period and stalled in their post-war development due less to historical reasons than to post-war abuse and

---

[57] For a discussion of these instructions at party plenums in 1948, see TsDAHOU f. 1, op. 24, d. 3648.
[58] See the numerous speeches at the same plenum: TsDAHOU f. 1, op. 24, d. 3648 (especially l. 18).

neglect from authorities.[59] It pays to trace the longer-term development of Raska and these poor farms together to better understand how abuse and neglect, especially through the theft of land and resources, had long-lasting costs beyond the suffering farms and *kolkhozniki* across the oblast.

Raska's farm, Pershe Travnia, was lucky to be reconstructed officially on the eve of the 1948 spring sowing season. The *kolkhozniki* were greatly enthusiastic about the prospects of improving conditions on their farm and in their village and worked extremely hard from the beginning of 1948 in anticipation of state assistance as stipulated by the reconstruction decree. As early as February that year the farm was set to receive a reconstruction loan of almost 35,000 roubles, a considerable sum at the time. The money was earmarked for spending on basic infrastructure to operate the farm or at least finish off construction previously stopped by *raion* authorities. This infrastructure included the cowshed to house the pre-war total of the 100 cows the *kolkhozniki* assumed would be returned to them, an aviary to house 100 birds, a grain storage warehouse with a capacity of 70 tonnes, a blacksmith's forge and a fodder station. This money was also supposed to pay for the purchase of seed, to rent machinery for ploughing and to pay *kolkhozniki* for their work in the sowing period.

However, of 120 hectares planned for sowing, only 25 hectares of grains and vegetables were sown before the period was cut short due to shortages of seed and equipment.[60] Part of the small harvest it did produce in the summer was destroyed by flooding from the nearby river, and the overall yield of that which survived was low, approximately half of what was expected across all crops.[61] Failure to till the less fertile soil of that returned to them and its broader mismanagement by appropriating institutions in previous years were primarily responsible for this low yield. For these reasons, the farm failed to deliver its foodstuff quotas to the state and its *kolkhozniki* failed to fulfil their work-day requirements. Their initial enthusiasm waned, and the farm chairman and leadership were sacked by the *raion* authorities.

The question remains: how could there be such a shortage in seed and machinery that the sowing period had to be cut short, when money had been allocated to purchase them? Quite simply, the farmers never received the entire loan. It seems that *raion* authorities backdated taxes on the farm upon its reconstruction and took money from the loan, and that this practice was part of a broader corruption in Ukraine. In other cases,

[59] DAKO f. 4810, op. 1, d. 33, l. 126.   [60] DAKO f. 4810, op. 1, d. 3, l. 2.
[61] DAKO f. 4974, op. 1, d. 15, ll. 6–8 ob.

authorities drove up farm debts by giving loans to farms for the purchase of services from corrupt providers that never delivered them, as in the previous chapter's examples. Collective farms were used in this way to launder state money and still allow *raion* authorities to demonstrate to their superiors that they had followed orders to assist farms, which ended up either with no assistance and/or even more debt.[62]

Perhaps the largest-scale example of this money laundering comes from the Vologda farms and the housing scheme in Kyiv Oblast discussed in the previous chapter, but the most relevant example to Raska comes from farms nearby with a similar historical trajectory. Much like Pershe Travnia in Raska, the poorest farm in Makariv *raion*, which borders Borodianka, Chervonyi Pluhatar, was also successful in the 1930s, destroyed completely by war and never managed to recover in the post-war period mainly due to the lack of support. Unlike in Raska, however, it did not adjoin a forest from which it could source timber to build infrastructure. It relied exclusively on state loans and other forms of assistance to operate. As it received little, it could hardly operate, paying less than 300 grams of bread wages per work-day to its *kolkhozniki*, which was still low by Ukrainian standards in 1949.[63] *Kolkhozniki* thus worked few days, surviving from their private plots mostly.

Another major problem the farm faced was the shortage of housing (most *kolkhozniki* lived in *zemlianki*), of farm implements for sowing and reaping, and of a warehouse for storing food. In 1947 its harvest was exceedingly poor in comparison to those of its neighbours, when the farm leadership finally acquiesced to the request of a nearby factory owner to give up some farmland in return for assistance in building the badly needed housing. Much of the land it gave up was to be used as *podsobnoe khoziaistvo* by factory workers, but *kolkhozniki* were also required to work sections of it and provide all of the food to the factory as payment. This was not an uncommon arrangement, but after the 1946 campaign to return collective farmland it became more difficult and time-consuming to engage in it through official processes, so the farm gave up almost 75 hectares of land to the factory unofficially. This meant the farm was still required to pay taxes on this land, that is, to meet the foodstuff quota requirements attached to it. The factory never completed the

---

[62] DAKO f. 4974, op. 1, d. 21, ll. 16–18. On the broader problem of swindling in the collective farm sector, see DAKO f. 4810, op. 1, d. 31, ll. 61–67.

[63] Average money and bread wages on Ukrainian collective farms were higher by the beginning of 1949, but only reached 1940 levels again from 1952. Pay and consumption data in Ukrainian collective farms can be found in RGAE f. 582, op. 24, d. 529.

building works it promised. When the farmers stopped providing their labour and food to the factory in response, the factory sued them for 107,000 roubles – the cost of the incomplete works. The *kolkhozniki* were left in the unenviable position of not only being unable to pay the money, but also having been found out for their illegal yielding of farmland.[64]

After the failed harvest of 1948, Raska's *kolkhozniki* too were forced to hire themselves out again as labour to the institutions that had appropriated their land and were still in possession of it, even after the 1948 decree. *Kolkhozniki* usually hired themselves out for labour or took up urban work in the low season. But in Vologda, Raska, Makariv and other cases, *kolkhozniki* were essentially producing hay or food from their own land to give to those who had illegally appropriated it. They were paid little or nothing at all for their work, losing both their time and their produce. In both Raska and Makariv, they were forced to pay taxes on land that was officially part of their farm, but which, in reality, remained in the hands of others. *Kolkhozniki* from both farms were forced into this labour by the worsening conditions on their farms and lack of assistance from authorities. They were most vulnerable to the empty promises of assistance by factories and institutions. Authorities knew about these corrupt schemes but did nothing about them. In fact, there were numerous other similar cases across the oblast in 1948, which oblast-level authorities denied were taking place, as Comrade Moskalets did in 1949.

Moskalets was lying. Farms having to pay tax on land that was officially part of their holdings but was in the hands of others who paid no tax on it and kept its produce was still an oblast-wide problem in 1949, likely affecting hundreds of farms. It was not only the farms' participation in corrupt schemes that inhibited them from notifying authorities about this problem. Even when farms did notify them about 'legal' exchanges of land, authorities rarely responded to the notification and did not adjust farms' tax burdens until years afterwards, if at all. By this time the damage had been done to the farms, including punishment of *kolkhozniki* for failing to meet their artificially inflated foodstuff quotas and other taxes. In the *raion* bordering Borodianka, Kyiv-Sviatoshin, where other cases of farm liquidation were also noted, numerous other farms exchanged land with industries in 1946 and 1947. This was usually less than 100 hectares in each case, but with the

---

[64] Collective farms tended to struggle to use the court system to their advantage in any case, especially in securing the return of their land that had been taken during the war by institutions. See DAKO f. 4810, op. 1, d. 33, l. 128.

required requests sent to the oblast-level agriculture department at the time. As a Council on Collective Farm Affairs report noted, by 1949, none of the numerous requests had been answered by the department:

> There are plenty of such cases on farms across the oblast, where, due to the failures of the *obliispolkom* and oblast-level agricultural department, numerous organisations have begun using collective farmlands without authorisation, though this land remains counted as part of the farm. The farms are still paying the foodstuff quotas and a range of other taxes attached to this land to the state.[65]

The impact of such schemes and the broader problem of land, labour and tax exploitation on farms was massive, especially for the poorest where this issue was most prominent. Farmers worked less on the farms and even on their private plots because of their labour duties to others. In 1948 more than half of the *kolkhozniki* in Raska fulfilled only half their work-day minimums, and each year after that fulfilled less and less in line with their reduced food production. For these transgressions against collective farm rules, they were punished with fines and threats of imprisonment.[66] These punishments were especially hard to bear for Raska's *kolkhozniki*, who were now being punished officially for the consequences of their poor treatment at the hands of officials. For the first time since *kolkhozniki* launched the fight to reconstruct the farm and village in 1945, they began to leave it. By the end of 1949, of the 150 able-bodied *kolkhozniki* present at the beginning of the previous year, 109 were left.[67]

As on the farms around Bila Tserkva, problems with agricultural production from previous years snowballed into the next. Labour losses and the failure to access machinery to properly plough land and rejuvenate soil led to a drop in the anticipated sowing area. The harvest yield from this smaller area for grain dropped in 1949 to only 370 kilograms per hectare in comparison to the 1949 average for Ukraine of 870.[68] Raska's entire vegetable crop, the primary crop, failed.[69] The farm's debt was high and rising in comparison to others. The changes in farm leadership in 1948 in response to the poor harvest, as was the usual response of *raion* authorities, clearly made things worse. The farm survived only because of its successful livestock breeding until 1950, when, after another poor harvest in that year

---

[65] DAKO f. 4810, op. 1, d. 31, l. 62.   [66] DAKO f. 4974, op. 1, d. 27, l. 1.

[67] DAKO f. 4974, op. 1, d. 21, ll. 20–21.

[68] The original measurements are in *tsentners*, where 1 ts. equals 100 kg: DAKO f. 4974, op. 1, d. 25, l. 12. For Ukraine figures based on barn yield in 1949, see RGAE f. 1562, op. 324, dd. 5295–5301.

[69] DAKO f. 4810, op. 1, d. 25, l. 12.

it acquiesced to the request of *raion* authorities and amalgamated with the neighbouring farm in Piskivka, Chervonyi Khliborob. This was the same farm it had been ordered to join from 1946 onwards. It was no coincidence that Comrade Petrov, the head of the Borodianka *raikom* who had led the initial attempts to liquidate the farm in 1946, was present at the meeting where the villagers signed the amalgamation agreement. He survived Khrushchev's public embarrassment at the 1949 Kyiv *obkom* CP(b)U Plenum to conclude his initial liquidation of Raska, launched in 1945. This was his final victory, although it was a pyrrhic one.[70]

Unlike in other cases of amalgamations, the larger farm did not swallow up what remained of Raska's farmland, nor did its *kolkhozniki* move to the new farm. Raska's *kolkhozniki* travelled daily to the new farm kilometres away to work and returned home each night. Only a small section the farmland of Pershe Travnia remained under cultivation in the 1950s. The continued occupancy of the village and small amount of cultivation never freed up the area for the type of industrial expansion anticipated by *raion*-level authorities. Its failure as a stand-alone collective farm gave no impetus for *raion* authorities to invest in it either. The area was caught between two stools. This lack of investment endured into the later Soviet period, which helps to explain the area's relative destitution to others (see next chapter).

The exploitation of land and labour and improper taxation in Raska and other poor farms flourished under the wilful negligence – or deliberate strategy – of the oblast-level agriculture department. Poorer and vulnerable farms were made more so by giving up land they could not cultivate properly for promises of goods and services they desperately needed, but could not afford to buy or garner from *raion*-level authorities. This finding leads us to the bigger issue of the impact of the return of land and increased taxation on other poor farms beyond Raska and Bila Tserkva. On these other farms, collective and private farm work were more mutually exclusive; that is, officials pressured *kolkhozniki* to work on collective farmland land rather than private plots. Less commonly, as in Raska and Bila Tserkva, officials illegally appropriated both types of land, often the most fertile, which *kolkhozniki* used for both collective and private purposes, limiting their capacity to work on both. The situation on many poor farms was thus more complicated than that of simply the return of illegally appropriated land in the 1946 campaign and afterwards, imposing a greater tax burden on the farms they were unable to meet because they

---

[70] It was not common for *raion* secretaries to visit farm meetings like this, but Petrov clearly had an interest in Raska: DAKO f. 4974, op. 1, d. 27, ll. 6–7.

could not properly cultivate the land. Clearly, most of these farms were incapable of properly cultivating the land already in their possession due mainly to lack of support from *raion* authorities, let alone cultivating additional land that was returned to them. The excess tax burdens of the returned land were probably one of the reasons why farm leadership eventually exchanged it with factories and institutions. They did this in much the same way that they had done during the war, when there was less state oversight on the countryside, and before the 1946 campaign.

For the poorest farms, giving up their land did not necessarily relieve them of their tax burdens: it could actually increase them. As the 1940s came to a close, the avenues for survival narrowed for them and widened for the better-performing farms that grew at their expense. The return of land to farms mostly accelerated, rather than diverted, the performance trajectories of poor farms and, indeed, rich ones. Well-supported and - performing farms could usually deal with the extra pressure of higher collections from expanded sown areas to make up the shortfalls from poor farms because they were well resourced and paid their *kolkhozniki* comparatively well for their work. These farms were celebrated by officials and, as the overall *raion*-level production figures indicate, delivered more food to the state than their quotas required.[71] This was especially the case after the 1947 harvest when central collection relaxed, and increased grain production in Ukraine generally improved food consumption levels on these farms and in these localities.

The rate of food collections from the farms after the 1946 harvest, then, was not the key determinant for the well-being of farms and their *kolkhozniki*. It was more the rate of support offered by *raion*-level officials to operate the farm properly. Their investment in some farms and localities as opposed to others made sense, as they received few funds or resources from their superiors to invest back into the collective farm sector. Capital investment in the sector in Ukraine was always too small to restore what had been destroyed by war and continued to lag exponentially in comparison to the amount of food, labour and other resources extracted from the sector afterwards.[72] Although the purpose of this sector had always been to facilitate the extraction of these resources, doing so without anywhere near sufficient investment in the infrastructure required to produce these

---

[71] DAKO f. 4810, op. 1, d. 33, ll. 134–135. See also the numerous speeches given at Kyiv *obkom* CP(b)U Plenums specifically on the successes of implementing the decrees issued by the February 1947 Central Committee Plenum on Agriculture, in TsDAHOU f. 1, op. 51, d. 3648.

[72] See Chapter 1 on the disparity in state investment in the Ukrainian agricultural sector in relation to wartime damage.

resources remained one of the sector's fundamental post-war problems. As mentioned earlier, by 1949 millions of *kolkhozniki* responded to these problems by permanently leaving the sector.

The problem with *raion*-level authorities' response to this overall shortage of investments was that it was targeted to the same farms over many years. The same farms did not get anything year on year; neither did the villages and sometimes neither did the towns in which they were located. Authorities developed the attitude that these poor areas were backwaters, that an investment in them (and they had hardly anything to invest) would be a waste of time and resources and possibly cost them their jobs, given that they anticipated no return on their outlay for which they could be punished. This attitude is best represented again by Dvornikov's epithet about Raska and its 'rotten' people at the beginning of this book and Comrade Tkachenko's retort to the Kyiv *obkom* CP(b)U Plenum in 1948 cited in the previous chapter, about the infeasibility of rebuilding farms with so few (and bad) *kolkhozniki*. The cost to the farms of this conduct was immense, not only in terms of stopping their operation and failing to improve the living standards of *kolkhozniki* therein, but also in rendering them more vulnerable to abuse from officials and others that exacerbated what problems they faced, be they taxes or debt. *Raion*- and oblast-level authorities' 'wagering on the strong' in agriculture helped lay or entrench the framework for disparity in economic development across the oblast for decades to come. This cost of this disparity was both material and psychological for those who paid it, and shaped their subsequent generations in Raska and Bila Tserkva, which is the main subject of the following chapter.

CHAPTER 5

Then and Now: The Shaping of Contemporary Ukraine in the Post-War Crises

Strong traces of collective farming remain in Raska today, although they are hidden under the weighty evidence of its collapse. Its sowing fields are overgrown with long grass and its livestock fodder pits are filled with long-rotting rubbish dumped by local businesses (see Figures 2 and 3). There are no *kolkhozniki* left, but some of the former ones still live there among a few, mostly related families and continue cultivating their private plots. There are few such traces left in Bila Tserkva. Decades of successful urbanisation have swallowed up the rural outskirts of the city where the farms were located, while many of the people who lived there have moved to other places. One of the farm's towns, Zarichia, is now an indistinguishable part of the city. The consequences of the past under study in this book and the present thus remains visible in Raska among its landscape and remaining inhabitants, both of which are largely absent in Bila Tserkva. This chapter traces the historical trajectories of these places from the 1950s onwards to explain this divergence and, where possible, connects their past to the present.

A key factor accounting for these divergent historical trajectories was the ability of *kolkhozniki* to stay on their land from the 1950s onwards and stop it from changing under their feet from rural to urban space. This was an incredibly difficult task even after the 'reconstruction' of the farms in 1948. Policy changes in the collective farm sector instituted from the 1950s forcibly relocated millions of *kolkhozniki* from their ancestral lands, and the broader process of rapid industrialisation transformed the landscape in which the farms were located and, indeed, the people who remained on them. Following the trajectory of these farms into the post-war decades tells us a great deal about why and how people fought to maintain physical and symbolic attachments to their land and to the pasts tied up in it, in the face of massive political, social and economic transition.

The historical trajectories of the farms diverged most sharply from 1950 onwards in response to the new policy on amalgamating small collective

147

2 Former sowing fields of the Pershe Travnia collective farm in Raska

3 Rubbish pits at the Pershe Travnia collective farm

farms. Spearheaded by Khrushchev, this policy sought to reduce the number of collective farms but increase their size to enable a more efficient employment of scarce resources and labour. Having larger and less numerous farms, and therefore having more *kolkhozniki* concentrated in one central place, also promised to be easier to manage. This policy usually entailed the joining of two small farms, which was already happening at the time in farming areas that were struggling. An often pernicious innovation of the policy was to force the 'amalgamation' of smaller farms to larger ones, to which they lost their lands and to which the *kolkhozniki* were often required to relocate. This usually entailed a reduction in the size or at least the quality of private plots. Though amalgamations were officially voluntary, in most cases *kolkhozniki* had little choice. *Kolkhozniki* reluctant to amalgamate may have been assured by state promises that doing so would improve their lot, especially in terms of greater access to technology, machinery and livestock.[1]

Imeni Lenina amalgamated with an adjacent small farm in 1950, much to its benefit. Its food production and overall sustainability improved markedly and more so when it amalgamated again in 1959 with a group of other small farms nearby. This group operated as a 'mega collective' until the end of the Soviet period and then as a commercial farm afterwards. The two other farms, Tretii Vyrishal'nyi and Peremoha, were forced to join with much larger farms numerous times – a process that continued into the 1970s. *Kolkhozniki* relocated to these farms and no longer enjoyed automatic access to their old farmland or private plots. *Kolkhozniki* on Tretii Vyrishal'nyi were a little luckier than those on Peremoha. By the late 1960s they became part of the major *sovkhoz* in the area where pay and conditions were generally much better than on the *kolkhoz*.[2]

Despite the different economic outcomes of the amalgamations, the common impact was to weaken traditional bonds between *kolkhozniki* and their land. Some historians see amalgamations as the final step in this process, which began with collectivisation in the 1930s.[3] In Bila Tserkva it was more the population shifts and broader urbanisation required or enabled by amalgamations that severed the final bonds of *kolkhozniki* to the land. Industry and suburban housing expanded along with the urban population in the farms' towns of Zarichia, Rotok and Oleksandriia at

---

[1] Postanovlenie TsK VKP(b), 'Pro ukrupnenie melkikh kolkhozov i zadachakh partiinykh organizatsii v etom dele' (30 May 1950), to be carried out by *obkom*s and *obliispolkom*s. As a result of the implementation of this decree, at the end of 1950 the number of collective farms in Ukraine had fallen to 19,295 from 28,374 in 1940. See Kul'chyts'kyi, *Chervonyi vyklyk*, 121.

[2] Peremoha amalgamated with another farm in 1951 and, as in the above case, became part of another, larger farm in a different location in 1971. In some of the towns today, many houses maintain some form of *podsobnoe khoziaistvo*. See AV BRDA (*predisloviia opis'ei*), f. 105, op. 1, f. 2810, op. 1, and f. 78, op. 1.

[3] On the severing of traditional bonds between land and *kolkhozniki*, see Verbitskaia, *Rossiiskoe krest'ianstvo*, 29.

different rates, as it did across large parts of the Soviet countryside, often breaking the human links between past and present in these places.

Unlike in Bila Tserkva, the amalgamation of Raska's farm Pershe Travnia in 1950 was most important in keeping the *kolkhozniki* connected to their land and to their past. They were permitted to keep their homes and maintain parts of their former farmland for personal use when they agreed to join the neighbouring farm, Chervonyi Khliborob, in the nearby town of Piskivka.[4] They travelled daily to the new farm to work and returned home each night to their sacred land. Chervonyi Khliborob and then Nove Zhyttia, as it was renamed, survived the Soviet Union's collapse in 1991 as a community farm. It did not survive long in the disastrous Ukrainian economy that followed: it folded in 1995, joining the other dots in the ruined agricultural landscape of the post-Soviet period.

The *kolkhozniki* who remained in Raska survived this collapse like many others did, by turning mostly to subsistence farming on their former private plots in their village, though this may be what is killing them now. Less than 100 kilometres south-west of the Chornobyl Exclusion Zone, the contamination of Raska's soil by radioactive material from the fallout of the 1986 nuclear disaster, residents suspect, is likely contributing to the abnormally high rate of cancers among them.[5] Recent scientific investigations conducted into the impact of the fallout strengthen this suspicion – warning of the specific danger posed by nuclear radiation to farmers who consume food produced by their livestock, particularly dairy. Raska's *kolkhozniki* had long survived by consuming milk from their cows and other dairy products. Even if they had been warned of this connection between food and ill health in the wake of the disaster, it is unlikely they could have stopped consuming it as they had few alternative food sources and were too poor to purchase food elsewhere.[6]

[4] DAKO f. 4974, op. 1, d. 27, ll. 6–7; f. r-880, op. 9, d. 17, ll. 170–171.
[5] The following report stresses the significant dangers for subsistence farmers close to Chornobyl who owned cattle and consumed dairy products, such as those in Raska. See Chornobyl Forum Expert Group (Environment), 'Environmental Consequences of the Chornobyl Accident and Their Remediation: Twenty Years of Experience', *International Atomic Energy Agency* no. 3 (2006), 3. However, the IAEA does not draw a direct connection between radiation exposure as a result of the accident and current cancer rates in Ukraine, but attributes these rates more to growing poverty and unhealthy lifestyles. Ukrainian medical organisations, by contrast, draw a direct connection between radiation levels and the much higher cancer rates among residents in areas surrounding the exclusion zone, particularly the National Research Centre for Radiation Medicine of the National Academy of Medical Sciences of Ukraine. See the centre's publication, Dimitry Bazyka, *Health Effects of Chornobyl Accident – 30 Years Aftermath* (Kyiv: National Academy of Medical Sciences of Ukraine, 2016).
[6] Valentin Dem'ianovich Koval'skyi, interview by Filip Slaveski (11–21 October 2016).

Raska's *kolkhozniki* thus paid dearly for their continued attachment to the land and to farming: first in terms of the enduring economic destitution discussed in the previous chapter, then through the succeeding generations continuing their legacy and consuming the fruits of their labour poisoned by Chornobyl. Conversely, the forced detachment of *kolkhozniki* from their land in Bila Tserkva allowed them to escape this fate. It was key to the eventual improvement of economic conditions there (even if all *kolkhozniki* did not share in this) through the transition from small to large collective or state farming. This transition bore fruit by the late 1960s, and then through the expansion of urban/industrial fringe in the former collective farm areas that had eventually given in to the demands of the city.

The divergent historical trajectories of Raska and Bila Tserkva raise numerous questions addressed below: what explains the enduring attachment to land and to collective farming among *kolkhozniki* in Raska and Bila Tserkva after the war, when so many others were leaving the land to become urbanites at this time? What does this attachment tell us about how some *kolkhozniki* understood themselves as Soviet citizens in post-war Stalinism? How do the enduring legacies of people's attachment to land here influence how they understand and commemorate their pasts and live today in post-Soviet Ukraine?

There were both practical and symbolic reasons for the attachment to land in Raska and Bila Tserkva at the end of the war. *Kolkhozniki* from both locations were not keen to become workers or urbanites. Their limited experience of work outside the farm had been uniformly negative. They wanted to continue what they were good at and what they understood they were born to do – cultivate their land. Their support for the reconstruction of collective farming and demonstrable patriotism when dealing with the authorities, as evident in Chapter 3, was the key method to sustain their right to do so. But *kolkhozniki* also demonstrated patriotic attitudes 'in private', deriving some value from their place in post-war Soviet society as *kolkhozniki*, veterans and, at least in Raska's case, the bearers of martyrdom. All of the farms' good pre-war performance in the late 1930s, furthermore, continued to inspire them to recreate it in the post-war period along with, perhaps, what remained of their pre-war lives.

Clearly, then, practical and symbolic reasons for the attachment to the land are entwined, especially in Raska. Ethnic Poles had been cultivating this land and living in Raska for generations, since the tsarist period. Their attachment to this land was the constant feature of life under different regimes and, as the *kolkhozniki* understood, the key defence against the whims of these regimes to punish, exploit and displace them in different waves of anti-Polish or broadly anti-peasant repressions. Protecting the graves of their loved ones provided further incentive to remain on the land in the post-war period at whatever cost, which remains strong among Raska's residents today.

Practical Reasons for Staying on the Farms

Becoming workers and urbanites, or, as one scholar of the Soviet countryside described it, becoming 'people of the first sort' in Soviet society,[7] was more than a work and residence change for *kolkhozniki*. It was a transformation of their status and general improvement of their well-being. The post-war mass migration of rural dwellers to the cities has thus attracted significant scholarly interest for its impacts on the countryside.[8] Despite this literature, we know little of how the expansion of city limits into farm areas affected those who remained on the land in the post-war period. Many of these people remained, not only due to their inability to migrate to the cities for a range of factors, but also because of their willingness to 'make a go' of collective farming in conditions unpropitious to its success.

For *kolkhozniki* in Raska and Bila Tserkva willing to 'make a go' of it, becoming workers and de facto urbanites did not carry the same allure as it did for other *kolkhozniki*. The illegal appropriation of their collective farmland initiated industrial and urban expansion in their area, the negative consequences of which they felt more keenly than the positive. Even leaving the unattractive nature of industrial work for these *kolkhozniki* aside, the factories offering it were the same ones that had appropriated their land. In some cases, they were the same factories in which the *kolkhozniki* had been forced to work by the Germans under occupation. After the war, these factories paid Raska's *kolkhozniki*, if at all, a miserly wage for the agricultural work the *kolkhozniki* had done for them on the very land that they had appropriated from the farms. Ongoing employment with these factories and institutions in industrial work was unlikely to be more profitable than the destitution they faced as *kolkhozniki*. In Bila Tserkva, many *kolkhozniki* used the offers of employment from appropriating institutions and factories as an excuse to flee the destitution of the farms and live as part of the *okolonaselenie*. But *kolkhozniki* who remained on the collective farms in Bila Tserkva and Raska feared that leaving the

---

[7] Verbitskaia, *Rossiiskoe krest'ianstvo*, 86.
[8] Ibid.; Zubkova, *Russia after the War*; Popov, *Rossiiskaia derevnia*.

farms and accepting offers of permanent rather than temporary industrial employment required forsaking their claims to both farm and village.

At least it seemed so in Raska until January 1948. The promise of taking up industrial work while remaining on their land should have made the offer from *raion* leader Shidaev and then *sel'sovet* chairman Marchenko to Raska's *kolkhozniki* in January 1948 most appealing. As discussed earlier, these officials offered the *kolkhozniki* work in the nearby industries without having to give up residence in their village, which would become part of a workers' settlement that would be built around them; alternatively, they would simply live in their village as workers. All they would need to do is give up trying to reconstruct the collective farm. This appeared to be an exceedingly generous offer at the time. The state was offering to bring the benefits of industrial work and urban life to the village, at the same time that more and more *kolkhozniki* were fleeing the villages to access these benefits in the cities, sometimes illegally.

The situation was worse in the west of Ukraine, which was still in the grip of a violent anti-Soviet insurgency. Forced collectivisation began in earnest around this time in 1948 in these areas, which had only recently come under or returned to Soviet rule. Collectivisation was an often violent process that included displacing peasants from their ancestral lands.[9] Moreover, although the 1947 harvest was considerably better across the Soviet Union than the previous year, this was less the case in the areas of Kyiv Oblast studied here, which lacked the necessary assistance during the sowing and harvesting periods from authorities to enable them to join in the successes of the sector. This made the harsh winter of 1948 even harder to bear. It would seem that Raska's farmers had good reasons to accept these offers of industrial work, but they did not find them appealing in the least.

The reasons why *kolkhozniki* rejected these offers were both deeply personal and practical. *Kolkhozniki* distrusted Marchenko for his part in attempting to liquidate the farm and the village, for his intimidation of farm chairman Kuriata, and because of their widespread belief that he was protecting collaborators who had taken part in the 1943 massacre. The sole survivor of the massacre still living in Raska today remembers only Marchenko among numerous officials who had tried to destroy her farm and village.[10] The *kolkhozniki* understood too that, in a practical sense, by shifting to another farm or becoming workers, they were in greater danger of losing legal claims of residence in their village. As *kolkhozniki*, they were

[9] David Marples, *Stalinism in Ukraine in the 1940s* (New York: St Martin's Press, 1992), ch. 7.
[10] Zosia Adol'fovna Lisovska, interview by Filip Slaveski (18 August 2018).

bound to the farm located on their hallowed village land, unable to leave it without legal authorisation from the authorities – as Marchenko himself had reminded Kuriata in his warning not to travel to Kyiv to seek assistance from oblast-level authorities. Working at another farm or simply residing in a workers' settlement, they would enjoy no greater privileges than other farmers or workers who would join them; they would also be more vulnerable to labour mobilisations to other areas, especially after 1946, when such mobilisations began to become more prevalent.[11] Unlike millions of their fellow *kolkhozniki* for whom being bound to the land reduced their capacity to survive in the miserable conditions of the post-war countryside, for those in Raska, these bonds were key to their survival.

These bonds had also been key to their initial capacity to reconstruct the village and farm before they were obstructed from doing so by *raion*-level authorities. In 1945, Raska's *kolkhozniki* drew on their membership of their farm to access state credit from those institutions that were unaware of its 'liquidation' by authorities. This 'liquidation' became official at the oblast level only in 1947. *Kolkhozniki* negotiated to receive reconstruction loans from state institutions in 1945 that operated from pre-war records indicating that Raska's farm was still operational. This included a 45,000-rouble loan from the oblast-level education department to purchase materials to rebuild the local school, and building authorities responded to their petitions and began drawing up architectural plans for rebuilding the village.[12]

Membership of the farm and entitlements as war veterans were key to negotiating the webs of bureaucratic confusion in order to rebuild at a time when citizens with legitimate claims were competing for scarce state resources across Ukraine. That the *raion* authorities confiscated building materials as soon as they became aware of the loan and tore down the school, plank by plank, only reinforced the sense among the *kolkhozniki*

---

[11] Before then, Moscow was reluctant to mobilise labour from the state labour recruitment agency (*orgnabor*) to rebuild Kyiv. Housing needed to be assigned to *orgnabor* workers before they could be given permits to live in a city and begin work, thus further encouraging Kyiv city officials to get their passport system and broader population movements under control. Adding to the problem was that, even if *orgnabor* labour had been approved by central authorities, this did not mean that it would arrive, as local authorities and industry then needed to negotiate with separate institutions to allocate the labour. Of course, Moscow also assigned a low priority to the rebuilding of Kyiv. In Kyiv Oblast, Moscow required its *kolkhozniki* to remain on the collective farms rather than be mobilised for other work, unlike other *kolkhozniki* in other 'lower-priority' agricultural regions, who were regularly mobilised for industrial work. Moscow's position significantly remained steadfast at least until late 1946: Blackwell, *Kyiv as Regime City*. For mobilisations of *kolkhozniki* from Bila Tserkva to the Donbas in 1947, see DAKO f. r-880, op. 9, d. 17, ll. 174–175.

[12] DAKO f. 4810, op. 1, d. 3, l. 23.

that collective farm membership, and the assistance from superior authorities it enabled, was key to their survival under the tyranny of local officials.[13] There was no way they were going to give this up for the promises of the same officials whom they distrusted, especially by January 1948, after they had met Gordienko, who said he would take their case for reconstruction to his superiors in Moscow. The *kolkhozniki* were perhaps savvy enough to understand that local officials would not have made such a 'good offer' to them had they not realised the failures of their coercion to displace them and now feared intervention from superior authorities.[14]

Kolkhozniki in Bila Tserkva who remained on the farms also understood that they had to sustain their collective farming efforts to keep residence of their land.[15] The situation was a little more complicated here given that former *kolkhozniki* were leaving the farms or farm work while retaining access to their private plots. However, *kolkhozniki* remaining on the farms clearly anticipated that these law-breakers would be prosecuted for their actions and eventually returned to the farms. The June 1948 reconstruction decree stipulated both, but neither was carried out. In any case, Council on Collective Farm Affairs representatives had been pushing for this outcome since early 1948, when they had their first conversations with *kolkhozniki* who had remained on the farms.[16]

Beyond this relationship between farming and residence on the land, many *kolkhozniki* in Raska and Bila Tserkva's farms were especially keen to resume collective farming because, by the late 1930s, it had become relatively profitable for them. It was the profitability of Pershe Travnia in relation to neighbouring farms around Raska that further encouraged authorities to conduct the anti-Polish operation against them with such ferocity in 1937.[17] The pre-war landholdings attached to the three farms in Bila Tserkva were large and exceptionally fertile for the growth of vegetables, which the farms were able to sell to the city at *kolkhoz* markets after meeting their procurement targets for the state.[18] This longing for pre-war prosperity was especially strong in times of severe crisis after the war.

---

[13] See farm meetings in DAKO f. 4974, op. 1, dd. 15–30, for Raska, and AV BRDA f. 280, op. 1, d. 15, and f. 105, op. 1, dd. 24–27, for Bila Tserkva.
[14] There is a wide literature on state coercion in the countryside during collectivisation. Briefly, for peasant resistance to the state, see Viola, *Peasant Rebels under Stalin,* and for post-collectivisation relations between the state and the peasantry, see Fitzpatrick, *Stalin's Peasants.*
[15] See farm meetings referred to in n. 13.   [16] DAKO f. 4810, op. 1, d. 3, ll. 2–14, 8–10.
[17] See Chapter 1.
[18] On Khrushchev's difficulties in reviving the pre-war policy of rural peripheries of cities and towns providing vegetables to them as part of food deliveries to the state in 1946, see Chapter 3.

Rather than leave the farms in these periods, like most other *kolkhozniki*, those who remained redoubled their efforts to rebuild what they had lost. This sentiment was shared widely among the *kolkhozniki* across all the farms and was articulated well by the chairman of Tretii Vyrishal'nyi, Nesterenko, in conversation with Gordienko in early 1948:

> In the years before the war, there were times when our *kolkhozniki* received 5 kilograms of bread per work-day. We flooded the city with vegetables and provided much food to the state. And yet they have been trying to liquidate us for three years![19]

Chairman Krugliakovskyi of Peremoha echoed Nesterenko's sentiment in his conversations with Gordienko at the time:

> Everything is collapsing around us, the harvests are failing, our houses are falling apart and only thirty-nine families are left on the farm ... but before the war we paid three kilograms of bread per work-day and two roubles! We have given so much bread [and so many] vegetables and meat products to the state.[20]

The chairmen were clearly putting forward a case that their farms deserved to be reconstructed with state assistance given their pre-war histories of good agricultural performance in service to the state. As discussed in earlier chapters, *kolkhozniki* on all farms were skilled in putting forward these cases; likewise, Gordienko was skilled in framing their cases for farm reconstruction to his superiors as examples of executing current central policies. In Raska, reconstruction was the proper response to martyred Soviet citizens in a region where collective farming was planned for expansion, while in Bila Tserkva reconstruction was a proper outcome of the 1948 Exile Campaign.

The farm chairmen and the *kolkhozniki* thus appear much like other Soviet citizens studied by historians who mobilised popular Soviet language and policy terms in their dealings with officials to curry favour and gain access to scarce resources. Stephen Kotkin's study of Magnitogorsk in the 1930s helped establish in the literature this explanation for the seemingly mass support for the Soviet regime that is evident in the sources. According to Kotkin, for Stalin's subjects to survive and thrive under Stalinism, they needed to display public loyalty to the regime. It was the public display that was important, not whether those making it really meant it or not. Such displays included participating in public events celebrating the regime; speaking out in favour of the regime in public

---

[19] RGASPI f. 17, op. 122, d. 316, l. 157.   [20] RGASPI f. 17, op. 122, d. 316, l. 158.

fora, such as the farm meetings; and using phrases and words whose meaning was set by the regime – what Kotkin calls 'speaking Bolshevik'.[21] But for understanding the reasons behind the enduring attachment to land and to farming it among *kolkhozniki*, even when it appeared not to be in their 'self-interest', we need to find out whether or not they really meant what they said. In order to understand this attachment, especially how it has continued in Raska and its impact on how people live there today, we need to look beyond Kotkin, to see, as some of his critics suggest, how Bolshevism engaged 'with the soul' of individuals.[22]

Symbolic Reasons for Staying on the Farms

Bolsheviks had engaged with the souls not only of the farm chairmen, but also of the *kolkhozniki*. Chairmen were not simply using Soviet language and mobilising the energy of campaigns to get what they wanted from the state. Records from farm meetings on the three farms in Bila Tserkva suggest that *kolkhozniki* agreed among themselves, both with officials present and alone, that, with the right state assistance, they could resume the farms' pre-war trajectories and live well and honourably as good Soviet citizens. As in Raska, they were hopeful that the reconstruction decrees would initiate this process. But they did not. As conditions on the farms worsened after the reconstruction decrees and hopes faded, these meetings indicate that – despite growing recriminations among the *kolkhozniki* and consternation over the viability of continuing farming and the value of staying on the land – ultimately, most sought to remain. Although these farm meetings were usually recorded and *kolkhozniki* may have been wary of what they said or may have chosen to say nothing at all, analysed carefully, these records are the best indication of how illiterate or semi-literate *kolkhozniki* thought about these issues at the time.

One of the common reasons *kolkhozniki* stayed on the farms was that they took great pride in themselves being 'good peasants' and 'honest citizens',[23] in contrast to '*okolonaselenie*' and 'collaborators'. On all farms, *kolkhozniki* certainly understood themselves in opposition to corrupt, callous local authorities who, in the *kolkhozniki*'s thinking, undermined

---

[21] Stephen Kotkin, *Magnetic Mountain: Stalinism as a Civilization* (Berkeley: University of California Press, 1995), ch. 5. On the complexities of public interaction in war and post-war Stalinism, mostly in urban areas of Ukraine and a broader development of Kotkin's thesis, see Serhy Yekelchyk, *Stalin's Citizens: Everyday Politics in the Wake of Total War* (New York: Oxford University Press, 2014).

[22] Halfin and Hellbeck, 'Rethinking the Stalinist Subject', 459.

[23] See farm meetings referred to in n. 13.

rather than represented central authorities, who would help when they found out what was going on. This thinking runs deep in tsarist history.[24] In the post-war period this thinking among *kolkhozniki* was part of a broader sense of being a member of the post-war Soviet community beyond the limits of their villages, and even past the neighbouring villages, with which some *kolkhozniki* had good relations, borrowing seeds and other resources when they were hungry, further explaining their desire to remain in place. This sense of community extended symbolically to others who had survived the war fighting on the Soviet side. As historians of the period have noted, this was a broad phenomenon across the Soviet Union, where people rephrased their long-standing desires and attachments in a new language and broader context of post-war Soviet patriotism in the wake of victory.[25]

Gaining membership to this community – and to all of the social and material benefits it afforded members in terms of status, greater protection under the law and access to state resources – was not as straightforward in Ukraine as it was in territories that had not been occupied during the war. Millions of Ukrainians remained under German occupation and thus under suspicion/derision by post-war Soviet authorities. Ukrainians reflected this suspicion/derision back towards Soviet power for numerous reasons, not least because of collectivisation and its consequences in the 1930s (and 1940s in the western territories), which did not dissolve after the war.[26] The path to gaining membership was even more crooked in Raska given the remaining stigma of pre-war anti-Polish repressions by the state. But in both Raska and Bila Tserkva, for both similar and different reasons,

---

[24] Note that peasants often referred to the tsar as 'little father', particularly Nicholas II, and certainly some *kolkhozniki* continued to refer to Stalin in similar ways. See Lévesque, 'Exile and Discipline', 17.

[25] On this growing sense of sense of community in Ukraine, see Weiner, *Making Sense of War*. On the other hand, on enduring discrimination against those who did not fit into these communities, such as former collaborators and other 'marginal' people in post-war Soviet society, particularly former 'eastern workers', see Pastushenko, '*V'izd repatriantiv do Kyïva zaboronenyi . . .* '.

[26] On public sentiments towards Soviet power in post-war Ukraine in the wake of the 1946–7 famine and during the 1950 amalgamations, see operational reports (*svodki*) gauging the 'public mood' and mail censored by NKVD/MVD in the Archive Department of the Security Service of Ukraine (Haluzevyi derzhavnyi arkhiv Sluzhby Bezpeky Ukraïny – HDA SBU) f. 16, op. 1, d. 614. This entire *delo* is full of *svodki* on the negative mood of the population towards Soviet power sent to Kaganovich. On the amalgamations in 1950, *svodki* contain evidence of much more positive moods towards Soviet power on this issue and broadly: d. 769, ll. 152–168. On the methodological challenges of analysing *svodki*, see Andrea Graziosi, 'The New Soviet Archival Sources: Hypotheses for a Critical Assessment', *Cahiers du monde russe* 40, nos. 1–2 (1999), 13–64; broadly on the challenges of using archival material, see Jan Plamper, 'Archival Revolution or Illusion? Historicizing the Russian Archives and Our Work in Them', *Jahrbücher für Geschichte Osteuropas* no. 51 (2003), 57–69.

kolkhozniki joined this community in the post-war period and valued their membership.

In Raska and Bila Tserkva, pledging allegiance to this community came not only in the form of *kolkhozniki* rebuilding their farms and their positive attitude towards Soviet power, but also denouncing those who they believed were wartime collaborators with the Germans and, in Raska, had been party to the 1943 massacre of their loved ones. In Bila Tserkva, *kolkhozniki* named both individuals who had left the farm and local authorities as collaborators. They specifically accused the *zemleustroitel'*, responsible for enlarging the private plots of former *kolkhozniki* at the expense of those who remained on the farm, of being a German collaborator (*prispeshnik*), establishing a link (which would prove useful to them) between the attacks on collective farming with collaboration. Oblast-level authorities were aware of these allegations, though there is no evidence that they took any action against the alleged collaborators.[27]

In Raska, *kolkhozniki* could not identify collaborators to their immediate local officials or in public fora where they were present, such as farm meetings, for it was these very officials, according to the *kolkhozniki*, who were protecting the collaborators. At farm meetings in Raska where these officials were not present, *kolkhozniki* charged Marchenko and the head of the local party organisation (*pervichnaia partiinaia organizatsiia*), Comrade Somov, with protecting collaborators. In this case, the collaborator was Marchenko's lover, the same woman whose son, *kolkhozniki* claimed, had served in the local police force under the Germans along with Marchenko's brother. At the end of May 1949, when Gordienko's deputy, Comrade Komoev, was the only official present, *kolkhozniki* sought to blame the 'wrecking activities' of these people, in part, for the second successive poor sowing period and thus dim prospects for the summer harvest:

KOLKHOZNIK 1: We have people who undermine work discipline on the farm, like [the accused],[28] who calls all honest *kolkhozniki* Banderites and is supported by Marchenko, whose brother also served in the police [along with the accused's son] and the secretary of the party organisation, Somov ... a drunk who does no party work.

KOLKHOZNIK 2: In 1949 our work discipline collapsed ... we have not received our loans for the purchase of livestock because [the accused] connives with Marchenko to deny us. She calls us all sort of obscene names like Banderites.

---

[27] RGASPI f. 17, op. 122, d. 317, l. 10. On denunciations among industrial workers in 1930s, see Goldman, *Inventing the Enemy*.

[28] Names of accusers and accused private citizens are withheld.

> Who is this woman? She is the mother of a policeman who took part in the massacre in Raska. She herself worked for the Germans, and now she mocks honest *kolkhozniki*. No one takes any measure against her.[29]

Accusations of collaborators engaging in 'wrecking' and other Bolshevik terms such as 'sabotage' were rife in the post-war Ukrainian countryside. Their veracity was often less important than their utility in explaining the poor performance of a farm or factory or discrediting an opponent, such as Marchenko in Raska and the *zemleustroitel'* in Bila Tserkva. Denunciations were a major problem in Stalinism: they had peaked in the Great Terror in the 1930s and now hit another high after the war.[30] During the Exile Campaign in 1948, these sorts of allegations were important in removing unpopular *kolkhozniki* or non-farm members from villages.[31] Much of the relevant literature analyses denunciations as a social phenomenon and is less concerned with assessing their veracity, which may be infeasible in any case. But establishing the veracity of these accusations or at least the enduring belief in them, again, is key to understanding that *kolkhozniki* valued their membership of the post-war Soviet community. In Raska, this was primarily because it afforded *kolkhozniki* protection from the axis of collaborators who had hurt them in war and were now allied to the post-war officials who continued to do so in the aftermath.

Soviet military authorities tried only some of the German officers and local collaborators responsible for the massacres in Raska and elsewhere in a military tribunal in Kyiv during January 1946. The only adult survivors of the massacre, two women, testified at the trial. The village head (*starosta*) under occupation was hanged along with the Germans for his part in the massacre in the centre of Kyiv.[32] However, broader collaboration among

---

[29] DAKO f. 4974, op. 1, d. 21, ll. 16–18.

[30] Goldman, *Inventing the Enemy*, and Lévesque, 'Exile and Discipline'.

[31] Some 'collaborators' did remain or move to other villages after the war and found protection from those members of local authorities also implicated by a sketchy wartime record. Together they were able to evade the worst tribulations that plagued collaborators in post-war Soviet society, partly by denouncing others for similar crimes. The state-led prosecutions of collaborators were less widespread here than Soviet authorities claimed, and the protection offered to them by local officials was much greater both than authorities conceded at the time and than historians note in their studies of other regions. On the difficulties of 'enemies of the people' in post-war Ukrainian society, see Danylenko, ed., *Povoienna Ukraïna*, 272–91; and on conditions in Ukrainian villages, see ibid., 339–51.

[32] Zosia Adol'fovna Lisovska, interview by Filip Slaveski (18 August 2018). Lisovska's mother was asked to identify the perpetrators from photographs by, Lisovska claims, NKVD agents. Raska's residents discussed the trial in their recollections of the massacre gathered by Soviet poets in 1973. These perpetrators included the head of the German military detachment located in Borodianka and a range of others. The Raska massacre was one of the crimes with which the perpetrators were charged at the trial which is recorded in the official chronicle of daily events in 1946. See Horlach and

party/state members, exceedingly embarrassing for authorities, was not explored at the trial. Neither, of course, was the contradiction between central authorities delivering justice to those killed, but local authorities denying it to their relatives who wanted to rebuild what the Germans had destroyed. Instead, Marchenko's 'protection' of the woman accused of collaboration, as alleged by *kolkhozniki* in the archival record, is corroborated by contemporary sources. The official currently occupying Marchenko's position as chairman of the village council (*sel' sovet/sil'ska rada*) in Piskivka, more than seventy years later confirms that Marchenko and the woman were lovers, or, in his words, 'used to walk together', though he claimed he knew nothing of the woman's or her son's alleged collaboration.[33]

Zosia Lisovska (Lisowska) also reiterates Marchenko's role in protecting the woman accused of collaboration today and the role of her son, the policeman, in the massacre.[34] She was one of the only children to survive the massacre and the only remaining survivor alive in the village today. She and her mother ran from the pit while her relatives were shot, escaping amid the madness of the massacre as dawn broke. Lisovska remembers significant particulars of the massacre and post-war reconstruction that confirm and add important detail to those in various other sources. She remembers how those destined to be killed remained mostly calm. Some were praying to God; they were shot in the Easter period.[35] Another survivor, besides her mother and herself, hid in the wall space behind the stove in her cottage and then fled across the nearby meadow when the Germans set it on fire. She escaped the encirclement of the village by the perpetrators only because a 'conscientious'[36] Ukrainian collaborator standing guard let her through.[37] The trauma of this massacre endures:

LISOVSKA: I was a child then and did not understand . . . what is happening . . . what is happening before our eyes . . . [crying]. They lead families and shoot . . . Maybe our turn will be next . . . And now, when I remember . . . I am not sleeping at night, I am crying all night long . . . How many of our people died there. Three sisters of my mother, her brother . . . with their families [crying].[38]

Pal'chik, *Dzvony pam'iati*, 189–90, and Oleh Rabenchuk, '29 sichnia 1946 (vivtorok)', in Instytut istoriï Ukraïny NAN Ukraïny, ed., *Ukraïna: Khronika XX stolittia. Roky 1946–1960: Dovid. Vyd. 1946–1953*, vol. I (Kyiv: Instytut istoriï Ukraïny NAN Ukraïny, 2005), 12.

[33] Anatoli Nikolaevich Rudnichenko, interview by Filip Slaveski (10 and 14 October 2016).

[34] Ibid.   [35] Zosia Adol'fovna Lisovska, interview by Filip Slaveski (11 October 2016).

[36] Lisovska used the term *sovestlivyi*.

[37] Zosia Adol'fovna Lisovska, interview by Filip Slaveski (18 August 2018).   [38] Ibid.

The fear of 'non-conscientious' collaborators stretches across memory into Lisovska's daily experience, as some of these collaborators continued to live freely in Ukraine and, at times, visited near Raska decades later. Lisovska relates her meeting with the policeman, of the woman Marchenko protected, in the late 1960s or early 1970s:

LISOVSKA: I am standing at the crossroads with my boy and I say: 'Son, there is a red car turning from Teteriv, we will stop it.' It drives closer. It was a disabled driver. I say: 'No, we are not stopping it.' He stops himself. 'Where are you going?' 'To Borodianka'. 'Have a seat, I'll give you a lift.' We sat down. He moves the car and asks: 'Where are you from?' I say, 'We are from Raska'. He puts on his black glasses and says: 'It is interesting to look at Raska now.' And I say, 'When have you seen Raska, before the war or after the war?' He says, 'I know Raska from those days when it was burned and shot' . . . I was shocked, I was scared. I asked, 'Where are you from?' 'From Makarevichi. I'm a policeman. I now live in Kherson, I had my holidays in Vorzel, and now I came to see my sister. When will you go back? I will pick you up and go to see Raska.' I say, 'I do not know when I will go back' . . . *Certainly, he was the policeman.*[39]

Around the same time in 1973, Soviet poets gathered recollections from Raska's residents on the massacre. These recollections were similar to Lisovska's but concerned more the horror of digging up their relatives thrown into the pit by the Germans and their collaborators in the vain hope that they might still be alive.[40] This is because those interviewed were not located in Raska on the day of the massacre, but nearby. The major difference in their recollections is that these residents, sometimes the same people recorded making accusations against Marchenko and the collaborators he protected in the late 1940s, did not mention them now. In fact, they did not mention any collaborators apart from the *starosta* who was hanged after the trial and a village resident executed by local partisans for his part in the massacre. That is, they mentioned only those collaborators to whom 'justice' had already been served by the state and whose representatives were collecting their statements:

The executioners got what they deserved . . . Our partisans killed ******, the traitor from our village. The former village head was also hanged by the state. He fled after the massacre and changed his name . . . but when he came back, our people quickly told him: 'A new surname will not save you, you executioner!' It was with their help that the Nazis burned 111 residential buildings and 99 non-residential premises of Raska – they wiped it off the face of the earth.[41]

This omission in 1973 is unlikely to be due to residents forgetting or overcoming the fears of corrupt local authority a generation after the

[39] Ibid. (my emphasis).   [40] Horlach and Pal'chik, *Dzvony pam'iati*, 186–91.   [41] Ibid., 189.

massacre. Marchenko, or at least his successors, may still have held power in the locality. As we have seen, the policeman and others like him could return to the village. This omission is more likely due to the limitations imposed by the Soviet-era wartime commemorations which applied less to *kolkhozniki* at farm meetings in 1948 and no longer apply to Lisovska. Within these limitations, the most dangerous collaborators, those who found ways to punish the same people under both regimes in local party/state positions of power, were rarely discussed publicly or became the subject of journalistic interest or academic works. This not only served to hide both the embarrassment for the state of the widespread collaboration among its own representatives, but also of the limitations of its own purges to weed them out from party state/structures in the immediate aftermath of liberation, especially local officials and policemen.[42]

The weight of this evidence suggests that Raska's residents clearly believed in the veracity of the same denunciations they had made at farm meetings in the late 1940s and that Lisovska reiterates today, across Soviet-era constraints. Residents thus had good reason to continue to fear that the axis of local officials and former collaborators would continue to harm them into the post-war period, well after the 1948 reconstruction, and continually sought ways to protect themselves from this threat. Whereas in the immediate post-war period they did so by naming the collaborators (carefully), in 1973 they achieved this by omitting mention of this embarrassing problem for the state. Either way, it helped to shift the official view of Raska's *kolkhozniki* from being anti-Soviet and 'rotten' to being bearers of a Soviet martyrdom, at least among central authorities, which was key to the survival of the village and farm.

---

[42] There is a difference of opinion on the effectiveness of the purging the ranks of state and party bodies after the war. For the view that the purges were effective, see Weiner, *Making Sense of War*; specifically for the rapidity of purging Communist Party members upon liberating territory from German occupation, see Vanessa Voisin, 'Caught between War Repressions and Party Purge: The Loyalty of Kalinin Party Members Put to the Test of the Second World War', *Cahiers du monde russe* 52, nos. 2–3 (2011), 341–71. On the trials against collaborators primarily in Ukraine and Belorussia as a small cross-section of overall perpetrators brought to justice, see Alexander Prusin, '"Fascist Criminals to the Gallows!" The Holocaust and Soviet War Crimes Trials, December 1945– February 1946', *Holocaust and Genocide Studies* 17, no. 1 (2003), 1–30; Tanja Penter, 'Collaboration on Trial: New Source Material on Soviet Postwar Trials against Collaborators', *Slavic Review* 64, no. 4 (2005), 782–90; and Diana Dumitru, 'An Analysis of Soviet Postwar Investigation and Trial Documents and Their Relevance for Holocaust Studies', in Michael David-Fox, Peter Holquist and Alexander M. Martin, eds., *The Holocaust in the East: Local Perpetrators and Soviet Responses* (Pittsburgh: University of Pittsburgh Press, 2014), 142–57.

Commemorating the Dead Today

There is little sense of the rural past of the immediate post-war period in the spaces where the farms in Bila Tserkva once stood, given the severing of ties to land, population changes and broader urbanisation of the farms' former towns over seven decades.[43] Unlike in Raska, it is less feasible in Bila Tserkva to connect the past under study to the present through unbroken intergenerational experience. In Raska, this connection is most prescient in the annual wartime commemoration of the 1943 massacre, which has continued since the immediate post-war period, at least in part, as a way for its residents to maintain their social standing and protection from corrupt authority. Their commemorations of the massacre in the Soviet period affirmed their martyrdom for the Soviet cause and did so in a manner that was sensitive to changing state narratives of wartime commemoration, most evident in the 1973 example. In the post-Soviet Ukrainian community, this cause has less value for some sections of the population and, in the main, is no longer supported unambiguously by the state. Now the threat from which protection is required is less the physical harm and displacement from the village and more the devaluing of the martyrdom of their loved ones and the displacement of their memory.

This threat comes from state-sponsored narratives of Ukrainian history in which ethnic Poles are considered, at best, not full-fledged members of Ukrainian society or, at worst, historical enemies of Ukraine. These narratives have blurred clear distinctions between 'good' people who supported the Soviet side in the war and 'bad' people who did not. They have attempted to invert the old Soviet terms of 'collaborators' for Ukrainians who fought with the Germans against the Soviets and, indeed, took part in the murder of Poles, making them into heroes who fought for Ukrainian independence. This attempt has encouraged their public commemoration across large parts of Ukraine, even in Raska's neighbouring village.

Raska and its neighbouring village Myhalky should be typical of how competing wartime commemorations represent and contribute to the pressing contemporary political and social polarisation tied up in how the wartime past is remembered in Ukraine. Victims of German forces and Ukrainian collaborators are commemorated each year in Raska. Next door in Myhalky, soldiers who died fighting against the Soviets in 1944 from the Ukrainian Insurgent Army (UPA) are commemorated annually as

---

[43] Some elderly locals who remain in Zarichia remember little of the immediate post-war period they experienced as children, other than that there used to be collective farming there but 'it was hard going and unproductive': group interviews at AV BRDA by Filip Slaveski (August 2018).

heroes who fought for an independent Ukraine, the UPA's responsibility for the murder of at least tens of thousands of ethnic Polish civilians in western Ukraine notwithstanding. Yet Raska is unique in how its successive generations have found ways to deal with the inversion of moral codes to renegotiate their membership to this new community according to 'new rules', and to find new ways to commemorate the dead to protect effectively the memory from erasure or displacement. That is, villagers in Raska – in co-operation with their neighbours – have found ways to balance the commemoration of their dead with the commemoration of their symbolic murderers. These new practices may help sustain communities, rather than drive them apart, as has been common across Ukraine over the past thirty years.

There is a vast scholarship on these types of changing wartime commemorations and the broader transition in the politics of Soviet to post-Soviet historical memory in Ukraine concerning World War II.[44] This scholarship has exploded in size and urgency since the Maidan Revolution and Russia's 'hybrid war' with Ukraine in 2014, as many scholars have sought to highlight how some of the current war's deeper historical causes may be rooted in memory and identity-making from both Russia's and Ukraine's Soviet past.[45] We have a unique capacity to understand Raska's commemorative practices from the 1940s onwards within this literature and how the same place connects its pasts and its present intergenerationally. This not only helps make sense of the anomaly of co-operation between Raska and Myhalky, but also establishes an important exception to this trend in the scholarship that may provide an example of how other places can ameliorate the contemporary conflicts that their pasts may anticipate.

The renarration and reinterpretation of war memories in Ukraine from the late 1980s and especially since the collapse of the Soviet Union in 1991 are a response, mainly from sections of the Ukrainian political elite and intelligentsia, to the previous Soviet policy of wartime commemoration. This Soviet policy stressed the commonality of Russian, Ukrainian and

---

[44] Edited works on these topics are good starting points, see U. Blacker, A. Etkind, and J. Fedor, eds., *Memory and Theory in Eastern Europe* (New York: Palgrave Macmillan, 2013). On the relationship between memory and nation building in post-Soviet Ukraine, see Yaroslav Hrytsak's works: *Strasti za natsionalizmom. Stara istoriia na novyi lad* (Kyiv: Krytyka, 2011) and *Narysy istorii Ukraïny*. For more recent studies on this development in Ukraine and in Poland and Russia, see A. Portnov, *Istoriia dlia domashnioho vzhytku. Esei pro polsko-rosiisko-ukraïnskyi trykutnyk pamiati* (Kyiv: Krytyka, 2013), and Portnov, *Istoriia istorykiv. Oblychchia i obrazy ukraïnskoi istoriohrafii XX stolittia* (Kyiv: Krytyka, 2011).

[45] Julie Fedor, Markku Kangaspuro, Jussi Lassila and Tatiana Zhurzhenko, eds., *War and Memory in Russia, Ukraine and Belarus* (New York: Palgrave Macmillan, 2017).

Belarusian wartime experiences of shared victory over fascism under the liberating Red Army in World War II rather than the distinctive, complex and contradictory experiences of war among these countries, as a way of promoting ties among this Slavic block in the retention of the Soviet Union. This policy entailed the reduction of Ukrainian identification from a nation to an ethnic group, devoid both of its own political aspirations and of its own history which did not serve this aim, and more so of ethnic minorities within Ukraine.[46] Ukrainian historical figures who fought against the Soviets were banished from public discussion or were distorted by Soviet historiography and commemorative practices.

Intellectuals and political elites in the early 1990s began publicly reimagining Ukraine's position in World War II as primarily a victim nation that heroically resisted both Nazism and communism. Soviet victory was now not a liberation from German rule, but a reintroduction of Soviet occupation that curtailed the emergence of an independent Ukrainian state. These repressed figures under Soviet rule became the historical material from which these people sought to connect and legitimate a historical trajectory of curtailed Ukrainian independent nation building with their own attempts at such schemes after the collapse of the Soviet Union. Other elites sought a balance between amending former Soviet narratives of Ukrainian history and adopting new ones, while others opposed the valorisation of the UPA and other Ukrainian 'independence' figures, helping to entrench the divisions in Ukrainian society that remain, roughly, today.[47]

For those elites who reimagined Ukraine's past, the key point of connection in historical and contemporary Ukrainian nation building as well as its greatest stumbling block remains, arguably, the UPA. This was the chief military organisation that fought for the establishment of an independent Ukrainian state in an internecine conflict with Soviet, German and Polish forces during and after World War II, as the military arm of its parent body, the Organisation of Ukrainian Nationalists (OUN). The problem with the UPA for ethnic Poles, especially in Raska, other Ukrainian elites, large sections of the Ukrainian population and Ukraine's neighbours in Poland and Russia is that the UPA not only fought to 'defend' Ukraine against Soviet/Russian and Polish forces during and after World War II; the UPA also fought to establish an ethnically

---

[46] Julie Fedor, Simon Lewis and Tatiana Zhurzhenko, 'Introduction: War and Memory', in Fedor et al., eds., *War and Memory in Russia, Ukraine and Belarus*, 8–9.

[47] Hrytsak, *Strasti za natsionalizmom*, 264–5.

'pure' Ukrainian state free of ethnic Russians, Poles, communists and Jews, and slaughtered thousands of these civilians in the process while, at times, allied to German forces. They slaughtered many of them not necessarily for what they had done or what they thought they had done, but for who they were – *a priori* enemies of the Ukrainian nation they were trying to build.[48] The UPA fought conventional military battles against Polish and Soviet military forces mostly until 1944 and then in a guerrilla war until the end of the decade, but the murder of civilians was key to the UPA's ultimate aim. This extermination included ethnic Ukrainians suspected of not supporting the UPA,[49] but was especially directed against ethnic Poles, whose physical destruction and physical relocation were the key methods used by the OUN/UPA to facilitate their removal from 'Ukrainian soil'.[50]

State-sponsored narratives pursued by different governments have tended to valorise members of the UPA as heroic military figures and state builders without due acknowledgement of their crimes. Alternatively, they have denounced the UPA as a fascist collaborator responsible for civilian deaths without acknowledgement of its fight for independence. There have been some state-led attempts to offer a more balanced view, and recent years have seen a growth in academic works that offer a much more sophisticated understanding of this complex issue.[51] But they have had generally little impact in the public

[48] Statiev, *The Soviet Counterinsurgency*, ch. 6.
[49] In the post-war period, ethnically Ukrainian rural dwellers became overrepresented as OUN/UPA victims, especially those who the OUN/UPA claimed had collaborated with the Soviets or other groups. This is explained, in part, by the depletion of their ranks 'under the weight of Soviet operations as well as by incentives created to attract their members to the Soviet side'. This turned 'the remnants of these movements ... toward naked terrorism against civilian "collaborators", demonstrating their transition from competitors for state authority to simple insurgents'. See M. Edele and F. Slaveski, 'Violence from Below: Explaining Crimes against Civilians across Soviet Space, 1943–1947', *Europe–Asia Studies* 68, no. 6 (2016), 1027.
[50] At times, this was also the aim of Polish forces seeking to rid what they considered to be Polish territory of Ukrainians, though the scale of their actions against civilians was much smaller and this 'conflict' was broadly characterised by a significant asymmetry in violence against civilians: Igor Iliushin, *UPA i AK. Protyvostoiannia u Zapadniy Ukraini (1939–1945 gg.)* (Kyiv, 2009). For an analysis of broader debates over UPA massacres of Poles in western Ukraine, especially well-known massacres such as Volhynia in 1943, see Portnov, *Istoriia dlia domashnioho vzhytku*, 134–46; and, for Polish perspectives, see Władysław Siemaszko and Ewa Siemaszko, *Ludobójstwo dokonane przez nacjonalistów ukraińskich na ludności polskiej Wołyni 1939–1945*, vol. II (Warsaw: Wydawn. von borowiecky, 2000).
[51] The findings of a Government Commission launched in 1997 to investigate the OUN/UPA led by historian Stanislav Kul'chyts'kyi did attempt to offer a more nuanced view of the OUN/UPA and often sought to avoid the binary and politicised interpretations of this issue. See S. V. Kul'chyts'kyi, *Organizatsiia ukrainskykh natsionalistiv i Ukrainska povstanska armiia* (Kyiv: Instytut istorii Ukraïny NAN Ukraïny, 2005). See Jeffrey Burds, 'The Early Cold War

sphere and have done little to upset this enduring binary understanding and the broader lack of honesty among elites in attempting to come to terms with this complex history objectively. This failure has exacerbated deep divisions within Ukrainian society between people who relate differently to the wartime past; it has eroded the broader base for political compromise and consensus nationwide, commonly required for the nation building which adherents of these narratives claim to pursue. Valorising the UPA without acknowledgement of its crimes against Poles and Jews in the Holocaust has also complicated Ukraine's international relationships with Poland and the European Union. As historians have noted, 'reclaiming' Ukraine's past from the Soviet shadow without 'coming to terms' with it honestly replicates Soviet methods of memory making which endure in the post-Soviet space, keeping Ukraine isolated culturally and politically in this space from which pro-European Ukrainians are desperate to emerge.[52]

This main division within Ukrainian society on which these competing historical narratives have operated, at least in geographical terms, lies roughly between the west and the east of the country and in different regions therein. Competing political forces that represent these areas mobilise these divisive historical narratives in an interplay with academic and cultural industries in their bids for local and national power, influence and legitimacy. In some parts of the country, particularly the west, support for the UPA as fighting heroically against Soviet and Polish occupying forces in World War II is deeply ingrained. Leading proponents of this narrative in key state positions have either ignored, downplayed or justified the atrocities they committed against Poles and other civilians.[53] In eastern Ukraine, the Soviet-era image of the UPA as fascist collaborators responsible for civilian deaths remains widespread, while its victims continue to be identified primarily as Soviet citizens rather than ethnic Poles or Jews.

in Soviet West Ukraine, 1944–1948', *Carl Beck Papers in Russian and East European Studies*, no. 1505 (Pittsburgh: University of Pittsburgh Press, 2001); John-Paul Himka, 'War Criminality: A Blank Spot in the Collective Memory of the Ukrainian Diaspora', *Spaces of Identity* 5, no. 1 (April 2005); David R. Marples, *Heroes and Villains: Creating National History in Contemporary Ukraine* (Budapest: Central European University Press, 2007); Prusin, *The Lands Between*; and Serhy Yekelchyk, *Ukraine: Birth of a Modern Nation* (New York: Oxford University Press, 2007).

[52] Hrytsak, *Strasti za natsionalizmom*, 256–9.

[53] Jared McBride, 'Who's Afraid of Ukrainian Nationalism?', *Kritika: Explorations in Russian and Eurasian History* 17, no. 3 (2016), 657.

The UPA's defeat is generally celebrated as part of Ukraine's liberation from German bondage by the Red Army.[54]

These are not finite divisions, and there are shared and positive attitudes towards the past among Ukrainians that cross them.[55] The historical narratives that reflect and exacerbate these divisions can be more nuanced than their unambiguous representations in media and politics. How people understand and respond to these narratives on the ground can also help to shape them on a broader level in an interplay of local and central actors.[56] As leading historians of historical memory have noted, this is how it is actually produced. This interplay is evident in how residents in Raska and Myhalky have responded to competing historical narratives peddled by different governments with their commemorative practices since the early 1990s. In this interplay, residents interpret state-sponsored historical narratives with which they identify to neutralise the polarisation that they anticipate on the local level in ways that have not been successful nationally. Two historical moments on either side of the current war provide the clearest evidence of this neutralisation: first, the seventieth anniversary of the Raska massacre on 11 April 2013 and, second, the commemoration of UPA soldiers killed by Soviet forces in 1944 in Myhalky on 14 October 2016. State officials gave speeches at these commemorations in 'support' of the dead, which reflected the then-predominant historical narratives of Ukraine's wartime past, under the governments first of Viktor Yanukovych (2010–14) and then of Petro Poroshenko (2014–19).

At the 2013 commemoration, the visiting politician from Kyiv referred to the war dead in his speech as 'Soviet citizens and soldiers', continuing the Soviet-era practice of omitting their ethnic Polish heritage. Remaining residents in Raska and Polish visitors to the commemoration were deeply disappointed by the official's reversion to this type of commemoration in 2013, but not surprised. They did not voice this disappointment publicly at the time, but accepted the politician's actions as part of a deeper problem of anti-Polish discrimination by local officials who would have briefed the visiting politician about the commemoration. This official from the city

---

[54] Hrytsak, *Strasti za natsionalizmom*, 66–7; Yuliya Yurchuk, *Reordering of Meaningful Worlds: Memory of the Organization of Ukrainian Nationalists and the Ukrainian Insurgent Army in Post-Soviet Ukraine* (Stockholm: Stockholm Studies in History, 2014), ch. 3. On the intersections of language, identity and nationalism in post-Soviet Ukraine before the Maidan Revolution – again, a broad literature – see Taras Kuzio's works: 'Competing National Identities and Democratisation in Ukraine: The Fifth and Sixth Cycles in Post-Soviet Ukrainian History', *Acta Slavica Iaponica* 33 (2013), 27–46; and 'Nationalism, Identity and Civil Society in Ukraine: Understanding the Orange Revolution', *Communist and Post-Communist Studies* 43, no. 3 (2010), 285–96.

[55] Hrytsak, *Strasti za natsionalizmom*, 273–4. [56] Ibid., 262–3.

4 Dual-language memorial plaque at the grave of honour in Raska
Translation: On this site in April 1943, fascists executed 613 innocent villagers, ethnic
Poles from the village of Raska, who supported the partisan movement in the fight
against the Hitlerite invaders. Among those killed were 120 children. Eternal glory to
the sons and daughters of our Fatherland. Immortal is the memory of the fallen.
Their names are inscribed in eternity.

most likely did not know or care about the ethnically Polish history of the
village, which Raska's Poles reclaimed in the early 1990s. Although they
erected a plaque commemorating the dead at the grave with a dual
Ukrainian–Polish inscription (see Figure 4), the politician still laid a
memorial wreath on it with a message in Russian. They had to pay the
'price' of forgoing their ethnicity for admission to the Soviet and post-
Soviet community decades apart.

The politician's ignorance, wilful or not, reflected the broader pro-Soviet wartime remembrance policies regarding victims of fascism held by some political parties and by the Yanukovych government.[57] This policy clearly facilitated the use of commemorations more as a platform to peddle historical narratives than to honour the victims. In the early 2000s, the Ukrainian Communist Party erected some of the first monuments to victims of the UPA in Simferopol (Crimea) and Luhansk (eastern Ukraine) referring to them only as 'Soviet citizens'. In 2010, commemorations under the new Ukrainian and pro-Soviet/Russian president Yanukovych seemingly changed course. 'Russian-speaking Ukrainians' under the patronage of Yanukovych's 'Party of Regions' organised an exhibition to honour Polish and Jewish victims of the UPA and their liberators in the Red Army. But this exhibition did little to honour the victims as Poles or Jews. It used their deaths as evidence to demonstrate how the UPA, unlike the Red Army, was a fascist ally committed to the extermination of civilians. The UPA was an aberration, not a part of Ukraine's shared history. Conveniently, neither the Molotov–Ribbentrop pact of 1939, which divided Poland between Germany and the Soviet Union, nor the Soviet massacre of 20,000 Poles in the Katyn Forest in 1940 received mention at the exhibition.[58]

The situation changed dramatically when the new Poroshenko government replaced Yanukovych's on the wave of enthusiasm from the Maidan Revolution and massive anti-Russian sentiment from the Donbas conflict in 2014. In 2015, the government passed numerous laws establishing an anti-Soviet and pro-nationalist narrative of Ukraine's wartime past that encouraged not a disregard of but a focus on ethnicity in Ukraine. Many proponents of this narrative in media, politics and academia highlighted the historical antagonism between Ukrainians and Poles, dismissed or diminished the importance of massacres committed against Poles by Germans or Ukrainians on Ukrainian soil and, broadly, gave little indication that they understood ethnic Poles as legitimate members of Ukrainian society.[59]

Locals in Myhalky had been commemorating the dead UPA fighters for some time at a monument dedicated to them, a large yellow and blue cross above their sandy graves (see Figure 5). Across the way there is an updated

[57] For the pro-Soviet narrative of Ukraine's past under Yanukovych, see T. Kuzio, 'Viktor Yanukovych's First 100 Days: Back to the Past, But What's the Rush?', *Demokratizatsiia* 18, no. 3 (2010), 208–18.

[58] Portnov, *Istoriia dlia domashnioho vzhytku*, 137.

[59] McBride, 'Who's Afraid of Ukrainian Nationalism?'

5 UPA grave in Myhalky

6 UPA monument in Myhalky
Translation: To the heroes of the UPA. Eternal memory to the soldiers who perished
here in the unequal battle for Ukrainian independence on 30 March 1944. Glory to
Ukraine! Glory to Heroes!

stone moment with an inscription as well. This type of monument is quite
common, but less numerous in central Ukraine than in the west (see Figure
6). The commemoration on 14 October 2016 was now of special importance, as in the previous year the Poroshenko government passed a law that

included the UPA and the OUN on a list of 'defenders of Ukraine' along with numerous historical organisations and individuals in the pantheon of Ukrainian historical heroes. These defenders would all be celebrated on the 'Day of the Defender', a national holiday on 14 October every year; public criticism of any of these defenders could now be prosecuted by law.[60] These laws formed part of a broader suite of 'decommunisation' legislation, the result of more than a decade of interplay between historians and politicians, which saw a broader celebration of OUN/UPA leaders for their military service in fighting for Ukraine's independence against the reintroduction of Soviet occupation.

The government's passing of these laws at the time was clearly a response to the Donbas conflict, highlighting the continuity between the historical Soviet occupation of Ukraine and the current annexation of Crimea and occupation of eastern Ukraine by Russia and Russian-backed forces. In the context of war and the spread of anti-Russian sentiment, this continuity and a more positive image of the UPA became more prominent in public conversations on a national level than its crimes and proto-fascist roots.[61] But these laws also hardened antagonism on the part of those who rejected this continuity, domestically and internationally. Including proto-fascist guerrilla forces in this pantheon of Ukrainian heroes offended millions of Ukrainians whose own family members had fought against them and, broadly, for the Soviet forces. Their grievance was that these relatives and they themselves, by implication, were being transformed, *ex post facto*, from liberators to occupiers as part of this reimagining of their country's past, despite Poroshenko's concessions to them in proclaiming that Ukraine should celebrate all veterans who fought for Ukraine on whatever side.[62]

Internationally, the response from Poland was swift; the government condemned these laws in the same spirit as it had condemned, four years earlier, the move of President Viktor Yushchenko (2005–10) – who began

---

[60] Law No. 2538–1, 'On the legal status and honouring of fighters for Ukraine's independence in the twentieth century'.

[61] Y. Yurchuk, 'Reclaiming the Past, Confronting the Past: OUN–UPA Memory Politics and Nation Building in Ukraine (1991–2016)', in Fedor et al., eds., *War and Memory in Russia, Ukraine and Belarus*, 126.

[62] Poroshenko announced at the Tomb of the Unknown Soldier in Kyiv on 8 May 2015 that: 'We bow to all veterans – those present here, in this holy place, those who celebrate in other streets and squares of Ukraine.' This attempt had little success on a national level: as reported in the Ministry of Defence website in Ukraine on 8 May 2015, www.mil.gov.ua/en/news/2015/05/09/president-may-9 -will-always-be-the-red-letter-date-in-the-ukrainian-calendar-%E2%80%93-the-day-of-victory -remembrance-and-reconciliation.

the mass valorisation of the OUN/UPA in the national political arena – to bestow upon Stepan Bandera, an OUN leader, the title of Hero of Ukraine in 2010. Though Bandera was more the figurehead than operational leader of the OUN in the war (he was detained from 1941 by the Germans) Poles hold him responsible for OUN/UPA massacres against Polish civilians, famously in Volhynia in 1943, where the UPA killed at least 60,000 Poles.[63] In 2015, the Polish president, Andrzej Duda, warned his counterpart in Kyiv about the necessity of open and honest dialogue about the past if Ukraine was to move forward into Europe, while ethnic Poles in Ukraine, as in Raska, braced for trouble.[64]

Broadly, then, the law enshrining these groups as 'defenders of Ukraine' and responses to it have hardened opposing positions in Ukrainian politics and society, specifically over the OUN/UPA and how the nation should commemorate its wartime past. These competing commemorations and the rituals performed to enact them across the country on anniversary days have been the site of contestation since the 1990s and have now taken on new meaning since these laws and the broader conflict in the Donbas.[65] A recent work explores current commemorative rituals in Ukraine, Russia and Belarus and how they

> serve to delineate the boundaries of post-Soviet identities, and often to identify and construct 'enemies' ... that advance our understanding of the mechanisms of collective mobilization in times of political crisis ... [and how] historical myths and visions of the past projected onto the present can make people see the current war as an unfinished battle of World War II, even motivating some of them to take up arms.[66]

The 'contesting' commemorations in Raska and Myhalky, by every expectation, should conform to this prescription, which is widely applicable across Ukraine. UPA supporters would demonise ethnic Poles who supported Soviet power. Ethnic Poles faced with this local state-supported threat would be expected to respond by referring to UPA supporters as enemies as well.

[63] Portnov, *Istoriia dlia domashnioho vzhytku*, 136–7.
[64] Valentin Dem'ianovich Koval'skyi, interview by Filip Slaveski (11–21 October 2016 and 18 August 2018).
[65] The war has further blurred the relationship between historical memory and national identity in Ukraine. For contemporary analysis of shifting attitudes among Donbas residents especially, see O. Haran, M. Yakovlyev and M. Zolkina, 'Identity, War, and Peace: Public Attitudes in the Ukraine-Controlled Donbas', *Eurasian Geography and Economics* 60, no. 6 (2019), 1–25.
[66] Fedor, Lewis and Zhurzhenko, 'Introduction: War and Memory', 7.

However, commemorations in Raska and Myhalky and those who conduct them do not follow this prescription. Here commemorative rituals have served not to delineate the boundaries of post-Soviet identities, but to blur them. Not enemies, but contemporary allies, are constructed among those demonised by the broader historical narratives that fuel these commemorations. It is exactly the local history of the area in the context of current war that encourages locals to come together to sustain community, at the expense of ideological alignment to the narratives they support. Attendance at each other's commemorations is about displaying good manners and maintaining good peaceable relations among neighbours, which is more important than the ideological contradictions and, indeed, personal trauma that attendance may entail. This is especially the case for the ethnic Poles, who, as we have seen, have sought to remain part of changing communities as a survival mechanism. Commemorations are celebrated on relevant anniversary days with public speeches, songs and food by people from both villages and the town. Ethnic Poles are invited and attend the UPA celebration and return the gesture to UPA celebrants who may attend the Polish remembrance of the massacre. Schoolchildren, officials and locals attend together and, although what is being commemorated is very different, the rituals performed to do so are very similar, from children singing folk songs to the speeches made by officials.[67] This commemorative space is not contested, but shared.

Sharing physical or symbolic space in this way is rare in Ukraine. Conflicting commemorations have turned violent and often provide a platform for antagonists to demonise their opponents, and ignore or exploit victims, as in the exhibition about the UPA's victims in 2010 described earlier.[68] Historians have noted a difference between such commemorations on a national level and those at the local level, as the state by no means controls exactly how adherents of the historical narratives it supports commemorate their important dates.[69] Local commemorations

---

[67] Recent work on the similarity of commemoration rituals from opposing narratives, albeit enduringly antagonistic ones unlike those here, demonstrates that this occurs because these narratives borrow from one another to establish themselves. Opposing narratives thus can display similar commemorative practices, even though the content of their commemoration is very different: A. Portnov, 'Bandera Mythologies and Their Traps for Ukraine', *Open Democracy Russia and Beyond* (22 June 2016).

[68] Yurchuk, 'Reclaiming the Past', 124.

[69] For the sometimes strained relations between grassroots and state commemorations in Russia over contested issues from the Stalin era, see Markku Kangaspuro and Jussi Lassila, 'From the Trauma of Stalinism to the Triumph of Stalingrad: The Toponymic Dispute over Volgograd', in Fedor et al. eds., *War and Memory*, 141–70.

can be less politicised and thus more capable of observing greater nuance in their practice and of opening dialogue about the past with 'opponents' rather than closing it. There have been some joint celebrations of the UPA and Red Amy veterans and, specifically relevant to Raska, memorials to Polish victims of German massacres have been erected in western Ukraine close to UPA commemorative sites. Some of these memorials have been constructed by joint efforts of Polish and Ukrainian officials at massacre sites close to Rivne. This effort reflected local sentiment and a desire to stress positive histories of Ukrainian and Polish co-habitation in these areas, with a view to the improvement of Ukrainian and Polish relations.[70]

These elementary steps in this direction in commemorative practice from the 2000s, however, have been limited in the capacity to 'share' space, and the dialogue that has been opened with others has not been completely honest. As one historian notes about these commemorations, they are 'governed by strategic forgetfulness that renders the memory of the inter-ethnic conflict full of silences and innuendos'.[71] These silences in UPA commemorations are their refusal to acknowledge their civilian and especially Polish victims, while commemorations of Polish victims of German massacres ignore the suffering of ethnic Ukrainians killed along-side them. Much like those at the national level, these commemorations, whatever their initial intentions, can end up being used for broader polit-ical purposes to further polarise social divisions by politicians and elites.[72]

Raska's and Myhalky's commemorative practices too are characterised by a strategic forgetfulness of UPA crimes, even silences about them. But this strategy renders memory of the inter-ethnic conflict less replete with innuendos, and instead reshapes it to the specific conditions of time and place to promote co-operation among, not divide, ethnic Polish and Ukrainian neighbours. The 2016 UPA celebration was attended by Ukrainian troops from volunteer battalions fighting in the Donbas, locals

---

[70] Specifically the monument to a UPA commander in Rivne (Klym Savur) and Polish civilians killed in the German massacre in the village of Borshchivka, some thirty kilometres from Rivne offered as case studies in chs. 3 and 4 in Yurchuk, *Reordering of Meaningful Worlds*.

[71] Ibid., 184.

[72] Other studies of commemorations or broader remembrance in other countries have noted the 'sharing' of space and argued against commemoration or remembrance as a zero-sum game, where one remembrance necessarily comes at the expense of another in the limited real estate of the public square. But this approach concerns historical narratives and identities that are not diametrically opposed, i.e. Holocaust versus slavery remembrance, as part of a broader argument about how the growth of Holocaust memory has encouraged others to emerge, such as those of other genocides, rather than crowding them out. This approach, clearly, has limited applicability to Ukraine. See M. Rothberg, *Multidirectional Memory: Remembering the Holocaust in the Age of Decolonization* (Stanford: Stanford University Press, 2009), 6–7.

(a)

(b)

7a, 7b October 2016 'Day of the Defender' commemoration at Mykhalky

from Myhalky, Raska and Piskivka, schoolchildren, local historians and politicians (see Figures 7a and 7b). Speakers made no explicit mention of UPA crimes against civilians or collaboration with German forces, referring more to the 'complicated' nature of the conflict in which they were engaged. The speakers noted that ethnic Poles had long been part of the Ukrainian community in Kyiv Oblast, represented by those from Raska present at the commemoration.

A major difference here in comparison with other commemorations was that the speakers also called for a figurative alliance with those in the audience, including the Poles, against the 'real enemies' of Ukraine on this 'Day of the Defender'. They should delineate these enemies carefully, not cast all Russians, Germans or Poles as enemies, but specify only the pernicious among them who had caused Ukraine harm. For most of the speakers it was clearly the *NKVDisty* (the Ukrainian colloquial term for members of the Soviet secret police, the NKVD)[73] who were responsible for the killing of the UPA fighters on the site in 1944, the same people responsible for anti-Polish purge in Raska in 1937. *NKVDisty* were represented as the common historical enemy of Poles and Ukrainians, now morphed into Russian special forces which had invaded Ukraine.

This subtle approach calling for a union of local Poles and Ukrainians against the historical/contemporary foe represents a revision of both historical OUN/UPA ideology and its popular contemporary application to the commemoration of its fallen fighters. This ideology was always diverse and contested among its adherents in the 1940s.[74] The UPA even concluded strategic agreements with Polish forces to battle the Soviets. But these agreements were the exception: it was more usual for them to fight each other and for Soviet–Polish alliances to be formed against the UPA. There was little real disagreement in the OUN/UPA in the 1940s about the ultimate aim of excising Poles from Ukrainian soil and little disagreement now in most contemporary commemorations by the UPA about Poles and Russians as Ukraine's historical enemy to the west and the east, respectively.[75]

Redefining enemies and inviting Raska's ethnic Poles to be allies against them is more feasible in Kyiv Oblast than in western Ukraine and especially during, not in spite of, the current war. Ethnic Poles in Raska had lived as a small enclave among a broader Ukrainian community since the 1800s, not – like Polish communities in western Ukraine – on territory historically contested by Ukraine and Polish forces seeking to expand their

[73] Russians tend to use the term *chekisty*, derived from Cheka, their shorthand reference to the original Soviet secret police and progenitor of the NKVD, the All-Russian Extraordinary Commission.

[74] Myroslav Shkandrij, *Ukrainian Nationalism: Politics, Ideology, and Literature, 1929–1956* (New Haven: Yale University Press, 2015).

[75] Statiev, *The Soviet Counterinsurgency*, 45–56, 51, 85–6.

own borders in the internecine conflict of the 1940s. The main vector of UPA violence towards Poles developed there, not in Kyiv Oblast, as have the enduring legacies of violence and forced deportation of both Ukrainians and Poles in war's aftermath. There are few Poles left in western Ukraine because of post-war deportations, making the need for balancing commemoration with promoting contemporary co-operation less salient than in Raska.

The historical trajectory of Raska discussed in this chapter is important, too, in encouraging its residents take up this invitation. Inclusion into the community and maintaining the memory of their dead have been the main aims of successive generations of Raska's Poles. Each generation has paid a price for this admission. In the Soviet period, it was forgoing their ethnicity. As we have seen, even though they have reclaimed it, this is not always recognised by the post-Soviet state, although it is by their neighbours in Myhalky. Some participate in the 11 April commemorations in Raska where the Polish ethnicity of the victims is highlighted, most evident in the dual-language memorial plaque erected on the grave (see Figure 4) and the dual-language speeches, both in Ukrainian and in Polish. This recognition also carries a price, that of treating UPA violence towards Poles in western Ukraine 'as a complex problem' rather than mass killing, and remaining silent on specific Ukrainian collaborators who participated in Raska's massacre.

But, just like in 1973, remaining silent about collaborators and the broader failure to 'come to terms' with this uncomfortable aspect of the past is part of a much longer tradition of navigating contemporary social and political norms to achieve social inclusion, status and protection. Silence is not always the same as dishonesty. It does not necessarily lead to the social polarisation seen in western Ukraine discussed above and documented widely in the literature.[76] When people have to deal with each other on a daily basis as neighbours, they can have greater incentive to balance their commemorative practices between honouring the past and living in the present. There is clearly less incentive to do this in places where the victims and perpetrators and their children no longer live side by side, as is mostly the case with Ukrainians, Poles and Jews in western Ukraine. There commemorations have more to do with contemporary

---

[76] In their analysis of Ukraine, some historians borrow German concepts of social memory such as 'coming to terms with the past' that '[emphasise] a critical view on the difficult aspects of the past, on the other'. See Yurchuk, 'Reclaiming the Past', 108.

identity and politics without the deeply practical implications that are present in Raska and Myhalky.

Striking this balance here is not always easy or pleasant.[77] The UPA and the Raska commemorations can be awkward and uneasy at times for locals. Contradictions in historical narratives may be assuaged publicly by speeches and politeness, but continue to jar those in attendance, who are affected emotionally, as is evident in the uneasy shifting in places and later reflections.[78] This is especially the case for survivors like Lisovska whose haunting image of the policeman, allied to the German occupiers, can morph into that of UPA fighters, all responsible for the murder of her relatives and of other ethnic Poles in Ukraine. But it is Lisovska and fellow villagers who provide most insight into how, beyond the practical considerations, they are reconciled morally to attend the celebrations. She is most adamant that Ukrainian society was and remains defined by an incredibly complex set of intersecting pasts and presents. Her relatives fought for the Soviets and the Poles. Her neighbours were collaborators, and some participated in the massacre, but 'there were those with consciences' who allowed others to escape it.[79] Like those who commemorate the UPA in Myhalky, she delineates enemies and finds allies not only among national groups, but also among perpetrators. Reserving moral judgement in reflecting on those who ended up on different sides in wartime, she said, 'I don't know who is guilty and who is innocent; only God can decide.'[80]

Reflecting on collaboration and resistance along a spectrum, rather than as a dichotomy, is less common in Ukraine than in west European countries that also suffered under German occupation. Later post-war generations there have come to terms with the complex legacies of collaboration in different and sometimes more sophisticated ways.[81] Some

---

[77] On the broader difficulties of post-war communities striking a balance between silence about traumatic histories, and seeking public acknowledgement of them but not fixating on their past so to jeopardise them living in the present, see Marc Silberman and Florence Vatan, eds., *Memory and Postwar Memorials: Confronting the Violence of the Past* (New York: Palgrave Macmillan, 2013), 2.

[78] Valentin Dem'ianovich Koval'skyi, interview by Filip Slaveski (11–21 October 2016 and 18 August 2018).

[79] Zosia Adol'fovna Lisovska, interview by Filip Slaveski (18 August 2018).

[80] Ibid. On the complexities of 'choosing sides' and surviving in wartime Ukraine and the political mobilisation of these identities in post-Soviet Ukraine, see Marples, *Heroes and Villains*. For Ukrainian–Polish conflicts, see ibid., 203–38.

[81] This is a massive scholarship. See review article of the state of the field: T. Cole, 'Review: Scales of Memory, Layers of Memory: Recent Works on Memories of the Second World War and the Holocaust', *Journal of Contemporary History* 37, no. 1 (2002), 129–38; and, more recently for case studies and theoretical approaches, see Aleida Assmann and Sebastian Conrad, eds., *Memory in a Global Age: Discourses, Practices and Trajectories* (Basingstoke: Palgrave Macmillan, 2010); and Aleida

scholars have drawn out significant similarities and differences in these memory cultures and those in eastern Europe.[82] It is at least clear from this chapter that such a reflection is more difficult to adopt in Ukraine – indeed, more difficult in some parts of it. This is clearly due to exterminatory nature of Germany's war in the East and the continuation of monochrome and repressive state-led narratives of remembering it imposed across the Soviet and post-Soviet periods.

At the same time, this type of reflection is all the more urgent in Ukraine because of these issues. The legacies of war, occupation, collaboration and repressive memory are enduring, indeed, prominent in contemporary Ukraine and the post-Soviet space, so much so that some scholars claim the current conflict in the Donbas is, at least partly, fuelled by them.[83] The way these legacies have converged around Raska has threatened to suffocate its residents from all sides, either physically as in the immediate post-war period or symbolically thereafter, requiring them to adapt how they remember the past in order to survive and live peaceably in the present. They have shown how to do so with their neighbours by reshaping broader historical narratives to reduce their polarising impacts and by paying different 'prices' for the sake of keeping the memory of their dead alive and for their children's futures. Their commemorative practices might serve as a new example of what sharing space of competing historical narratives can look like in parts of Ukraine. These intelligent local practices require a moral courage and fortitude born from immeasurable suffering that are difficult to replicate, though urgently needed on a national level. This village, a backwater a few hours from Kyiv, may have much to teach the city.

Assmann, *Shadows of Trauma: Memory and the Politics of Postwar Identity*, trans. S. Clift (New York: Fordham University Press, 2015).
[82] Silberman and Vatan, *Memory and Postwar Memorials*.   [83] Fedor et al., eds., *War and Memory*.

Conclusion

RAIKOM SECRETARY: I would like to say something about the massive upsurge in patriotic feeling that we are seeing in the *raion*. Before the war, I have to admit, it was so difficult to conduct some of the campaigns that we are conducting so easily now. *Kolkhozniki* have already signed up for two million roubles worth of state loans in just two days. Before the war, we would have struggled a great deal more to achieve that sum.

KHRUSHCHEV: Yes. The Germans taught them to love us. Even those who were against Soviet power before the war (audience laughter).

Kyiv obkom CP(b)U Plenum, 15 March 1944[1]

Despite the devastation of Ukraine upon its liberation from German occupation by 1944, the country's political leaders were greatly optimistic about the prospect of rebuilding it. *Raion* leaders from Kyiv Oblast took turns at this plenum proclaiming how enthusiastic *kolkhozniki* were about the return of Soviet power and their commitment to working hard to supply the Red Army with food to aid in the final defeat of the German enemy. They supplemented their speeches with colourful examples of *kolkhozniki* spontaneously swearing oaths to Soviet power and to Stalin personally, just like their forebears had done to the tsars.

These positive sentiments, widespread in the territories of eastern and even central Ukraine originally part of the Soviet Union, generally diminished the further west that the Red Army travelled. Many Ukrainians did not welcome the Red Army as liberators when they reached west Ukrainian territories that had only come under Soviet control briefly in 1940 and remained in the grip of a massive anti-Soviet insurgency by 1944.[2] But for

---

[1] TsDAHOU f. 1, op. 50, d. 2866, l. 86. 'State loans' refers to loans the state pressured collective farms to take during the war and the post-war period. These loans were essentially another form of taxation to raise food and monetary revenues from the countryside using the demands of the war and post-war reconstruction to cajole *kolkhozniki* into paying up.

[2] TsDAHOU f. 1, op. 50, d. 2866, l. 86; see the numerous speeches of the two-day plenum above by *raion* leaders. Not only *raion* leaders, but also Soviet secret police agents reported along similar lines

political leaders reading reports from the east and centre of the country amid this euphoria of liberation in late 1943 and early 1944, it seemed that the war had solved many of the old problems that had beset the Ukrainian countryside. The primary problem had been the fear and loathing large sections of the Ukrainian peasantry held for Soviet power, collectivisation and its ills, not least than the mass famine of 1932–3. Most *kolkhozniki* displayed an enduring intransigence about forced collective farm work. These problems did not dissolve upon liberation and then victory in war, as the leaders had thought, but were joined by new fears and even hopes among *kolkhozniki*.

Many who had remained civilians under German occupation feared the returning Soviet state might punish them for failing to evacuate or fight as the Germans advanced in 1941 – the only two options the Soviets accepted. *Kolkhozniki* hoped that demonstrating their allegiance to the state might save them from possible retribution. Alongside this fear, hope of a new life was also widespread. If the war was won, the state might repay its citizens who had won it, or at least suffered from it, with a better life. Therefore, working hard for victory would demonstrate their allegiance to the state and enable them to partake of the anticipated better life in the countryside, with improved working and living conditions even if collective farming remained.[3] Whether it came from fear or hope, Khrushchev thus had good reason to speak of 'love' in a cynical tone. For all of the relief of being saved from the Germans' genocidal occupation and the chance to rebuild their lives, the 'love' of *kolkhozniki* for the state was conditional on the realisation of this better life. The state's love for *kolkhozniki* was conditional on their accepting the resumption of the harshness of their pre-war life.

This 'love' waned soon after victory in 1945, as neither of these incongruous hopes was realised. Soviet leaders measured the love of *kolkhozniki* for the state by their willingness to give up their grain to it and follow the draconian collective farm rules it enforced as part of its broader reassertion of control over the countryside in 1946. On both counts, *kolkhozniki* failed. Leaders would be hard-pressed to find examples of positive attitudes towards the state anywhere in Ukraine during the 1946–7 famine that

to Moscow from their intelligence gathering on attitudes towards Soviet power in the rear of the Red Army's advance across Ukraine. Some areas were still rife with remaining German forces, agents, collaborators and anti-Soviet military forces. The NKVD launched a massive operation to 'clear' these areas of such people, and there were more of them the further west the NKVD travelled in Ukraine. Oblasts were liberated progressively mostly from October 1943 for eastern oblasts and by April 1944 for southern and western oblasts. On positive Union-wide sentiment (although focused on Russia) upon liberation and victory, see 'Introduction' in Zubkova, *Russia after the War*.
[3] Zubkova, *Russia after the War*; Danylenko, ed., *Povoienna Ukraïna*, 204.

kolkhozniki understood, quite correctly, had been accelerated by state policies. Its rapacious collections of grain from the countryside had pre-cipitated famine from the failed harvest, while its reduction in the size of *kolkhozniki*'s private plots limited their capacity to reproduce the food taken from them. Now there was less hailing and more cursing of Stalin, as starving *kolkhozniki* increasingly left the collective farms in search of food and, eventually, a better life.[4] This 'love' had evaporated for both *kolkhoz-niki* and their leaders by this time.

It was exactly at this time that love began to blossom between the *kolkhozniki* in Raska and Bila Tserkva and 'their leaders' – the Council on Collective Farm Affairs representatives on the ground, their superiors in Moscow, and the republican leadership in Kyiv, not least Khrushchev himself. They loved these *kolkhozniki* because the latter fought tooth and nail to stay on the farms in times of crisis when others left them. If the interests of the state and *kolkhozniki* were inherently opposed in the collective farm system, here they coalesced, or both parties thought they did. However, this uniqueness was the problem. Few *kolkhozniki* under-stood their interests as being in re-entering the collective farm system and reclaiming ownership of land stolen from them in order to perform better within it. The *kolkhozniki* who fought for the return of this land were unique in that they had more to lose by not getting back into the system when the majority had more to gain by leaving it.

This key disparity helps further explain the post-war demographic evisceration of the countryside launched by the war. As in other rural out-migrations in European history, mostly the old, infirm and women, and a few unique souls who understood their fate as tied to the land, remained on it.[5] Many of the young who had left to make new lives in the cities after the war settled there, taking their families out of the village by the end of the 1940s.[6] The difference in the Soviet case was that this process was not gradual, but incredibly rapid, which exacerbated its devastating impact on the countryside and the people left behind.

If the state's and *kolkhozniki*'s interests in Raska and Bila Tserkva coalesced, namely, reconstructing collective farming and staying on the land, then so did both their interests coalesce in fighting against a common

[4] HDA SBU f. 16, op. 1, d. 614. This entire *delo* sent to Kaganovich is full of *svodki* on the negative mood of the population towards Soviet power in 1947.
[5] On concurrent urban–rural migration from the 1950s and 1960s across Europe, see W. J. Serow, 'Recent Trends and Future Prospects for Urban–Rural Migration in Europe', *Sociologia Ruralis* 31, no. 4 (1991), 270.
[6] See Chapter 3 and Zima, *Golod*, ch. 8.

enemy – the local official. Central authorities were always disappointed with the performance of officials at the lower level in their management of the countryside. The perennial problem that central authorities faced was that it was only through these local officials that they could assert control over the localities and, therefore, the former needed to cede much of their control to the latter. Local officials exercised control in many different ways, but often it was to reconcile the impossible demands of fulfilling the laws and central policies their superiors demanded with the local reality before them. It was the impossibility of this reconciliation that often fostered the very types of behaviours at the local level that central authorities most despised, though they rarely reflected on this irony.

We have a good understanding of this fundamental problem of Soviet governance in the literature, but until now not of how it changed at the pivotal point of war to post-war transition in the countryside – the launching of the 1946 Campaign on Collective Farm Rules. When central authorities ramped up the pressure to deal with officials' failures and corruption in the collective farm sector, some officials bit back. A major change from the pre-war period was that now officials used their control not to reconcile central demands with local realities, but to challenge the central authorities that had afforded them this control.

What made this challenge so pernicious for the *kolkhozniki* caught up in it, and so hard to defeat for the state, was that it was fuelled not only by the callousness or vice of local officials, as the *kolkhozniki* complained, but also by officials' visions of improvement. Officials were convinced that what they were doing in self-supply – continuing to turn *kolkhozniki* into workers and collective farms into workers' plots after it became illegal – was in the best interests of the *kolkhozniki* and their localities just as it had been during the war. It was in the best interests of the *kolkhozniki*, even if the officials had to beat and starve them in order to convince them of it. And the more 'rotten' the *kolkhozniki* were, the harder the beating and starving needed to be, until 1948 in Raska and at least until 1950 in Bila Tserkva. As was often the case in Soviet history, officials' visions for improvements could be much more dangerous for the people being improved than the malicious policies directed against them.

Central authorities' attempt to put an end to self-supply in a context of mass drought, with famine looming, provided the greatest impetus for officials to continue it and thus precipitated this challenge to central authorities. The attempt to punish local officials for this challenge criminalised survival, in the same way that punishment for expanding private plots criminalised survival among *kolkhozniki* and made surviving so much harder. Those officials who continued self-supply were mostly those who had made illegal appropriations in war and especially egregious ones, as in Raska and Bila Tserkva, and tried to avoid the exposure of their illegal actions. They did this by employing violence against the whistle-blowers and also liquidating and/or inhibiting the operation of their farms. In this way, not only did Soviet policies encourage illegality, as the literature tells us, but the 1946 campaign and related policies in the countryside bred a violent criminality out of a relatively benign wartime illegal activity of land appropriations. This violent criminality was much more pernicious for *kolkhozniki* and now injurious to the state.

Making criminals out of people for surviving was a widespread practice in Soviet history and, in the immediate post-war period, not unique to it. Post-war Europe was rife with black market activity conducted by people who needed to supplement their poor or non-existent rations to survive.[7] What was different in the Soviet case again was not just the extremeness of this criminality, or that even officials needed to engage in criminal actions to do their jobs and make the system work, as scholars have noted.[8] The real difference in the post-war period was the way in which this criminality was conducted and protected, and punishment avoided, through the conspiratorial networks that were not an aberration of the political system, but formed part of its fundamental post-war foundation.

In some ways, then, the war had made the state's problems with local officials in the countryside worse than they had been in the 1930s and done little to improve its problems with *kolkhozniki* after the euphoria of liberation and victory evaporated. In the post-war period, the Stalinist state might have been all-powerful. Other than insurgency in western Ukraine and, in a much more minor way, the Baltic republics, its position was undisputed both at home and, with some exceptions, even in its new

---

[7] On black market problems in Germany exacerbated by the food crisis and porous borders between occupation zones in Berlin in 1945, see P. Steege, *Black Market, Cold War: Everyday Life in Berlin, 1946–1949* (New York: Cambridge University Press, 2007), 255. For Soviet soldiers taking part in black market activity in Germany in defiance of the law and generally making the enforcement of the black market laws more difficult for authorities, see State Archive of the Russian Federation (Gosudarstvennyi arkhiv Rossiiskoi Federatsii – GARF) f. r-9401, op. 2, d. 97, ll. 307–308; f. r-7103, op. 1, d. 22, ll. 3–10. On urban dwellers travelling out to rural areas to steal crops from fields in post-war Germany and the limitations of policing this crime, see Slaveski, *The Soviet Occupation*, 91. On the pervasiveness of the black market in occupied Europe and especially occupied France in World War II, as well as the difficulties of enforcing laws against it, see L. Taylor, 'The Black Market in Occupied Northern France, 1940–1944', *Contemporary European History* 6 no. 2 (1997), 175–6.

[8] The 'psychology of circumvention' thesis as in Filtzer, *Soviet Workers*, 250, and Gill, 'The Communist Party', 123.

empire in eastern Europe. But it exercised much less control than it had anticipated on the local level in the Soviet countryside. The state's attempts to recover this control were largely unsuccessful, and sometimes they backfired.

The key reason for this backfiring, revealed by this book, was that the war had provided new avenues for local authorities to keep exercising greater control than central ones once the war was over, despite pressure from the centre to shut such avenues down. Scholars have long noted that the war forearmed the generation of veterans who flooded into positions in the post-war party and Soviet government with skills and viewpoints that shaped the development of the country until its demise.[9] What we see here is that the wartime experience also imbued in those pre-war officials who survived the war in the rear a sense of how to operate successfully in a context of extreme food pressure. This context endured after the war had ended, and the officials continued to operate in the same way as they had in wartime, especially in terms of self-supply. They did not make the transition to 'peace' that Zhdanov had demanded in 1946 because they were still facing similar wartime pressures and were dealing with them with the tools that had proved successful so far, despite changes in state policy that now outlawed such tools. There remained significant tension between old officials who 'sat out the war in the rear' and new officials coming back from the front to replace them.[10] The state's continually shifting officials to other positions as punishment for their poor performance continued to inhibit their improvement and compounded the problems that required their shifting in the first place. But new officials coming back from the war and those transient officials also learned how to operate these tools from the officials already there, establishing a degree of continuity in policy practice that helps explain how self-supply endured. Such continuities are easily obscured in the massive ruptures in personnel and practice in the war-to-post-war transition.

Central authorities managed to finally defeat the challenge of self-supply in Kyiv Oblast not by the campaign designed to do so or by punishing

---

[9] Zubkova, *Russia after the War*, and E. S. Seniavskaia, *Frontovoe pokolenie, 1941–1945. Istoriko-psikhologicheskoe issledovanie* (Moscow: Institut Rossiiskoi Istorii RAN, 1995).

[10] Many veterans believed that officials, the same ones who were denying them their entitlements, had sat out the war in the rear to enrich themselves while they themselves had risked their lives at the front. But this clear polarisation became blurrier soon after the war as millions of war veterans became party members, so that increasingly it was veterans who 'found work in precisely those administrative positions such as district housing … which their former comrades found so disagreeable'. The social fabric created by shared wartime experience among veterans mattered little in the battle for survival in post-war scarcity according to Dale, *Demobilised Veterans*, 88, 56.

officials for it, but only by removing the impetus for officials to mount it. Reducing the amount of grain collections in relation to the total amount produced after the 1947 harvest left more food in the countryside, and thus there was less impetus for self-supply, at least among officials. Relaxing the anti-corruption drive on officials also discouraged them from employing violent and criminal methods used to conceal illegal appropriations, as they feared less punishment from above. But this entrenched broader and more flagrant abuses in the collective farm sector by emboldening offending officials. Through relaxing its exercise of power over the countryside, in terms of reducing the impetus but also the punishment for self-supply, the state thus reclaimed some control over parts of it, but continued to lose it in others. The complexities of seeking control by force or relaxation at this time demand further scholarly attention in terms of how self-supply and other abuses developed elsewhere, if we are to acquire a more accurate picture of the post-war evisceration of the Soviet countryside.

In as much as this book adds to this picture, clearly the policy of amalgamations in 1950 put a final, though crooked nail in the countryside's coffin. It is clear why the state pursued this policy. The loss of agricultural labour encouraged the more efficient use of what remained as well as of resources, which meant centralising them in larger, less numerous farms where more people could use them to cultivate more land. Fewer and larger farms would also be easier to manage. But if *kolkhozniki*'s attachment to land was keeping some committed to working in the servitude of the collective farm sector, as in Raska and Bila Tserkva, while millions of others were fleeing it, then severing this connection through amalgamations made little sense. Severing these ties only accelerated the process of *kolkhozniki* leaving the land and exacerbated the labour shortages the policy was supposed to combat. This paradox was especially galling in Raska and Bila Tserkva, as it was the *kolkhozniki*'s attachment to the land that had aroused enough sympathy among central authorities to help them keep their farms in 1948, not least from Khrushchev himself. By 1950 he was spearheading the policy that either liquidated their farms, removed *kolkhozniki* from their lands, or both. The 'long benevolent hand' of central authorities into Raska and Bila Tserkva in 1948 turned out to be quite short and cruel.

In some ways, this hand was crueller towards Bila Tserkva than Raska. City authorities had finally 'won' in Bila Tserkva by the 1970s, making a reality of the 1946 rezoning of these lands from rural to urban through numerous farm amalgamations. By the 1970s the area was much richer than it had been before the war. But the price paid by *kolkhozniki* for this enrichment, like in most other places, was either losing attachment to their land symbolically or, worse, being forced to move away from it physically. Raska stayed poor in material terms, but its more unique amalgamation meant its *kolkhozniki* remained rich in keeping their ancestral lands and graves of their loved ones and entering into the post-war Soviet community. It is important to stress these more symbolic gains, as these are what the *kolkhozniki* themselves have held dearest, and to stress the uniqueness of its amalgamation that ensured they would retain these gains into the present.

Zosia Lisovska, and some of the children of the post-war *kolkhozniki* who remain in the village today, look back fondly on their lives in Kyiv Oblast or in Nove Zhyttia. Life had always been hard for them, especially as children, but by the time they were young adults the farm worked reasonably well, and they made a decent living beyond the imagination of their parents' generation.[11] They were members of a more inclusive society that valued them as bearers of Soviet martyrdom and, one which, they all remember, was characterised by a greater egalitarianism and generosity among citizens than now. As Lisovska reflects:

> Yes, those were very difficult years. Oh, how hard it was to live. It was very hard to live ... But our people were so friendly. They used to share a piece of bread. If I have and you don't have – I gave you. If I don't have and you have – you gave me. There were very friendly people. Very. One believed and trusted. One sympathised with the other ... Today it is not like that. No, it is not like that. Now there is everything ... bread in abundance, but there is no life.[12]

There are significant similarities between Lisovska's nostalgia for the Soviet past and the contemporary assessment of life in the village made by residents in 1973.[13] We have already seen how their recollections of the massacre and especially of Ukrainian collaborators' role in it were distorted by the constraints of Soviet-era publications. But it would be unwise to assume that any positive statements they made about life under Soviet rule were also automatically distorted or, indeed, manufactured. As some scholars of Soviet history remind us, we should avoid replicating this long-standing tendency in the literature 'to treat only negative, resisting

---

[11] Valentin Dem'ianovich Koval'skyi, interview by Filip Slaveski (11–21 October 2016 and 18 August 2018).

[12] Zosia Adol'fovna Lisovska, interview by Filip Slaveski (18 August 2018).

[13] On the complexities of nostalgia for the Soviet past in contemporary Russia, see David Satter, *It Was a Long Time Ago, and It Never Happened Anyway: Russia and the Communist Past* (New Haven: Yale University Press, 2012).

statements as indices of a true speaking out' or of what people actually thought, rather than assessing those statements supporting the regime as possibly genuine as well.[14] This advice is particularly pertinent here as Lisovska's nostalgia connects further with the evidence we have of *kolkhozniki*'s sentiments from the late 1940s, establishing a continuity of how life was felt and state policies experienced in one village over seventy years rarely seen in this scholarship.

The 'love' of some *kolkhozniki* for the state or, better, its society, then, clearly survived the euphoria of liberation not only in Raska but likely elsewhere as well. It was not only cynical, as Khrushchev suspected, but complex and endured well beyond him and the collapse of the Soviet Union. Another of Lisovska's positive recollections of the post-war period could well have been voiced by many others who survived the war as children, who remember its horrors rather than Stalin's of the 1930s, and who understand their survival as a result of Soviet victory:[15]

> I guess what I'm telling you that although it was hard to live, people were optimistic. They were striving for something. They were striving for some goal. People were alive. People go to work and sing, go from work and sing. At work, they sit down for a rest and sing . . . [16]

These songs have changed in post-Soviet Ukraine. For Lisovska and other ethnic Poles in Raska, some can be hard to sing, particularly those venerating their 'symbolic murderers' sung at the UPA grave on 14 October every year in Raska's neighbouring village of Myhalky. But some ethnic Poles still attend these commemorations every year out of respect to their current neighbours, just as some from Myhalky attend the commemoration of Raska's massacre on 11 April each year. The neighbours' attempts to sing each other's songs in commemoration of their respective dead, or at least listen to them, is a figurative call for a hopeful future, born from a terrible past.

---

[14] J. Hellbeck, 'Speaking Out: Languages of Affirmation and Dissent in Stalinist Russia', *Kritika: Explorations in Russian and Eurasian History* 1, no. 1 (2000), 85. On the deeper roots of this approach of treating negative statements more seriously than positive ones especially the Western literature, see A. Krylova, 'The Tenacious Liberal Subject in Soviet Studies', *Kritika: Explorations in Russian and Eurasian History* 1, no. 1 (2000), 119–46.

[15] Yurchak's study of the (last) post-war generation in Soviet history focuses on those born after the war, unlike Lisovska. But there are significant continuities in how she and other members of her generation, not far removed from the following one, both understood the values, ideals and realities of Soviet socialism as relevant and genuinely important to their lives. This was especially the case with regard to life in the 1960s and 1970s, which was a more dynamic period than established understandings of it as politically, culturally and socially stagnant under Brezhnev. See A. Yurchak, *Everything Was Forever, Until It Was No More: The Last Soviet Generation* (Princeton: Princeton University Press, 2013), 6–7.

[16] Zosia Adol'fovna Lisovska, interview by Filip Slaveski (18 August 2018).

APPENDIX

Archival Source Locations and Guide for Further Research

The Council on Collective Farm Affairs in the USSR Council of Ministers (Sovet po delam kolkhozov pri Sovmin SSSR) operated from 1946 to 1953. Particularly during 1946–7, this was a powerful body that helped to drive the re-establishment of central control over the countryside. Its numerous document repositories at central and local levels provide us with further insight into this process and, broadly, into conditions in the collective farm sector. At the local level especially, reports provide 'on the ground' assessments of conditions by officials who established close relationships with the area and with locals, in some cases more so than local party/state officials. The Council also operated as an investigative agency on the operations of local government. Unlike party and state investigative agencies, which generally stood apart from the levels of power they were investigating, Council representatives were embedded in these structures and worked together with local officials, sometimes towards the same goals. Their reports are less 'exposés' of incompetence and corruption at these levels and more investigations into the mechanics of numerous problems riddling local governance in the countryside, of which incompetence and corruption were only part. Council representatives' reports, in addition to other sources, thus can present different and comprehensive perspectives of both local conditions in the countryside and the difficulties of establishing effective rule over them.

Given representatives' correspondence upwards through their hierarchy of power, scholars also have a unique opportunity to trace central (republican and all-Union) decision making in response to the very local problems at the village level at which representatives sought resolution. As with all sources, these need to be treated carefully, though when read with other sources from competing agencies of power, they offer a rich addition to knowledge available. Scholars may do well to investigate further these

191

sources at the central/local nexus in different areas of the former Soviet Union, especially the liberated territories where the Council's work was generally most difficult.

On the ground, the Council was made up of 'representatives', that is, heads of working groups distributed in each oblast of the Soviet Union for which they were responsible. They reported up the hierarchy to the central body in Moscow, which, though operating out of Sovmin, also operated out of the Central Committee secretariat given that its Head was the Central Committee secretary, Andrei Andreev. Sources from the Council were thus widespread in the government/party apparatus and, therefore, now widespread in the archive repositories of these agencies. The repository at the central level is located in RGAE (*fond* 9476). This contains reports and correspondence sent from Council representatives organised by oblast, as well as the internal correspondence and reporting of the Council's central apparatus.

Many reports from Council representatives in the oblast were addressed to Andreev or forwarded to his office, so they now are held in Central Committee *fond*s in RGASPI, along with copious correspondence. The most fruitful location of documents lies within the *opis'* belonging to the Upravlenie po proverke partiinykh organov TsK VKP(b) (Department for the Inspection of Party Organs of the Central Committee of the VKP(b)), where especially egregious abuses in the collective farm sector revealed by the Council were sent to the investigative department and then distributed among Central Committee sectaries for review (f. 17, op. 122).

In Ukraine, large folders of Council reports and correspondence with the Ukrainian government (Sovmin) are found in TsDAVOU, especially concerning late 1946–7 (the famine period). These reports – sent from oblast to republican level and vice-versa – form numerous *dela* in f. r-2, op. 7, and either concern Ukraine as a whole or are divided by oblast. Council representatives also wrote directly to officials with both party and state roles on the republican level, but sent urgent reports to these officials in their party roles, because they concerned 'political' problems in the countryside. Again, serious abuses of a political nature often made it all the way to highest echelons of power in Moscow and thus to the Central Committee, and can be found in RGASPI f. 17, op. 122.

Perhaps the most valuable, though underutilised, resources of the Council are at the individual oblast level. It is here that the need for more research is most pressing. In Kyiv Oblast, it was clear that from the original sign-in sheet attached to each *delo* in DAKO (located in their subsidiary depository in the basement of TsDAVOU), which scholars are supposed to sign upon accessing them, that few had consulted them since the original archivists declassified them. Sometimes the rule requiring scholars to sign them is not strictly enforced, or scholars, myself included, forget to sign their name. These elusive sheets fixed to the folders can also be lost, removed or replaced. But these were the original sheets from 1989 onwards in at least forty *dela*. Nor could the attendant archivists remember retrieving these *dela* for review over a number of years. There may be a similar situation in other oblast archives. *Raion*-level archives in Bila Tserkva and documents from the *sel'sovet* in Piskivka which covered Raska and other villages were also incredibly useful sources, though they present different access and, as in my case with private documents, citation constraints.

Accessing all of these local sources in other oblasts may enable scholars to connect a vertical hierarchy of power from village to central authorities in Moscow. With enough research in enough oblasts, we could connect this research 'horizontally' across the Soviet Union to provide much greater insight into the operation or dysfunction of the post-war collective farm sector, the political system that operated it, the eventual evisceration of both, and the enduring consequences of this history in people's lives and the post-Soviet space.

Bibliography

Archives

Archive Department of the Bila Tserkva Raion Administration (Kyiv Oblast) (Arkhivnyi viddil Bilotserkivs'koi raiderzhadministratsii Kyïvskoï oblasti – AV BRDA)

Archive Department of the Security Service of Ukraine (Haluzevyi derzhavnyi arkhiv Sluzhby Bezpeky Ukraïny – HDA SBU)

Central State Archive of Public Organisations of Ukraine (Tsentral'nyi derzhavnyi arkhiv hromadskykh ob'iednan' Ukraïny – TsDAHOU)

Central State Archive of Supreme Bodies of Power and Government of Ukraine (Tsentral'nyi derzhavnyi arkhiv vyshchykh orhaniv vlady ta upravlinnia Ukraïny – TsDAVOU)

Russian State Archive of Socio-Political History (Rossiiskii gosudarstvennyi arkhiv sotsial'no-politicheskoi istorii – RGASPI)

Russian State Archive of the Economy (Rossiiskii gosudarstvennyi arkhiv ekonomiki – RGAE)

State Archive of Kyiv Oblast (Derzhavnyi arkhiv Kyïvskoï oblasti – DAKO)

State Archive of the Russian Federation (Gosudarstvennyi arkhiv Rossiiskoi Federatsii – GARF)

References

Alexopolous, Golfo. *Stalin's Outcasts: Aliens, Citizens and the Soviet State, 1926–1936*. Ithaca: Cornell University Press, 2003.

Altman, I. A. 'Memorializatsiia Kholokosta v Rossii. Istoriia, sovremennost', perspektivy', *Neprikosnovennyi zapas*, no. 2 (2005), https://magazines.gorky.media/nz/2005/2/memorializaciya-holokosta-v-rossii-istoriya-sovremennost-perspektivy.html.

Arutiunian, Yu. V. *Sovetskoe krest'ianstvo v gody Velikoi Otechestvennoi voiny*. Moscow: Akademia Nauk SSSR, Institut Istorii, 1963.

Ascher, Abraham. *P. A. Stolypin: The Search for Stability in Late Imperial Russia*. Stanford: Stanford University Press, 2002.

Assmann, Aleida. *Shadows of Trauma: Memory and the Politics of Postwar Identity*, trans. S. Clift. New York: Fordham University Press, 2015.

Assmann, Aleida and Sebastian Conrad, eds. *Memory in a Global Age: Discourses, Practices and Trajectories*. Basingstoke: Palgrave Macmillan, 2010.

Baran, V. K. and V. M. Danylenko. *Ukraïna v umovah systemnoi kryzy (1946–1980-i rr.)*. Kyiv: Al'ternatyvy, 1999.

Barber, John and Mark Harrison. *The Soviet Home Front, 1941–1945: A Social and Economic History of the USSR in World War II*. London and New York: Longman, 1991.

Bazyka, Dimitry A. *Health Effects of Chornobyl Accident – 30 Years Aftermath*. Kyiv: National Academy of Medical Sciences of Ukraine, 2016.

Berkhoff, Karel C. *Harvest of Despair: Life and Death in Ukraine under Nazi Rule*. Cambridge, MA: Harvard University Press, 2004.

Bessel, Richard and Dirk Schumann, eds. *Life after Death: Approaches to a Cultural and Social History of Europe during the 1940s and 1950s*. New York: Cambridge University Press, 2003.

Biess, Frank and Robert G. Moeller, eds. *Histories of the Aftermath: The Legacies of the Second World War in Europe*. New York: Berghahn Books, 2010.

Blacker, U., A. Etkind and J. Fedor, eds. *Memory and Theory in Eastern Europe*. New York: Palgrave Macmillan, 2013.

Blackwell, Martin J. *Kyiv as Regime City: The Return of Soviet Power after Nazi Occupation*. Rochester: University of Rochester Press, 2016.

Bohn, Thomas M. 'Soviet History as a History of Urbanization', *Kritika: Explorations in Russian and Eurasian History* 16, no. 2 (2015), 451–8.

Boterbloem, Kees. *Life and Death under Stalin: Kalinin Province, 1945–1953*. Montreal: McGill-Queen's University Press, 1999.

Brown, Kate. *A Biography of No Place: From Ethnic Borderland to Soviet Heartland*. Cambridge, MA: Harvard University Press, 2003.

Burds, Jeffrey. 'The Early Cold War in Soviet West Ukraine, 1944–1948', *Carl Beck Papers in Russian and East European Studies*, no. 1505. Pittsburgh: University of Pittsburgh Press, 2001.

Cadiot, Juliette and John Angell. '"Equal Before the Law"? Soviet Justice, Criminal Proceedings against Communist Party Members, and the Legal Landscape in the USSR from 1945 to 1953'. *Jahrbücher für Geschichte Osteuropas* 61, no. 2 (2013): 249–69.

Chornobyl Forum Expert Group (Environment). 'Environmental Consequences of the Chornobyl Accident and Their Remediation: Twenty Years of Experience'. *International Atomic Energy Agency* no. 3 (2006), www.iaea.org/publications/7382/environmental-consequences-of-the-chernobyl-accident-and-their-remediation-twenty-years-of-experience.

Cohn, Edward D. 'Policing the Party: Conflicts between Local Prosecutors and Party Leaders under Late Stalinism'. *Europe–Asia Studies* 65, no. 10 (2013): 1912–30.

Cole, T. 'Review: Scales of Memory, Layers of Memory: Recent Works on Memories of the Second World War and the Holocaust', *Journal of Contemporary History* 37, no. 1 (2002): 129–38.

Dale, Robert. *Demobilized Veterans in Late Stalinist Leningrad: Soldiers to Civilians*. New York: Bloomsbury Academic, 2015.

Danilov, A. and A. V. Pyzhikov. *Rozhdenie sverkhderzhavy. SSSR v pervye poslevoennye gody*. Moscow: Rosspen, 2001.

Danylenko, V. M., ed. *Povoienna Ukraïna. Narysy sotsial'noï istoriï (druha polovyna 1940-kh–seredyna 1950-kh rr.)*. Kyiv: Instytut istoriï Ukraïny NAN Ukraïny, 2010.

Danylenko, V. M., ed. *Ukraïna XX st. Kul'tura, ideolohiia, polityka*, vol. XIII. Kyiv: Instytut istoriï Ukraïny NAN Ukraïny, 2008.

David-Fox, Michael, Peter Holquist and Alexander M. Martin, eds. *The Holocaust in the East: Local Perpetrators and Soviet Responses*. Pittsburgh: University of Pittsburgh Press, 2014.

Davies, R. W. and S. G. Wheatcroft. *The Industrialisation of Soviet Russia 5. The Years of Hunger: Soviet Agriculture, 1931–1933*. Basingstoke: Palgrave Macmillan, 2004.

Denisevich, M. N. *Individual'nye khoziaistva na Urale, 1930–1985*. Ekaterinburg: Institute of History and Archeology, 1991.

Denisov, V., A. V. Kvashonkin, L. Malashenko, A. Iu. Miniuk, M. Iu. Prozumenshchikov and O. V. Khlevniuk, eds. *TsK VKP(b) i regional'nye partiinye komitety 1945–1953*. Moscow: Rosspen, 2004.

Echternkamp, Jorg and Stefan Martens, eds. *Experience and Memory: The Second World War in Europe*. New York and Oxford: Berghahn Books, 2007.

Edele, Mark. 'A "Generation of Victors"? Soviet Second World War Veterans from Demobilization to Organization 1941–1956'. PhD dissertation, University of Chicago, 2004.

Edele, Mark. *Soviet Veterans of World War II: A Popular Movement in an Authoritarian Society, 1941–1991*. Oxford: Oxford University Press, 2008.

Edele, Mark. 'Veterans and the Village: The Impact of Red Army Demobilization on Soviet Urbanization, 1945–1955'. *Russian History* 36, no. 2 (2009): 159–82.

Edele, Mark and Filip Slaveski. 'Violence from Below: Explaining Crimes against Civilians across Soviet Space, 1943–1947'. *Europe–Asia Studies* 68, no. 6 (2016): 1020–35.

Efremov, K. I. 'Ekonomika Vologodskoi oblasti v gody Velikoi Otechestvennoi voiny'. *Istoriia narodnogo khoziaistva* 2, no. 10 (2010): 132–7.

Fainsod, Merle. *Smolensk under Soviet Rule*. Cambridge, MA: Harvard University Press, 1958.

Fedor, Julie, Markku Kangaspuro, Jussi Lassila and Tatiana Zhurzhenko, eds. *War and Memory in Russia, Ukraine and Belarus*. New York: Palgrave Macmillan, 2017.

Field, Daniel. *Rebels in the Name of the Tsar*. Boston, MA: Houghton Mifflin Co., 1976.

Filtzer, Donald. *Soviet Workers and Late Stalinism: Labour and the Restoration of the Stalinist System after World War II*. Cambridge: Cambridge University Press, 2002.

Fitzpatrick, Sheila. *The Commissariat of Enlightenment: Soviet Organization of Education and the Arts under Lunacharsky, 1917–1921.* Cambridge: Cambridge University Press, 1970.

Fitzpatrick, Sheila. 'How the Mice Buried the Cat: Scenes from the Great Purges of 1937 in the Russian Provinces'. *Review* 52, no. 3 (1993): 299–320.

Fitzpatrick, Sheila. *On Stalin's Team: The Years of Living Dangerously in Soviet Politics.* Princeton, NJ: Princeton University Press, 2015.

Fitzpatrick, Sheila. 'Revisionism in Soviet History'. *History and Theory* 46, no. 4 (2007): 77–91.

Fitzpatrick, Sheila. *Stalin's Peasants: Resistance and Survival in the Russian Village after Collectivization.* New York: Oxford University Press, 1994.

Friedrich, Carl J., ed. *Totalitarianism.* Cambridge, MA: Harvard University Press, 1953.

Friedrich, Carl J. and Zbigniew Brzezinski. *Totalitarian Dictatorship and Autocracy.* Cambridge, MA: Harvard University Press, 1956.

Fürst, Juliane, ed. *Late Stalinist Russia: Society between Reconstruction and Reinvention.* Abingdon, UK: Routledge, 2006.

Ganson, Nicholas. *The Soviet Famine of 1946–1947 in Global and Historical Perspective.* New York: Palgrave Macmillan, 2009.

Gatrell, Peter and Nick Baron, eds. *Warlands: Population Resettlement and State Reconstruction in the Soviet–East European Borderlands, 1945–1950.* Basingstoke: Palgrave Macmillan, 2009.

Getty, J. Arch. 'Pragmatists and Puritans: The Rise and Fall of the Party Control Commission'. *Carl Beck Papers in Russian and East European Studies* no. 1208. Pittsburgh: University of Pittsburgh Press, 1997.

Getty, J. Arch. '*Samokritika* Rituals in the Stalinist Central Committee, 1933–1938'. *Russian Review* 58, no. 1 (1999): 49–70.

Goldman, Wendy Z. *Inventing the Enemy: Denunciation and Terror in Stalin's Russia.* Cambridge: Cambridge University Press, 2011.

Goodhand, Jonathan. *Bandits, Borderlands and Opium Wars: Afghan State-Building Viewed from the Margins.* Copenhagen: Danish Institute for International Studies, 2009.

Gorlizki, Yoram. 'Ordinary Stalinism: The Council of Ministers and the Soviet Neopatrimonial State, 1946–1953'. *Journal of Modern History* 74, no. 4 (2002): 699–736.

GOSPLAN. *Posevnye ploshchadi SSSR v 1938.* Moscow and Leningrad: Gosplanizdat, 1938.

Graziosi, Andrea. 'The New Soviet Archival Sources: Hypotheses for a Critical Assessment'. *Cahiers du monde russe* 40, nos. 1–2 (1999): 13–64.

Gregory, Paul. *The Political Economy of Stalinism.* New York: Cambridge University Press, 2003.

Hachten, Peter. 'Property Relations and the Economic Organization of Soviet Russia, 1941–1948'. PhD dissertation, University of Chicago, 2005.

Halfin, Igal and Jochen Hellbeck. 'Rethinking the Stalinist Subject: Stephen Kotkin's "Magnetic Mountain" and the State of Soviet Historical Studies'. *Jahrbücher für Geschichte Osteuropas* 44 (1996): 456–463.

Hamburger Institut für Sozialforschung, ed. *Verbrechen der Wehrmacht. Dimensionen des Vernichtungskrieges 1941–1944: Ausstellungskatalog.* Hamburg: Hamburger Edition, 2002.

Haran, Olexiy, Maksym Yakovlyev and Maria Zolkina. 'Identity, War, and Peace: Public Attitudes in the Ukraine-Controlled Donbas'. *Eurasian Geography and Economics* 60, no. 6 (2019): 1–25.

Heinzen, James. *The Art of the Bribe: Corruption under Stalin, 1943–1953.* New Haven: Yale University Press, 2016.

Hellbeck, Jochen. 'Speaking Out: Languages of Affirmation and Dissent in Stalinist Russia'. *Kritika: Explorations in Russian and Eurasian History* 1, no. 1 (2000): 71–96.

Hessler, Julie. 'A Postwar Perestroika? Toward a History of Private Enterprise in the USSR'. *Slavic Review* 57, no. 3 (1998): 516–42.

Himka, John-Paul. 'War Criminality: A Blank Spot in the Collective Memory of the Ukrainian Diaspora'. *Spaces of Identity* 5, no. 1 (April 2005).

Hisamutdinova, R. R. 'Narusheniia kolkhoznogo zemlepolzovaniia na Urale v 1940–1950-e gg.'. *Vestnik Leningradskogo gosudarstvennogo universiteta im. A. S. Pushkina* 4, no. 1 (2014): 116–23.

Horlach, L. N. and I. M. Pal'chik et al. *Dzvony pam'iati. Knyha pro trahediiu sil Kyïvshchyny, znyshchenykh fashystamy u roky viiny.* Kyiv: Radyanskyi pys'mennyk, 1985.

Hrytsak, Yaroslav. *Narys istorii Ukraïny. Formuvannia modernoi natsii XIX–XX stolittia.* Kyiv: Heneza, 1996.

Hrytsak, Yaroslav. *Strasti za natsionalizmom. Stara istoriia na novyi lad.* Kyiv: Krytyka, 2011.

Iliushin, Igor. *UPA i AK. Protyvostoiannia u Zapadniy Ukraïni (1939–1945 gg.).* Kyiv, 2009.

Instytut istoriï Ukraïny NAN Ukraïny. *Holod v Ukraïni u pershii polovyni XX stolittia. Prychyny ta naslidky (1921–1923, 1932–1933, 1946–1947).* Kyiv: Instytut istoriï Ukraïny NAN Ukraïny, 2013.

Instytut istoriï Ukraïny NAN Ukraïny. *Istoriia mist i sil URSR. Kyïvs'ka oblast.* Kyiv: Instytut istoriï Ukraïny NAN Ukraïny, 1971.

Instytut istoriï Ukraïny NAN Ukraïny. *Ukraïna: Khronika XX stolittia. Roky 1946–1960: Dovid. Vyd. 1946–1953,* vol. I. Kyiv: Instytut istoriï Ukraïny NAN Ukraïny, 2005.

Jones, Jeffrey W. *Everyday Life and the 'Reconstruction' of Soviet Russia during and after the Great Patriotic War, 1943–1948.* Bloomington: Slavica Publishers, 2008.

Kessler, H. and G. E. Kornilov, eds. *Kolkhoznaia zhizn' na Urale, 1935–1953.* Moscow: Rosspen, 2006.

Khasianov, O. R. 'Khoziaistvennaia povsednevnost' kolkhoznoi derevni v poslevoennoe desiatiletie (na materialakh Kuibyshevskoi i Ulianovskoi oblastei)'. *Istoriia: fakty i simvoli,* no. 3 (2016): 35–43.

Khlevniuk, Oleg. *Khoziain. Stalin i utverzhdenie stalinskoi diktatury.* Moscow: Rosspen, 2010.

Khlevniuk, Oleg, ed. *Politbiuro TsK VKP(b) i Sovet Ministrov SSSR 1945–1953.* Moscow: Rosspen, 2002.

Khlevniuk, Oleg. 'Sistema tsentr–regiony v 1930–1950-e gody', *Cahiers du monde russe* 44, nos. 2–3 (2003): 253–68.

Kondrashin, V. V. 'Krest'ianstvo i sel'skoe khoziastvo SSSR v gody Velikoi Otechestvennoi voiny'. *Izvestiia Samarskogo nauchnogo tsentra RAN* no. 2 (2005).

Kotkin, Stephen. *Magnetic Mountain: Stalinism as a Civilization.* Berkeley: University of California Press, 1995.

Koval'skyi, Valentin Demianovich. Interview by Filip Slaveski. 11–21 October 2016 and 18 August 2018.

Krupyna, V. 'Osvitn'o-kul'turnyi riven' partiinoï nomenklatury UkSSR (druha polovyna 1940-kh–pochatok 1950-kh rr.)', *Ukraïnskyi istorychnyi zbirnyk*, no. 12 (2009): 207–14.

Krylova, Anna. 'The Tenacious Liberal Subject in Soviet Studies'. *Kritika: Explorations in Russian and Eurasian History* 1, no. 1 (2000): 119–46.

Kul'chyts'kyi, S. V. *Chervonyi vyklyk. Istoriia komunizmu v Ukraïni vid yoho narodzhennia do zahybeli,* vol. III. Kyiv: Tempora, 2013.

Kul'chyts'kyi, S. V. *Organizatsiia ukrainskykh natsionalistiv i Ukrainska povstanska armiia.* Kyiv: Instytut istoriï Ukraïny NAN Ukraïny, 2005.

Kulczycki, John J. *Belonging to the Nation: Inclusion and Exclusion in the Polish–German Borderlands, 1939–1951.* Cambridge, MA: Harvard University Press, 2016.

Kuzio, Taras. 'Competing National Identities and Democratisation in Ukraine: The Fifth and Sixth Cycles in Post-Soviet Ukrainian History'. *Acta Slavica Iaponica* 33 (2012): 27–46.

Kuzio, Taras. 'Nationalism, Identity and Civil Society in Ukraine: Understanding the Orange Revolution'. *Communist and Post-Communist Studies* 43, no. 3 (2010): 285–96.

Kuzio, Taras. 'Viktor Yanukovych's First 100 Days: Back to the Past, But What's the Rush?' *Demokratizatsiya* 18, no. 3 (2010): 208–18.

Leibovich, Oleg. *V gorode M. Ocherki sotsial'noi povsednevnosti sovetskoi provintsii.* Moscow: Rosspen, 2008.

Lévesque, Jean. 'Exile and Discipline: The June 1948 Campaign against Collective Farm Shirkers'. *Carl Beck Papers in Russian and East European Studies,* no. 1708. Pittsburgh: University of Pittsburgh Press, 2006.

Lewin, Moshe. 'Rebuilding the Soviet *Nomenklatura* 1945–1948'. *Cahiers du monde russe* 44, nos. 2–3 (2003): 219–52.

Lewin, Moshe. *The Soviet Century.* New York: Verso, 2005.

Lieberman, Sanford R., ed. *The Soviet Empire Reconsidered.* Boulder: Westview, 1994.

Lisovska, Zosia Adol'fovna. Interview by Filip Slaveski. 11 October 2016 and 18 August 2018.

Livshin, A. I., I. B. Orlov and O. V. Khlevniuk. *Pis'ma vo vlast', 1928–1939. Zaiavleniia, zhaloby, donosy, pis'ma v gosudarstvennye struktury i sovetskim vozhdiam*. Moscow: ROSSPEN, 2002.

Lovell, Stephen. *The Shadow of War: Russia and the USSR, 1941 to the Present*. Oxford and Malden, MA: Wiley-Blackwell, 2010.

Lovell, Stephen. *Summerfolk: A History of the Dacha, 1710–2000*. Ithaca: Cornell University Press, 2003.

Maksimenko, E. V. 'Istoriografiia problemy razvitiia individual'nogo i kollektivnogo ogorodnichestva i podsobnykh khoziaistv na iuzhnom Urale v gody Velikoi Otechestvennoi voiny i poslevoennyi period'. *Vestnik Orenburgskogo gosudarstvennogo pedagogicheskogo universiteta* 5, no. 1 (2013): 83–6, http://vestospu.ru/archive/2013/articles/maksimenko1-5.html.

Marples, David R. *Heroes and Villains: Creating National History in Contemporary Ukraine*. Budapest: Central European University Press, 2007.

Marples, David R. *Stalinism in Ukraine in the 1940s*. New York: St Martin's Press, 1992.

Martin, Terry. 'The Origins of Soviet Ethnic Cleansing'. *Journal of Modern History* 70, no. 4 (1998): 813–61.

McBride, Jared. 'Who's Afraid of Ukrainian Nationalism?' *Kritika: Explorations in Russian and Eurasian History* 17, no. 3 (2016): 647–63.

Milokhin, D. V. and A. F. Smetanin. *Komi. Kolkhoznaia derevnia v poslevoennye gody, 1946–1958. Sotsial'no-ekonomicheskie aspekty razvitiia*. Moscow: Nauka, 2005.

Montefiore, Simon Sebag. *Stalin: The Court of the Red Tsar*. London: Weidenfeld & Nicolson, 2003.

Moskoff, William. *The Bread of Affliction: The Food Supply in the USSR during World War II*. New York: Cambridge University Press, 1990.

Motrenko, T. V. and V. A. Smolii, eds. *Istoriia derzhavnoi sluzhby v Ukraini*, vol. II, *Holovne upravlinnia derzhavnoi sluzhby Ukraïny*. Kyiv: Nika-Tsentr, 2009.

Motrevich, V. P. 'Vosstanovlenie sel'skogo khoziaistva na Urale v pervye poslevoennye gody (1946–1950 gg.)'. *Agrarnyi vestnik Urala* 96, no. 4 (2012): 23–6.

Mukhamedov, Rashid and Evgeni Nikolaev. 'Priusadebnye khoziaistva kolkhoznikov v poslevoennyi period (1946–1953 gg.)'. *Obshchestvo: filosofiia, istoriia, kultura* no. 5 (2017): 86–90.

Musial, Bodan. 'The "Polish Operation" of the NKVD: The Climax of the Terror against the Polish Minority in the Soviet Union'. *Journal of Contemporary History* 48, no. 1 (2013): 98–124.

Nadkin, T. D. *Stalinskaia agrarnaia politika i krest'ianstvo Mordovii*. Moscow: Rosspen, 2010.

Pastushenko, Tetyana. *'V'izd repatriantiv do Kyïva zaboronenyi … ' Povoienne zhyttya kolyshnikh ostarbateriv ta viiskovopolonenykh v Ukraïni*. Kyiv: Instytut istoriï Ukraïny NAN Ukraïny, 2011.

Penter, Tanja. 'Collaboration on Trial: New Source Material on Soviet Postwar Trials against Collaborators'. *Slavic Review* 64, no. 4 (2005): 782–90.

Perekhrest, O. 'Sil'ske hospodarstvo Ukraïny v 1943–1945 rr. Problemy ta rezul'taty vidbudovy'. *Ukraïnskyi istorychnyi zhurnal* no. 3 (2010): 92–109.

Petrov, N. V. and A. B. Roginskiy. '"Pol'skaia operatsiia" NKVD 1937–1938 gg.', http://old.memo.ru/history/polacy/00485art.htm.

Plamper, Jan. 'Archival Revolution or Illusion? Historicizing the Russian Archives and Our Work in Them'. *Jahrbücher für Geschichte Osteuropas* no. 51 (2003): 57–69.

Polian, Pavel. *Zhertvy dvukh diktatur. Ostarbaitery i voennoplennye v Tret'em reikhe i ikh repatriatsiia.* Moscow: Vash Vybor Tsirz, 1996.

Popov, V. P. *Rossiiskaia derevnia posle voiny (iiun' 1945–mart 1953).* Moscow: Prometei, 1993.

Portnov, Andriy. 'Bandera Mythologies and Their Traps for Ukraine'. *Open Democracy Russia and Beyond* (22 June 2016).

Portnov, Andriy. *Istoriia dlia domashnioho vzhytku. Esei pro polsko-rosiisko-ukraïnskyi trykutnyk pamiati.* Kyiv: Krytyka, 2013.

Portnov, Andriy. *Istoriia istorykiv. Oblychchia i obrazy ukraïnskoi istoriohrafii XX stolittia.* Kyiv: Krytyka, 2011.

Pred, Allan. *Making Histories and Constructing Human Geographies: The Local Transformation of Practice, Power Relations, and Consciousness.* Boulder: Westview, 1990.

Prusin, Alexander Victor. '"Fascist Criminals to the Gallows!" The Holocaust and Soviet War Crimes Trials, December 1945–February 1946'. *Holocaust and Genocide Studies* 17, no. 1 (2003): 1–30.

Prusin, Alexander Victor. *The Lands Between: Conflict in the East European Borderlands, 1870–1992.* Oxford: Oxford University Press, 2010.

Qualls, Karl D. *From Ruins to Reconstruction: Urban Identity in Soviet Sevastopol after World War II.* Ithaca: Cornell University Press, 2009.

Raleigh, Donald J., ed. *Provincial Landscapes: Local Dimensions of Soviet Power, 1917–1953.* Pittsburgh: University of Pittsburgh Press, 2001.

Rendle, Matthew. 'Post-Revisionism: The Continuing Debate on Stalinism'. *Intelligence and National Security* 25, no. 3 (2010): 370–88.

Rothberg, Michael. *Multidirectional Memory: Remembering the Holocaust in the Age of Decolonization.* Stanford: Stanford University Press, 2009.

Rowney, Don K. and Eugene Huskey, eds. *Russian Bureaucracy and the State: Officialdom from Alexander III to Vladimir Putin.* Basingstoke: Palgrave Macmillan, 2009.

Rudnichenko, Anatoli Nikolaevich. Interview by Filip Slaveski. 10 October 2016 and 14 October 2016

Satter, David. *It Was a Long Time Ago, and It Never Happened Anyway: Russia and the Communist Past.* New Haven: Yale University Press, 2012.

Seniavskaia, E. S. *Frontovoe pokolenie, 1941–1945. Istoriko-psikhologicheskoe issledovanie.* Moscow: Institut Rossiiskoi Istorii RAN, 1995.

Serow, William J. 'Recent Trends and Future Prospects for Urban–Rural Migration in Europe'. *Sociologia Ruralis* 31, no. 4 (1991): 269–80.

Shearer, David R. *Policing Stalin's Socialism: Repression and Social Order in the Soviet Union, 1924–1953*. New Haven: Yale University Press, 2009.

Shkandrij, Myroslav. *Ukrainian Nationalism: Politics, Ideology, and Literature, 1929–1956*. New Haven: Yale University Press, 2015.

Siegelbaum, Lewis, ed. *Borders of Socialism: Private Spheres of Soviet Russia*. New York: Palgrave Macmillan, 2006.

Siemaszko, Władysław and Ewa Siemaszko. *Ludobójstwo dokonane przez nacjonalistów ukraińskich na ludności polskiej Wołynia, 1939–1945*, vol. II. Warsaw: Wydawn. von borowiecky, 2000.

Silberman, Marc and Florence Vatan, eds. *Memory and Postwar Memorials: Confronting the Violence of the Past*. New York: Palgrave Macmillan, 2013.

Slaveski, Filip. *The Soviet Occupation of Germany: Hunger, Mass Violence and the Struggle for Peace, 1945–1947*. Cambridge: Cambridge University Press, 2013.

Smolii, V. A. *Ekonomichna istoriia Ukraïny. Istoryko-ekonomichne doslidzhennia v dvokh tomakh*. Kyiv: Nika-Tsentr, 2011.

Snyder, Timothy. *Bloodlands: Europe between Hitler and Stalin*. New York: Basic Books, 2010.

Starodub, Oleksii, et al. *Budivel'na istoriia Biloï Tserkvy XI–XXI stolit'*, vol. II. Bila Tserkva, 2017.

Statiev, Alexander. *The Soviet Counterinsurgency in the Western Borderlands*. Cambridge: Cambridge University Press, 2010.

Steege, Paul. *Black Market, Cold War: Everyday Life in Berlin, 1946–1949*. New York: Cambridge University Press, 2007.

Subtelny, Orest. *Ukraine: A History*, 3rd ed. Toronto: University of Toronto Press, 2000.

Taylor, Lynne. 'The Black Market in Occupied Northern France, 1940–1944'. *Contemporary European History* 6, no. 2 (1997): 153–76.

Trifonov, A. N. 'Ogorodnichestvo i reshenie prodovol'stvennoi problemy na Urale v gody Velikoi Otechestvennoi voiny'. *Istoriko-pedagogocheskie chteniia* no. 9 (2005): 214–27.

Trifonov, A. N. 'Sel'skokhoziaistvennye podsobnye khoziaistva Urala v gody Velikoi Otechestvennoi voiny'. *Istoriko-pedagogicheskie chteniia* 10 (2006): 290–5.

Verbitskaia, O. M. *Rossiiskoe krest'ianstvo. Ot Stalina k Khrushchevu, seredina 40-kh–nachalo 60-kh godov*. Moscow: Nauka, 1992.

Veselova, O. M. 'Pisliavoienna trahediia. Holod 1946–1947 rr. v Ukraïni'. *Ukraïnskyi istorychnyi zhurnal* no. 6 (2006): 98–124.

Viola, Lynne. *Peasant Rebels under Stalin: Collectivization and the Culture of Peasant Resistance*. Oxford: Oxford University Press, 1999.

Viola, Lynne. *The War against the Peasantry, 1927–1930: The Tragedy of the Soviet Countryside*. New Haven: Yale University Press, 2008.

Voisin, Vanessa. 'Caught between War Repressions and Party Purge: The Loyalty of Kalinin Party Members Put to the Test of the Second World War'. *Cahiers du monde russe* 52, nos. 2–3 (2011): 341–71.

Vrons'ka, T. V. *V umovakh viiny. Zhyttia ta pobut naselennia mist Ukraïny (1943–1945 rr.)*. Kyiv: Instytut istoriï NAN Ukraïny, 1994.

Ward, Chris. 'What Is History? The Case of Late Stalinism'. *Rethinking History* 8, no. 3 (2004): 439–58.

Weiner, A. *Making Sense of War: The Second World War and the Fate of the Bolshevik Revolution*. Princeton: Princeton University Press, 2001.

Wheatcroft, Stephen G. 'The Soviet Famine of 1946–1947, the Weather and Human Agency in Historical Perspective'. *Europe-Asia Studies* 64, no. 6 (2012): 987–1005.

Wheatcroft, Stephen G. 'The Turn away from Economic Explanations for Soviet Famines'. *Contemporary European History* 27, no. 3 (2018): 465–9.

Yekelchyk, Serhy. *Stalin's Citizens: Everyday Politics in the Wake of Total War*. New York: Oxford University Press, 2014.

Yekelchyk, Serhy. *Ukraine: Birth of a Modern Nation*. New York: Oxford University Press, 2007.

Yurchak, Alexei. *Everything Was Forever, Until It Was No More: The Last Soviet Generation*. Princeton: Princeton University Press, 2013.

Yurchuk, Yuliya. *Reordering of Meaningful Worlds: Memory of the Organization of Ukrainian Nationalists and the Ukrainian Insurgent Army in Post-Soviet Ukraine*. Stockholm: Stockholm Studies in History, 2014.

Zima, V. F. *Golod v SSSR 1946–1947 godov. Proiskhozhdenie i posledstviia*. Moscow: Institut Rossiskoi Istorii RAN, 1996.

Zubkova, E. Yu. 'Mir mnenii sovetskogo cheloveka, 1945–1948 gg. Po materialam TsK VKP(b)'. *Otechestvennaia istoriia*, no. 3 (1998).

Zubkova, E. Yu. *Poslevoennoe sovetskoe obshchestvo. Politika i povsednevnost', 1945–1953*. Moscow: Rosspen, 1999.

Zubkova, Elena [E. Yu.]. *Russia after the War: Hopes, Illusions and Disappointments, 1945–1957*, trans. and ed. by Hugh Ragsdale. Armonk, NY: M. E. Sharpe, 1998.

Zubkova, E. Yu. and T. Yu. Zhukova, eds. *Na 'kraiu' sovetskogo obshchestva. Marginal'nye gruppy kak ob'ekt gosudarstvennoi politiki, 1945–1960-e gg.* Moscow: Rosspen, 2010.

Zubkova, E. Yu. et al. *Sovetskaia zhizn', 1945–1953*. Moscow: Rosspen, 2003.

Index

16th Central Committee Plenum of the CP(b)U
  January 1949, 75, 97

Andreev, Andrei, 18, 47, 96, 112, 192

Bakhchysarai, 133
Belogirsk, 133
Belous, Comrade, 76–7, 104
Bila Tserkva
  destruction of, 58
  destruction of, massacre, 2
  gorkom/gorsovet. *See* local authorities
  Oleksandriia, 149
  reconstruction of, 44–5, 87, 135–6
  Rotok, 149
  urbanisation, 135, 149–50
  Zarichia, 147
Borodianka raion, 97, 137, 142
  raikom/raiispolkom. See local authorities
Butenko, Hryhorii, 80

Campaign on Collective Farm Rules. *See* political
  campaigns, 'On measures to eliminate
  abuses of collective farm rules'
central authorities
  relaxation towards corruption, 112–4
  structure of, 15–6
Chornobyl, 150
collaborators
  destruction of Raska, 1–2
  moral reflections, 180–1
  protection from, 157–63
  trial of, 160–1
collective farms/farming
  '*otstaiushchie kolkhozy i raiony*', 140
  amalgamations, 87, 147–50,
    188
  besperspektivnye, 137–8
  cyclical problems, 86, 122
  'empty land', 74
  farm meetings, 66, 87, 103, 157–60, 163

Imeni Lenina. *See* Bila Tserkva
kolkhoz markets, 138
labour shortages, 38, 127, 128, 129–31, 139, 188
land appropriations (illegal), 53–83
land appropriations (wartime), 39–42
land appropriations, literature on, 23–5
land recovery, 12, 48–9, 124–7
land renting, 25, 60
liquidation of, 61–72
loss of farm documentation, 50–2
Nove Zhyttia. *See* Raska
okolokolkhoznyi element/okolonaselenie, 131–4
Peremoha. *See* Bila Tserkva
performance in Bila Tserkva, 127–9
Pershe Travnia. *See* Raska
pre-war performance, 155–6
reconstruction of, 58–9
rezoning land, 56–7
state loans, 140, 154
taxes, 140
Tretii Vyrishal'nyi. *See* Bila Tserkva
wartime damage, 44
Council on Collective Farm Affairs (Sovet po
  delam kolkhozov), 18
  discovery of conspiracy, 72–3
  loss of power, 105–6, 111–12
  structure/operation, 109

demobilisation, 25, 37, 40, 42–3, 45
Dvornikov, S. K., 16–19, 51–2, 92, 104,
  146

ethnic Polish discrimination, 22, 61–2, 90
  Katyn massacre, 171
Exile Campaign. *See* political campaigns, 1948
  Exile Campaign

famine, 4, 12–16, 26–7, 30–1, 51, 68, 90, 98, 124–6,
  137, 184
food rations, 4, 12, 14–16, 24, 39, 43, 46, 186
forced labourers, 1, 43

German 'anti-partisan' war, 2–3, 94–5
Gordienko, M., 63, 96
  as true believer, 121–2
  attacks on, 110–11
  communication with Khrushchev, 99, 110
  discovery of conspiracy, 99
  speech at May 1948 Kyiv *obkom* CP(b)U
    Plenum, 101–3
Gryza, A. A., 110–12

Kaganovich, Lazar
  as First Secretary, 49–50, 62
  response to famine, 15–16
Kherson Oblast, 67, 126
Khrushchev, N. S.
  as First Secretary, 49–50, 74–5
  on liberation, 182
  response to famine, 15–16
  support for expansion of collective farms, 97–9
kolkhozniki
  abuse of, 26, 140–3
  attachment to land, 147–81
  flight/post-war rural migration, 27, 46, 135, 184
  pay, 5, 23, 48, 122
  post-war hopes, 183
  private plots, 46, 66–7, 126
  punishment of, 143
  resistance by, 18–19
  truancy, 122
Koval'skyi (Kowalski), Leon, 6
Kuriata, S. I., 65, 96, 153, 154
  Marchenko dispute, 90–2
Kuznetsov, Aleksei, 19, 96
Kyiv, repopulation of, 42
Kyiv *Obkom* CP(b)U Plenum May 1948, 74,
  101–3, 146
  May 1949, 144
Kyiv Oblast
  Borodianka raion, 37, 137
  Korsun-Shevchenko raion, 76
  Kyiv-Sviatoshin raion, 137, 142
  Makariv raion, 137, 141–2
  repopulation of, 43

Lisovska (Lisowska), Zosia, 147–81
Local Anti-Aircraft Defence Organisation
  (MPVO), 63, 78
local authorities
  avoiding punishment, 114–15
  conspiracy, 17, 50–2, 63–4, 81–3
  jurisdictional synapse, 61
  money laundering by, 140–3
  punishment of, 65, 104
  structure of, 5
Luhansk, 171

Maidan Revolution, 165, 171
Malashkevich, Comrade, 86, 104
Malenkov, Georgii, 133–4
Marchenko, Comrade, 64–5, 153–4, 159–63
  Kuriata dispute, 90–2
martydom, 93–4
Myhalky, relations with Raska, 147–81
Mykolaiv Oblast, 50–1, 79–80

Nesterenko, E. P., 84–6

Odesa Oblast, 50–1, 79–80
ogorodnichestvo, 138
Oleinik, Z. F., 62–3, 92
Organisation of Ukrainian Nationalists (OUN),
  147–81

Petrov, Comrade, 74–5
Piskivka, 57, 144, 150, 161, 177, 193
podsobnoe khoziaistvo
  attempts to keep, 99
  conversion to, 17, 53–83, 84–117
  false conversions, 81–3
  no taxation, 134
  wartime, 43
  workers' loss of, 9–14
Polissia, 97
political campaigns
  1948 Exile Campaign, 84–6, 100–1, 105, 131–4
  'On measures to eliminate abuses of collective
    farm rules', 13, 47–8, 54, 124–7
Poroshenko, Viktor, 169–73
post-war transitions, 30–1
  Soviet/European comparison, 31–3

Raska
  massacre, 2, 37, 94
  massacre, recollections of, 161–3
  reconstruction of, 66
Riazan Oblast, 113–14

sel'sovet. See local authorities
self-supply, 10–11, 184–7
Serdiuk, Z. T., 103–4, 110–12
Serebniak, Comrade, 84–6
Shidaev, Comrade, 64–5, 153
Simferopol, 171
Somov, Comrade, 159
Sovol'ev, N. V., 133–4
'speaking Bolshevik'
Stalin, I. V., 15–17, 27, 29, 84, 98, 100, 107, 112,
  156, 182, 184, 190
Stalinism
  anti-rural bias, 25, 39, 138
  clash of local and central authorities, 14–17, 30

Stalinism (cont.)
  inherent problems in, 76–7, 107–8, 115–17,
    184–7
  localism, literature on, 27–9
Stolypin, Petr, 'wager on the strong', 137–8
supplications, 18
  literature on, 22–3
  reasons for success, 88–99

Tkachenko, Comrade, 101–3,
  146

Ukraine
  community, 158–9
  decommunisation, 171–4
  political divisions, 168–9
  wartime damage, 4
  wartime liberation, 183
Ukrainian Insurgent Army (UPA), 147–81

Vologda Oblast, 80–2

war veterans
  as moral force, 91–2, 95–6
  entitlements, 64
wartime commemorations, 147–81
western Ukraine
  collectivisation, 13
  ethnic Polish population, 179
  insurgency, 32, 44, 153, 166–7, 182,
    186
  population exchanges, 44
workers' settlement, 64

Yanukovych, Viktor, 171
Yarygin, Comrade, 104

zemlianki, 110, 130, 141
Zhdanov, Andrei, 30, 133–4

For EU product safety concerns, contact us at Calle de José Abascal, 56–1°, 28003 Madrid, Spain or eugpsr@cambridge.org.

www.ingramcontent.com/pod-product-compliance
Ingram Content Group UK Ltd.
Pitfield, Milton Keynes, MK11 3LW, UK
UKHW020352140625

459647UK00020B/2425

*9 7 8 1 1 0 8 7 9 4 1 8 3 *